BINT ARAB

*Arab and Arab American Women
in the United States*

Evelyn Shakir

Westport, Connecticut
London

E
184
.A65
S48
1997

Library of Congress Cataloging-in-Publication Data

Shakir, Evelyn, 1938–
 Bint Arab : Arab and Arab American women in the United States /
Evelyn Shakir.
  p. cm.
  Includes bibliographical references (p.) and index.
  ISBN 0–275–95671–7 (alk. paper).—ISBN 0–275–95672–5 (pbk. :
alk. paper)
  1. Arab American women—Social conditions—Anecdotes. 2. Arab
American women—Interviews. I. Title.
  E184.A65S48 1997
  305.48'8927073—dc21   96–50316

British Library Cataloguing in Publication Data is available.

Library of Congress Catalog Card Number: 96–50316
ISBN: 0–275–95671–7
    0–275–95672–5 (pbk.)

First published in 1997

Praeger Publishers, 88 Post Road West, Westport, CT 06881
An imprint of Greenwood Publishing Group, Inc.

Printed in the United States of America

The paper used in this book complies with the
Permanent Paper Standard issued by the National
Information Standards Organization (Z39.48–1984).

10 9 8 7 6 5 4 3 2

Copyright Acknowledgments

The author and publisher gratefully acknowledge permission to reprint the following materials:

From "Syrian-Lebanese Women Tell Their Story," *Frontiers* 7, no. 1 (1983). Copyright 1983
The Frontiers Editorial Collective, reprinted by permission of *Frontiers.*

Reprinted from Shakir, Evelyn. "Good Works, Good Times: The Syrian Ladies Aid Society
of Boston, 1917–1932." In *Crossing the Waters,* edited by Eric J. Hooglund (Washington, DC:
Smithsonian Institution Press), pages 133–143, by permission of the publisher. Copyright 1987.

From Albert Aboud, "Letter," *The Syrian World* 3, no. 7 (January 1929), pp. 46–47. Reprinted
by permission of *The Syrian World.*

From A. Hakim, "On the Marriage Problem Among Syrians," *The Syrian World* 3, no. 5 (No-
vember 1928), pp. 27–32; 3, no. 6 (December 1928), pp. 20–25; 3 no. 7 (January 1929), pp.
18–23. Reprinted by permission of *The Syrian World.*

For my mother
Hannah Sabbagh Shakir
1895–1990

CONTENTS

Acknowledgments   ix

Introduction   1

Part I: The First Wave, 1875–1925

1   Miriam   13

2   Katreen   17

3   *Syrian* Emigration   20

4   Women Immigrants   27

5   Peddlers   35

6   Mill Girls, Factory Hands, and Entrepreneurs   43

7   Students and Teachers   52

8   Clubwomen   59

9   Making a Match   65

Part II: From Second Generation to Third

10   Fighting "Political Racism"
     Paula   79

11   Reconnecting
     Linda   95

12   Women for Women
        Cheryl Qamar   104

13   Color and Religion
        Khadija   112

Part III: The Second Wave, 1945 to the Present

14   Palestinians
        Emily
        Ihsan
        Najeebi
        Suhair, Souad, Nuha, and Nawal
        Mona   125

15   Collage   165

Epilogue   195

Appendix   197

Notes   201

Bibliography   213

Index   219

ACKNOWLEDGMENTS

Over the last decade or more, in preparation for writing this book, I have interviewed dozens of Arab and Arab American women. Even though many of these women will not find themselves specifically referred to in the pages that follow, I want them to know that their contribution to this project has been important and has informed the writing at every stage.

I would also like to thank the many individuals who opened doors for me within the Arab American community, above all Helen Hatab Samhan, of the Arab American Institute, who referred me to women in cities throughout the United States. Thanks, too, to Elaine Hagopian and Evelyn Menconi, who always had names and telephone numbers to suggest. Camilia Odeh introduced me to young people in Chicago; Mary Kahedi, to teenagers in New York City. In Detroit, May Berry and Maha Freij provided access to women of diverse backgrounds. Evelyn Unes Hansen led me to wonderful story tellers in St. Paul; a phone call from Eva and Rob Higgins in Baltimore paved the way to my first interview with an Algerian woman; Kanan Makiya put me in touch with Iraqi women in several cities; Eric Hooglund extended my network of contacts in Washington, D.C. I am grateful also to Eric and to Martha Ramage for putting a roof over my head for several days, and to Carol Haddad for doing the same on my first visit to Detroit. Apologies and thanks to the many others whom I am no doubt overlooking but whose particular acts of kindness helped me map a route from one female narrator to another.

As I pursued my research, I also became acquainted with intriguing women of the past. I am grateful to Mary Mokarzel, daughter of the distinguished publisher Salloum Mokarzel, for first putting me on to the story of entrepreneur and socialite Marie Aziz El-Khoury. A more detailed biography was graciously provided by Gloria Barsa, whose father was an executor of El-Khoury's estate. My discovery of journalist Afifa Karam was facilitated by Alixa Naff. Michael Suleiman, a generous source of bibliographic data, called my attention to several other writers. Emily Hajar added detail to my sketch of Saleemie Yazgie.

I come now to the librarians and archivists. Without them, where would we be? Many thanks to Fawzi Tadros of the Library of Congress, who helped me track down articles in Arab American newspapers; to Amy Lewontin, Sheila Eckman, Robert Favini, and Janice Eastes of Bentley College, who did magical things with computers; and to Lindsey Carpenter, also of Bentley, who tirelessly reeled in books, articles, and dissertations from libraries across the country. I am especially grateful to Alice Chucri Deyab of Harvard's Widener Library, who offered me true Arab hospitality in her home and most generously shared with me her private collection of articles by early women immigrants.

Of course, those articles were in Arabic, but luckily I found Alex Baramki, a talented translator and patient advisor who helped me sort out and evaluate materials that I could not decipher. (Except where indicated otherwise, all translations are his.) Thanks also to Shirine Hamadeh for her translation of two articles.

Rounding up illustrations was not easy. For their help, thanks to Rola Nashef, Alixa Naff, Ann Kuebler, Evelyn Unes Hansen, Eric Hooglund, Eugene Nassar, Muayyad Qubbaj, Angelita Mireles, Ken Skulski, Roseanne McKeen, Bruce Harknes, and Pamela Yameen. For answering many questions on history and politics, thanks again to Elaine Hagopian.

Several institutions have helped me along the way. I have happy memories of the Virginia Center for the Creative Arts, where, amidst bluebirds and honeysuckle, I was first able to make major headway on my writing. Bentley College provided a series of grants that supported my work even when it seemed to be stretching on interminably. Thanks also to Rudolph Vecoli, Halyna Myroniuk, and other staff at the Immigration History Research Center (University of Minnesota), where I studied for the better part of a summer.

All students of the Arab American experience are indebted to the humane historical narratives of pioneer scholar Afif Tannous; I am grateful, too, for his personal kindness and encouragement. Precious moral support came also from Faye Chandler, Karin Cook, Anita Skeen, and Diane Weinstein, each of whom read (or listened to) sections of my manuscript and said all the right things, as did Paula Hajar, who nurtured this project along as if it were her own. Thanks also to John Harney for his good counsel.

Family, too, was always there to be relied on; I am grateful to my brother, Philip Shakir, and all the cousins who swapped stories with me about (and provided photos of) grandparents, aunts, and uncles.

Finally, my deepest gratitude is reserved for George Ellenbogen who read (with the eye of a poet), applauded (with the zeal of a friend), and stubbornly insisted (until he'd finally convinced me) that I could bring this book to pass.

INTRODUCTION

At first, most of us—both immigrants and children of immigrants—called ourselves "Syrians," a catch-all term for people from the eastern end of the Mediterranean. Later, as new states were formed in the region and political boundaries redrawn, more and more of us repackaged ourselves as "Lebanese." It is an awkward thing to change one's identity; it smacks either of duplicity or of stupidity. But we did it, we said, to avoid confusion—our ancestral villages *were* in Lebanon, once a part of *Greater Syria* but now an independent state. We had another motive, too. By the mid-1950s, it was more comfortable to be associated with Lebanon, a loyal if obscure American ally, than with Syria, a nation flirting with socialism and ever more bitterly at swords' point with the United States. Beginning in the late 1960s, a good number of us—both Lebanese and Syrian—added on the label "Arab."

Of course, among ourselves we had always been Arab, *bint arab* (Arab daughter) for females, *ibn arab* (Arab son) for males. To now assume that identity in English was again a political statement, a declaration of solidarity with Arab states that had been humiliated in the Six-Day War with Israel.

But the more I answered to Arab, the more I puzzled over the discrepancy between what most people believed about Arabs and what I knew of Arab Americans. The stereotypes just didn't fit. Terrorist, oil sheik, master of the seraglio—it was impossible to connect these terms with my uncle who baked blueberry muffins for his wife's breakfast and washed out her underthings by hand, or with my other uncle who belonged to the Rotary Club, voted Republican, and was a deacon in the Baptist church. Yes, there were also

*When italicized, *Syria* will refer to *Greater Syria*, the region out of which modern day Lebanon, Syria, and Palestine/Israel were carved; *Syrian* will refer to immigrants from that region, the majority of whom were natives of what is today the state of Lebanon. I have edited quotations to make them conform to this scheme.

overbearing, hot-tempered bullies among the men, just as there were women afraid to speak up for themselves or, at a different point on the same curve, a few who dressed like tarts and jangled their bracelets as provocatively as they jiggled their breasts and who could not keep their hands off the knees of other women's husbands.

But most women in the community—riding the streetcars to garment factories each day, playing whist with husbands and friends on Saturday night, keeping open house for family on Sunday—could not be confused with either harem girls or domestic slaves. Nor did the women of every age who danced at church picnics (and who remain in my memory as embodiments of perfect grace) conform to stereotype: the playful beckonings and sweet refusals they mimed were far removed from the sweaty grind of the nightclub belly dancer—a creature fashioned to meet Americans' lurid fantasies about the East. And when, as a child, I watched Arab girls waitress at Ladies' Aid dinners—laughing, proud, alive—all the English and Irish girls I had ever gone to school with paled into insignificance.

Of course, Arabs and Arab Americans were two different sets of people; I understood that. And though my parents and their generation had been born in the Arab world, decades spent in the United States had no doubt left their mark, turning them into people they would not have been had they lived out their lives at home. That made good enough sense, especially since most had emigrated while still young, sometimes no more than children. Then, too, they were almost all from Mount Lebanon (which even in the nineteenth century had frequent contact with Westerners) and so knew little or nothing of desert, tents, or camels, the usual appurtenances of the mythic Arab. Most important, my parents' generation of immigrants were Christian not Muslim, and thus not easily yoked with lascivious harems and bloody Saracens. In short, I could tell myself that the stereotypes of Arabs were not meant to apply to me and mine.

Yet every time I identified myself as *Arab* American, those stereotypes barged in again like uninvited guests. And, upon reflection, I found it wasn't just a trick of language connecting me with "Arabs." As far as I could tell, there really was a bedrock of common Arab culture—a holding dear of the same values (some of which I rejected)—that cut across religious and political boundaries, and reached even to the United States. I concluded that if the stereotypes didn't ring true to me, maybe it was not so much because the people I knew were a generation removed from the Arab world, and a fringe group at that, but because the stereotypes were caricatures that distorted the faces of all Arabs, men and women alike.

Edward Said's 1979 landmark study on Orientalism helped me place myth-making about Arabs in historical context and to understand it not as simple xenophobia, but as convenient justification for political, economic, and cultural exploitation of colonial lands. Matured in Europe, transplanted to the United States, Orientalism is a habit of mind that divides the world into polar opposites, East and West, them and us, and assumes that those exotic others are so benighted, depraved, or genetically disabled that they cannot run their own affairs or be trusted to know what is in their own best interests.

Since the same logic has universally been used to keep women in their place, I expected that American feminists, a group with whom I felt allied, would be quick to recognize and reject it even when applied to Arabs. But for the most part, they have not. Instead, they have sometimes seemed to have a vested interest in broadcasting stories of savage Arab men and perpetuating the stereotype of the passive, pathetic Arab woman, needing to be roused from her moral, intellectual, and political stupor. Such depictions may be well meaning, intended to denounce patriarchy in its starkest forms. But they become pernicious when, as often happens, they turn into sweeping statements about some generic "Arab woman." Thus, the complaints of Palestinian feminists that they have not only had to battle against foreign occupation and against reactionary forces within their own community but also have had to mount a third front against Western feminists who claim to speak on their behalf but wind up, in effect, lampooning them.

Humiliated and on the defensive, Arab women—especially in this country, where denigration of Arabs is still the rule—have sometimes responded by muting their own criticism of Arab society. In the early 1980s, Egyptian-born sociologist Leila Ahmed wrote about attending a women's studies conference in Bloomington, Indiana, at which a panel of Arab women presented what seemed to her "an unwarrantably rosy picture of women in Islam" (521). Later, after having lived for a time in this country, Ahmed came to understand why the women on the panel took the position they did. In her words,

If one is of Arabic or Islamic background in America, one is almost compelled to take that stand. And what compels one is . . . that Americans "know," and know without even having to think about it, that [Moslems] are backward, uncivilized peoples totally incapable of rational conduct. . . . [And Americans] know also with the same flawless certainty that Muslim women are terribly oppressed and degraded. And they know this not because they know that women everywhere in the world are oppressed, but because they believe that, specifically, Islam monstrously oppresses women. (521–522)

Barraged by such "knowledge" (which inextricably links Islam and Arabs) American women of Arab heritage yearn for new narratives about themselves, their mothers, their grandmothers, and for new readings of Arab culture. Ahmed has obliged by reinterpreting the harem (Orientalism's most charged emblem) as a sacrosanct female space that nurtures sisterhood and liberates the mind. Only partly tongue-in-cheek, she suggests that "some young commune-minded American feminists should go immediately to Saudi Arabia . . . not to study Arabian women as scientists study insects, but to study as apprentices and disciples of their women's world" (531).[1]

Ahmed's theory may sound like special pleading. But since the eighteenth century, as Billie Melman has recently shown, a number of Western women have also described the harem in glowing terms. In their writing, it has become an "autonomous sorority" (144), a *sanctus sanctorum* where women can be "safe from all intrusion" (140), a setting where "women of different classes, different age-groups, and, usually, different races" (154) are integrated into a single community. All this, of course, is a far cry from the Orientalist's notion of the harem as realm of male despotism and dirty secrets.

But that is Melman's point—that although Orientalism long reigned as the dominant Western discourse about the Middle East, it has not had the floor to itself. Even as Orientalism flourished, says Melman, there grew up alongside it another discourse most easily seen in the writing of certain European women. The jumping-off point for this alternative rhetoric was the reality that women—unlike men—had access to harems and to women's *hammams* and, if they wished, could even try on the anonymity conferred by the veil.

Armed with the authority that comes from seeing with one's own eyes, some women merely confirmed the prevalent Orientalist view of harem life. Others, however, consciously set about "correcting" it. Not only did they deny that Arab women were slaves to their husbands, they also pointed to advantages enjoyed, at least in theory, by Arab women (a married woman's right to her own property and to initiate divorce) but denied at the time to women in the West. Lady Mary Wortley Montagu (1689–1763), sometime friend of Alexander Pope, onetime wife of the British ambassador to Turkey, concluded, " 'Tis very easy to see [Muslim women] have more Liberty than we have" (in Melman 86)—(though she evidently had in mind the freedom to follow illicit inclination). In fact, Montagu soon learned that in the eyes of some Turkish women, she was an object of pity, not envy. In recounting her visit to a *hammam*, she writes,

After [the matron of the house] had slipped off my gown and saw my [corset] stays, she was very struck at the sight of them, and cried out to the other ladies in the bath: "Come hither and see how cruelly the poor English ladies are used by their husbands!"[2] (in Ahmed 525)

It would be foolish (as Melman herself points out) to conclude that Montagu and the iconoclasts who followed in her tradition were uninfected by Orientalist bias. At the least, however, they did demonstrate that there was more than one story to tell and more than one tone to adopt in speaking about Arab women and the circumstances of their life. If nothing else, that demonstration loosens the iron grip of Orientalism on the imagination.

And it is an iron grip. Or why, in the first place, was there so much attention to the harem? However large it loomed in the fantasy life of European men and women, the practice of taking multiple wives and of closeting womenfolk has always been totally alien to most immigrants from the Middle East, both Christian and Muslim. Certainly the harem, like the veil, played no part in my family history. If I want specific help, then, in imagining the lives of my grandmothers or great-grandmothers or even the childhood of my mother, it is no good relying on tales of female seclusion in upper-class families. I have had to search for stories about nineteenth-century peasant women living in the territories that now constitute Syria, Lebanon, Jordan, and Israel/Palestine.

As it happens, the lives of these women were documented by a number of Westerners who came to live and work among them, most notably anthropologists, missionaries, and—beginning in the 1840s—pioneers in the new technology of photography. Back in the West, there was a ready market for photos of the Holy Land (Palestine and its environs) and of its people, who seemed to be leading lives that hearkened back to Biblical days. Photographs of sacred landmarks and landscape and of natives (e.g., a young woman at a well, another gleaning in the fields) were used to illustrate new editions of the Bible as well as biblical histories and travel books. Slide shows of Palestine found their way into Sunday School classes and into fundraisers for foreign missions (Graham-Brown 47).

In their various ways, artists, archaeologists, and historians mined the same vein, traveling east to find a sacred world that had been theirs since childhood. All such enterprises, focusing attention on the Near East, proved useful not just to those Arabs who lived off the pilgrimage trade but, on this side of the ocean, to Arab immigrants looking for acceptance in the United States. Thus, in a 1929 text, Rahme Haidar (born in Mount Lebanon) introduced herself as a native of "that mysterious and most wonderful land of the Saviour" (9). Jesus was a *Syrian*, she asserted, as were all of Abraham's descendants (19). Even now, she promised, if her Western audience could but accompany her to Damascus, they would hear a poet strumming a *Syrian* harp like that "touched by the masterly hand of David" (43), and feast on a *Syrian* pottage of lentils and cracked wheat, "Esau's favorite dish" for which he sold his birthright (44).[3]

In his autobiography, Abraham Rihbany (author of *The Syrian Christ*) likewise assimilated to biblical story the customs, beliefs, and even household furnishings in his native village. Once, in describing his family's removal from that village to another, he writes,

The picture of my sad mother on that morning as she sat on the mule's back, the right end of her *mendeel* (long bead scarf) turned under her chin and thrown over the left shoulder, my baby sister in her lap, and one of my cousins walking by her side, stands in my memory as the original of "The Flight to Egypt." (72–73)

Typecasting Near Easterners as characters in a sacred text may ultimately be a sentimental dodge, reducing them to the level of the picturesque, but it is less offensive than the habit missionaries (among others) sometimes fell into, of branding that same population as corrupt and fallen. Writing in 1870, the American missionary Henry Jessup told of a village girl taken into the home of a fellow missionary's family in order to be educated and brought up as a Protestant. The girl's mother—not friendly to the Christians—was denied access to the home and prevented from seeing or speaking to her daughter (much as happens today to parents whose children join certain religious cults). Jessup reported that the distraught mother (whose major crime seems to have been that she was Muslim) stood outside the missionary's house crying and tearing her hair, but not because she cared for her daughter, Jessup reassured his readers, but simply out of shame at her daughter's defiance.

For nineteenth-century missionaries, it was not just the drive to capture souls, but the need (as they saw it) to save Eastern women from abuse and degradation that justified their efforts in the field and helped them raise funds at home. Thus, Jessup also returned again and again to the allegedly brutal treatment Muslim women received at the hands of their husbands, the scourging and beating and sometimes killing. "Nominal" Christians (Catholics and Greek Orthodox) behaved better to their wives, he wrote, but only marginally so. Fortunately, in Jessup's pages, every husband and wife who convert to Protestantism become a model couple.

Jessup is easy to mock. But there is no denying that Arab women— whether village or urban—lived in a society that was unabashedly and often oppressively patriarchal (though it does not seem to have occurred to Jessup that the same could be said of his own society). If they fell into bad hands, they could be exploited, demeaned, and physically abused; if they ran afoul of highly charged cultural taboos, they might—in extreme cases—be killed by members of their own family (though perhaps no more frequently than American women are killed by their husbands and boyfriends). But individual circumstance can mitigate or undermine cultural dictate, and custom often supersedes theory. My mother once put it to me this way:

Yes, in the old country, they respected the father. He had the say. But it doesn't work that way all the time. My mother used to boss my father more than he used to boss her. She would tell him "Do this" or "Don't do that." He would say, "She knows best."

It is a point insisted upon by Hilma Granqvist, the Finnish anthropologist of the 1920s, who studied the Palestinian village of Artas and drew most of her data from daily interviews with local women as well as from her own observation. After three years in Artas, Granqvist concluded,

It is difficult to answer the question, how does a man [in Artas] treat his wife. There are wedding ceremonies intended to impress upon the wife from the very beginning the fact that her husband is her lord and master and has power over his wife. But this need not signify that a man treats his wife badly. (2:167)

In fact, said Granqvist,

There are women in Artas who, far from being at all submissive in spirit, are really dominating personalities, with an imposing dignity, to whom their husbands must certainly very often give way. (2:169)

The consensus of writers on the Middle East is that village women (like those in Artas) often enjoyed a greater degree of freedom than urban women. For one thing, many restrictions were not workable in a rural setting. Diminutive village houses did not lend themselves very well to separate apartments for men and women (sometimes not even for parents and children). Nor was it practical for a busy village woman, who had to work in garden and field, to veil every time she stepped outside her door.

Moreover, the village wife was not a "kept" woman but rather an active contributor to the family's economy. And if she also had a commanding personality, her judgment and wishes were not easily ignored. Certainly there is evidence to suggest that an unlettered village woman of intelligence, capacity, and will could exercise considerable power within her family (especially in her post-menopausal years when she had achieved seniority in her household and was no longer in danger of dishonoring her family by means of an untoward pregnancy).

Take the remarks made in 1909 by the American archaeologist and anthropologist Frederick Bliss, who had grown up in *Greater Syria*. He cited the example of a

handsome, dignified matron, who serenely kept her face uncovered [and] had an authoritative air. . . . From her little booth she was regulating the varied work of her estates, which brought her in the princely income of twelve hundred to fifteen hundred dollars a year: the herding of cows and goats; the threshing of wheat; the culture of vines and tobacco; the cutting of wood. Her sons, all married or betrothed, obediently worked under her orders. Her husband I recall as a mild man, apparently in total eclipse. Such instances are not uncommon. (282–283)

In confirmation of his observations, Bliss offered the opinion of Phillipe Baldensperger, a nineteenth-century writer on peasant life in Palestine. According to Baldensperger, in Palestine

[Woman] is considered inferior. . . . But from this it does not follow that a man absolutely commands the house. On the contrary, the fellah [peasant] woman is just as often—virtually—the head of the family, and differs in nothing from women in the rest of creation. . . . I have known many fellah-women to manage everything better than the husband, and even scolding him to some degree for any mismanagement, or teaching him what to say in the men's assembly. (in Bliss 283)

If—under the right circumstances and endowed with the right character— Muslim women could achieve such status and wield such influence, it follows that Christian women could probably do as much or perhaps more. In fact, imposing matrons and matriarchs frequently appear in the first-person accounts of Christian *Syrian* immigrants, for instance the 1914 volume in which Abraham Rihbany described his mother as "the intellectual leader of the family—alert and resourceful . . . swift both to hear and to speak" (6–7).

A generation or two later, the American novelist Vance Bourjaily wrote a semiautobiographical novel in which his alter-ego, Quincy, visits his father's native village high in the Lebanese mountains. There (the time is World War II) he discovers that "once a woman is past child-bearing, she begins to come to power. Her place is still the kitchen, but she imposes her will from there on her entire immediate family" until eventually "her word becomes absolute" (266–267).

Quincy's great-aunt Naifi is such a woman. To her house, perched on a rise, half the village climbs each day, "either to take Naifi food and water or to ask advice, to carry gifts or seek judgments. . . . When she spoke it was brief, it was practical, and . . . it was binding." As Quincy watches her, "the mountainous old woman at peace," he wonders "how the Semites, which my people are, had ever hit upon the notion that God was male" (267, 268).

I have wanted to learn about peasant women of the nineteenth century and later, living in what used to be called the Near East, so that I could understand the life out of which my own life grew. I knew from the start that Orientalist depictions of Arab women were fictions, out of accord with any reasonable understanding of human nature, its complexity, quirkiness, irrepressibility. It didn't matter that the fictions were primarily of Muslim women, not Christian; no group of women anywhere in the world, I was convinced, could be such nonentities, so brain dead.

I wanted counter fictions, richer, more interesting, and more persuasive. And so I was glad to come across stories that did not conform to the Orientalist narrative and to encounter individual women who were neither as pathetic nor as decadent as the stock characters of that narrative. The formidable women described by Montagu, Bliss, Granqvist, and Bourjaily pleased me, too, because they called to mind flesh-and-blood women I had known since childhood. I could believe in them. But, though tempted to, I do not label such women "representative" because I am convinced that the very notion of representative women leads inevitably to caricature and distortion. And I know, too, that exceptional women are precisely the ones about whom stories are generated, and so they are likely to be over-represented in a body of narratives, whether written or handed down by word of mouth, just as horror stories and their victims are over-represented. Furthermore, the teller of a tale is always suspect. Whether they knew it or not, in spinning their stories, Orientalists were furthering the business of empire. And European women sometimes were seeing the Middle East through the filter of their own discontents. (After her divorce, Montagu was left without an income and with no claim on her husband's fortune. Had she been a Muslim woman of comparable social class, she would have had her own property and a prenuptial settlement to rely on.) As for missionaries of Jessup's stripe, they were mounting a holy war against Islam; and early Arab American autobiographers had their agenda, too. Rihbany, for instance, was writing at a time when hostility toward dark-skinned immigrants was gathering steam, together with the move to bar their entry into the United States. His goal was to show that *Syrians* were not so alien, after all.

Since Rihbany's day, American suspicion of Arabs (always equated with Muslims) has only intensified, as has American fascination with Middle Eastern women. Since the 1980s, a flood of material on Arab women has been published, much of it memoir and oral history, those first-person forms from which (although we know better) we are always hoping for unvarnished truth and always getting only a version of it. But, at least, these are versions of the women's own making. Today, as never before, if we are willing to listen, Arab women are telling us about themselves.

But once they come to this country, a great silence descends. Very little is available on what happens to them (or happened to their predecessors) and even less on the lives of their daughters.[4] And this despite a resurgence of immigration from the Arab world; since 1970 alone, nearly half a million Arabs have entered the United States. Slowly, however, texts written by Arab American women are beginning to accumulate—a limited body of poetry, a little fiction, a handful of autobiographies and memoirs. To this small library, those of us born in America turn with some eagerness, wanting to see our own experience reflected and that of those who came before us, as well as to learn more about the lives of recent immigrants. Different from us and yet akin, new immigrants help us in the quest for our heritage and provide living refutation of facile Orientalist stereotype. They are on the front line in the encounter with American society.

Though only a few Arab women in America, newcomers or not, have put their stories in writing, many have passed them on by word of mouth, certainly to their own children and grandchildren, and frequently to interested others. This book, in fact, is based largely on conversations conducted over the last few years both with recent immigrant women (who usually think of themselves as "Arabs living in America") and with second- and third-generation women (who mostly think of themselves as "Arab Americans" or as "Americans of Arab descent"). I have my own stories, too, some handed down within my own family. Part I begins with an account of my two grandmothers, much of it based on tales my mother told me; throughout Part I, she remains my collaborator, her voice alternating with my own, her narrative with my essay.

Thus, this book is not a solo performance—many voices join in. I have tried to recruit to the ensemble a good number of women representing various classes, religions, and national backgrounds. But early on, I gave up the idea of being comprehensive. In the most obvious omission, not every Arab country is represented. I have chosen instead to focus, though not exclusively, on Lebanon and Palestine, two lands that have yielded large numbers of immigrants to the United States.

Given their diverse backgrounds, it is no surprise that the speakers in the book do not all agree on matters of fundamental concern to women. I am glad of their variety and disagreement, since, just as I would like to help dismantle the notion of *the* Arab woman, I would like to avoid creating another monolith, *the* Arab American woman. It is true, however, that as one listens to story after story, certain subjects recur.

One is the difficulty—faced more by women than by men, more by younger women than by their mothers—of negotiating between sets of values and cultural ideals that often seem incompatible. So, for instance, in a culture where family honor has required that women be chaste and their demeanor impeccably modest, behaviors quite innocent by Western standards may be looked at askance. Dating is an obvious example, or talking to men on the street, or leaving home for any reason other than marriage, or in some cases, even laughing out loud (instead of acting demure) in the presence of men. The history of Arab families in this country shows that, over time, young women have gradually gained greater personal autonomy, but even so, a painful cultural lag has sometimes intervened between the old order and the new. In response, some women have engaged in outright rebellion against their parents' or husbands' authority. Others have been able to invoke traditional values to justify unconventional behavior; in the name of service to family and community, much has been permitted.

Another major conflict is grounded in ambivalence toward the United States, a country that may offer immigrant women new opportunities for self-direction and achievement, yet often seems dangerously hostile to the Arab world. For daughters and granddaughters, the conflict is similar, a tug of war between attachment to the land of their birth (the United States) and anger or frustration at American policies in the Middle East. Though men also face these conflicts, they take on special meaning for women; female and Arab, they may feel doubly victimized.

The following pages are peopled with women who have lived with osuch tensions and, more often than not, responded to them in creative and courageous ways. Their stories constitute what I have been searching for, personal testimony of what it has meant and what it means today to be an Arab or Arab American woman in the United States.

PART I

The First Wave, 1875–1925

1

MIRIAM

My grandmother Miriam used to eavesdrop on her chickens. Once, in the middle of Lebanon's long Mediterranean summer, when they had been shooed out of the terraced garden and into the earth cellar under the house, she overheard them trying to make sense of things.

"I wonder why She's cooped us up here."

"You know why. Because we pecked at the beans."

"No, you donkey! It's because we tasted the tomatoes."

Afterwards, when she acted it out for the children—her voice a cackle, her shoulders fluttering—they laughed and were glad she was their mother.

With livestock, Miriam kept the upper hand. But inanimate objects, just like children, had minds of their own. Dishes raised a shameful racket when she washed them—"How bold they are!" she'd complain, disclaiming all responsibility. In America, it was no better. "Curse this clock and its ill breeding," she'd mutter, bringing her sons their morning coffee in bed. "It doesn't slow down, it doesn't take a break, it doesn't stop to consider that Elias (bless his eyes!) and Litfallah (may his bride be beautiful!) and my baby Naseeb (may he bury me!) were up until midnight." Her indignation nursed them out of bed and reconciled them to the work day ahead.

Miriam bore the first of her six children in 1879, when she was twenty-three, which suggests that she married late. In her time and place, teenage marriage would have been the norm. But Miriam was needed at home; the only daughter in a family of five sons, she took on the chores that her own mother was inept at or overwhelmed by. She rolled grapeleaves and cooked lentils and rice for her brothers, mended their clothes, and did their laundry, heating water over an open wood fire in the yard. Twice a week she mixed and kneaded dough, shaped it into flat, round loaves, took it to the community oven for baking. Every morning she drew water from the village spring and bore it home in a tall jug balanced like a child on her shoulder. (When, eventually, she had a real little girl of her own, she bought her a miniature jug and taught her to move erect and confident beneath its weight. In America, that skill would be useless, but the superb carriage it engendered would last the little girl, my mother Hannah, well into her eighties.)

At night, her chores done, Miriam (if she is to be believed) could barely find a patch of floor to lay her bones on. Not that sleeping on the floor was itself a hardship. In her day, as in biblical times, most people slept on quilts spread on the clay earth each evening and rolled up again each morning. (Which explains what Jesus had in mind when he instructed the paralytic man to rise and take up his bed.) And so Miriam would squeeze in where she could in that sibling sea of elbows and knees, sleeping, as she liked to say, "in the crack between two mattresses and two pillows." No room for bedding of her own.

And no school for her either, because she had no time, and because she was a girl. Years later, when Hannah, who was shy, begged to skip school, Miriam would have none of it. "Listen," she told her, quoting an Arab adage: "a person who cannot read will be employed to deliver his own death warrant."

Jiryas, the local dyer Miriam finally married, had just enough schooling to read simple words, which he would spell aloud before sounding out. He was sixteen years her senior, a widower when he married her, and nearly forty when their first child was born. Of the two, she had the brains. But he had an idea that eventually got the better of him. He wanted to see America. Sometime in the late 1880s or early 1890s, the idea was planted, perhaps by his sister, who kept house for an American educator living in Beirut.[1] Or perhaps the idea took root as Jiryas saw men he knew returning from the West, enough money in their pockets to build fine houses with red-tiled roofs. True, they were often men half his age, but he was still strong, and he wanted to go. Wanted it wholeheartedly, unreasonably, as a child wants a toy the other children have. In his heyday, friends had called him *Abu Llayl*, father of the night, because he loved to party. He wanted to party still. Or perhaps just to feel young one more time.

At any rate, flight must have been a daily temptation, since from his tiny house in his tiny mountain village, he had a spectacular view of Beirut harbor, glistening blue and silver, traversed by ships that people said were bound for the United States. Or was it, after all, Miriam who prodded him—a woman greedy for her family's prosperity?

The certainty is that one day Jiryas made his way down the mountain and stowed away in a bright ship, after telling Miriam he would be back in six months. Two years later, he returned from Brazil, having somehow missed his mark. Unrepentant, he wanted to try again. And after a decent interval he did, but this time chaperoned by his middle son, seventeen years old, who spoke some English and, more to the point, had inherited Miriam's good sense. Together, they made their way to Maine, sent eventually for two more sons, then sought better opportunity and the company of their compatriots in Boston. With the boys working in factory and restaurant and living together in a rented room, Jiryas returned home, having finally gotten the hang of the thing.

Miriam was waiting and continued to wait until it got to be too much. With each year, traffic between Lebanon and America was swelling, not only in her family but among friends and acquaintances. Steamship agents were coming round to encourage it, and her own husband was full of his latest overseas adventures.

She missed her sons, she said, and on the basis of that claim, left Jiryas and her three youngest children at home while she came to see America for herself. Apparently she liked it well enough to stay for a year and to feel, once she was home again, a restlessness she could not shake. If nothing else, she must have realized that her oldest sons were in America to stay. When she announced to Jiryas that they must all emigrate, he replied, "Just as you wish."

In Boston, the two adults and four children—a cousin had come along— stood uncertainly outside South Station, valises strapped to their backs, oddly shaped bundles littering the sidewalk at their feet. Miriam was the first to collect herself and her belongings. As the one with the most recent experience of the city, she led the march up Essex Street, paused to ask a cop for directions ("Willya please?"), then spotted on her own the Atlantic Avenue el. Now she knew where she was, and with a small cry of triumph, hurried the others on into Oliver Place, the densest alley of the *Syrian* Arab enclave. It was 1907, and Miriam was fifty years old.

My mother died in 1990. Who remembers Miriam now? Only a couple of grandchildren (my cousins), each about eighty, and they never speak of her. Unless, somewhere in Lebanon, is an ancient neighbor or cousin in whose memory Miriam has clung like a burr for eighty years.

And *I* remember her, a woman I never knew, who died before my parents were married. With no children of my own to make the future real for me, I am always looking over my shoulder, trying to make out the shapes and faces of those who came before me. I see Miriam standing in the dappled shade of a mulberry tree, reaching up for leaves to feed the spring lamb; I see her hurrying down the hillside and out of earshot—a neighbor woman has come to pierce Hannah's ears, and if the child cries, Miriam does not want to hear. And I see her, too, in America, her realm reduced to a tenement flat, wearing one apron and over it another to keep the first one clean, for when company comes.

I know little enough of Miriam, but she knew nothing of me, and perversely enough, I find I resent that. And I am not grateful that, for whatever reason, she emigrated to America although I think I used to be. It seems to me that she gave up a lot, not so much for herself, I suppose, as for me. It is so easy to romanticize: to see myself gathering fragrant violets on a Lebanese hillside; picnicking under the Roman ruins at Baalbek; strolling along the Corniche with my artist friends, chatting in French or English or Arabic, as our mood or subject dictates; sipping Turkish coffee at a seaside cafe; wading with a lover in the moonlit Mediterranean. No, that was not Miriam's world. But for a good while and on good days, it was the world that Miriam's great-nieces and -nephews inhabited, those whose grandparents and parents stayed at home and prospered there more than mine ever did in America.

Of course, I know enough to know that their privileged world, for all its urbanity and grace, was built, in significant measure, on inequity, exploitation, and a neurotic hankering after European things. And I know, too, that as a woman born and bred in Lebanon, even in a progressive Christian family, wading in the moonlight with a lover would not necessarily have been a carefree way to spend the evening. Perhaps the romance of Beirut was always a delicacy best savored by foreigners—the tourist, the expatriate, the visiting professor, the junior diplomat, who were judged by different rules, as strangers always are, and allowed to shame themselves if they wished.

Still, I am hooked on the myth of Beirut as the Paris of the Arab world, on Beirut as I knew it in the summer of 1972, three years before a war that would create a new and terrible Beiruti myth. A war that would reach even to Miriam's mountain village with its grapevines, its pomegranate trees, and its tumbling stream where Miriam's children used to play.

2

KATREEN

Few places in Lebanon were spared. A hundred miles inland, on the other side of the mountains, where people look east to Damascus, rather than west to the sea, the war reached Zahle, a town so beautiful it is called the Bride of the Bekaa Valley. In Lebanon, brides are serenaded. "Ah, Zahle," its townspeople sing, with tears in their eyes and arak in their glasses; "you decorated bride, adorned by the deeds of your men!" "Oh, these men from Zahle," my mother would say when exasperated by my father, "who do they think they are?!"

In 1981, a right-wing Christian militia camped in Zahle was attacked and nearly surrounded by Syrian forces before a face-saving compromise was found. It was not half so bloody an encounter as occurred in 1860, the "year of the massacres," when throughout Mount Lebanon, Druse and Catholics, each backed by a European power, struck at each other, the Catholics getting the worst of it. In Zahle that year—so the story goes—Christian men were tricked into laying down their arms and gathering in a single building, on the pretext that their enemies wanted to talk peace. Once inside, they were mowed down, old and young, fathers and sons.

My grandmother Katreen, born eight years later, must have been brought up on the story of that bloody day when her grandfather and uncles were killed. Did it make her afraid, I wonder, or defiant or guilty just to be alive? I have no idea, because although she lived with us until her death when I was eight, took care of my brother and me while our parents went to work, I remember almost nothing about her. In pictures of her as an old woman, she is sweet of face, sitting behind my father, smiling over his shoulder at the camera. Or she is standing exposed and awkward, her arms dangling, her hands large and clumsy as mitts.

Staring at those hands, I remember that she slapped me once, whirling on me suddenly for something I had said that I didn't even know was wrong

and cannot now recall. Though there was another time—my only other
specific memory of her—when I was sick, crying because my infected ear
hurt so much, and she sat by my bed to comfort me. The throbbing pain
in my head competed with my gratitude at her surprising tenderness.

Every Sunday, my aunt and uncle (her children), would come to pay their
respects. She'd had three children in all, the oldest my father, born when
she was sixteen. All I know for sure about her husband is his name, Elias,
and that he was from a family smaller and poorer than hers. All I know
about her landowner father is that when he died, she was entitled to a daughter's portion, which amounted to half what a son would inherit. But Katreen
renounced even that, preferring it be added to her brother's share so that
he, the carrier of the family name, might prosper and increase in prestige.
It was a gesture made (hesitantly or not) by many Arab women, who looked
to their brothers, more than to their husbands, as their natural protectors
and as the source of their reflected glory.

So Katreen did the expected thing, and it might not have mattered much,
except that then her husband died, too. She was barely thirty, vigorous,
intelligent, but in her world there were few ways for women to earn even
pocket money and none that would not mortify the pride of her family. Ten
or twenty years earlier, her only option would have been to stay on as a
dependent in her brother's home, she and her children relying on his lar-
gesse and on the good will of her sister-in-law. But it was 1900, and Katreen
had another option.

For over a decade, Zahle had been a fountainhead of emigration; its young
men had helped lead the way to the United States, some going as far as
Montana to prospect for gold. More recently, women had followed. Katreen
took the chance. In the same year that Miriam's older sons sailed for America, Katreen left her mother, brother, and sisters behind as well as her in-
heritance and headed west with her children. Her destination was Boston,
partly because it already housed a community from Zahle and partly because
my father, her bookish son and now at fifteen the man of the family, had
read somewhere that Boston was the literary center of America. In Lebanon
he had been attending a residential school founded by Protestant missionaries and might have gone on to the American university if his father had
lived or his uncle had pleased. In Boston, he wound up earning a high school
diploma at night and in the day peddling notions and needlework. Eventually, he learned the printing trade and bought his own press; turning out
invoices and sales pads kept him in business, publishing the work of emigré
poets fed his soul. In his spare time, he read books on history and religion
and developed left-wing political views.

Pacing our living room, he would complain bitterly about Republicans
and Zionists, not about his own lot, at least not in my hearing. But in an
unusual outburst after his death, my mother waxed indignant at Katreen's
brother who had let her come to America to make her own way, or rather

to have her children make it for her, and at Katreen herself, too proud or family vain to claim from her brother what was rightfully hers.

Katreen's story puzzles me. How is it she had the gumption to emigrate, yet not the drive to support herself once here? Or the assertiveness before that to ask for money, if not for herself then for her children? Did the habit of deference to an older brother supersede even her ambitions for her sons? Or was my father calling the shots? Proud and headstrong, perfectly capable of cutting off his nose to spite his face, did he argue with his uncle over some real or imagined slight, then stalk off all the way to America, pulling his mother and the little ones in his wake, spurning his uncle's aid, forbidding her from seeking it?

And am I doing Katreen dirt? My older cousins, who remember her better than I do, say she was warm and sane, easy to be with, strict yes, but not stern. And even my mother used to claim that of all her in-laws, Katreen had the best understanding and was the most progressive.

I wonder now what she meant by that. There is no one to ask. I wish I had talked to Katreen about her life or to her cousin Hafeeza, who grew up with her. After they died and I was older, I wish I had been curious enough to mine the memories of my aunt or uncle or father for stories not only about Katreen's life but about their own. They are all dead now, my father for over thirty years. "We were never a family to gossip much about ourselves," says his oldest neice.

My mother's family were talkers, my mother herself a wonderful story teller who, even at the age of ninety, her voice still strong, her body limber, would spring from her chair to act out the punch line of a story. "Why don't you ride on my back?" was one of her favorites, a sarcastic rejoinder she delighted in. She would repeat it over and over to make sure I got it and to relish it fully herself, all the while bending over, hands on her knees, rear end in the air, offering her back to the buffoon of the story who had gotten his comeuppance.

Miriam was funny, said my mother, and I believe her because I see Miriam in her and in the stories she told. I see her vigor and originality. Katreen, who half raised me, seems far less real, which is too bad, because I suspect I may be more like her, a woman negotiating between lessons learned too well and the pleasures of recalcitrance. And not quite getting it right. Not yet.

3

SYRIAN EMIGRATION

In the fifty years bracketing the turn of the twentieth century, a quarter of
a million Arabic-speaking people picked up and took off for new homes
around the world, primarily in the Americas, Australia, and Africa. Of that
number, one hundred thousand entered the United States. Whatever their
destination, virtually all came from *Greater Syria* (a cluster of provinces that
had been ruled for centuries by the Ottoman Turks), some from its Palestinian sector or from Damascus, but most from the parts of *Greater Syria*
that today make up the state of Lebanon. In fact, it was Mount Lebanon,
home to both Miriam and Katreen, that started the mass migration. By the
1920s, that tiny dot on the map (2,000 square miles, half the size of Lebanon
today) had lost one-fourth of its population to emigration.[1]

That they were suddenly so footloose teases the imagination, these people
whose parents might have lived and died without ever traveling twenty miles
from home, for whom even the nearest cities were exotic destinations. (A
traditional village song begins with the compliment "Your husband, oh beautiful one, has gone to Damascus and come back, alone!") Some people, of
course, had always moved around because their livelihood demanded it. Itin-
erant weavers made the circuit of distant villages, and stone masons might
desert the mountains for months at a stretch.[2] In hard times, people had
even been known to leave for Egypt or other Arab lands. But never before
had so many traveled so far.

It would have been one thing if they were fleeing wretched conditions at
home, but by comparison with other parts of the Ottoman empire, Mount
Lebanon was not a bad place to live. After the bloodletting of 1860[3] sand
under pressure from European powers, it was granted a degree of autonomy,
and thereafter its young men were exempt from conscription and its people
protected from the exorbitant taxation and rampant lawlessness that plagued
most of *Greater Syria*. Now they had a chance to tend their crops in relative

peace, to ply their trades, and with the help of foreigners, to build roads, string telegraph wires, and start schools. Nearby, the harbor of Beirut (enlarged by the French) became a gateway through which Mount Lebanon could trade with the world. Among *Syrians*, the saying took root, "Happy is he who has even a goat's pen in Lebanon." But to say that Mount Lebanon was doing better than its neighbors is not to say that it was thriving.

By the 1880s, with an exploding population and not enough land to go around, a domestic market that increasingly preferred European goods to anything produced at home, and foreign markets that were proving equally fickle, Mount Lebanon's economy was faltering. Even silk production, its major industry, was in trouble, though two decades later Miriam was still raising silk worms at home. Every spring, a booth, its walls lined with shelves, would be built in the family orchard[4]; and clay trays, lined with straw, would be set on the shelves, ready to receive the tiny silkworm eggs.

The "seeds" came from France in little boxes. My mother would scatter them on the straw, and after a few days, you'd see these little black "threads" moving. Then she would gather tender mulberry leaves and chop them up fine, like tobacco, and sprinkle them two or three times a day for the worms to feed on. Quickly, quickly they would begin to grow and spread.

When the worms are about an inch long, they stop eating for a day or two. Then they start again. Now they begin turning white. Another few days and they fast again, then eat again. Now you have to work very hard to keep them supplied, not cutting the leaves but leaving them whole. You hear the worms feeding, like the sound of rain in the trees. A third fast, and they are hungry again. Now you have to get up at night to feed them. You're bringing whole branches in, with the leaves still on, and the worms are two inches long, fat and nice. Then you bring in [pine] shrubbery and tie it to the shelves, and after a fourth fast, each worm climbs into the shrubbery and begins to spin a silk thread from its mouth. After two or three days, there are white cocoons everywhere. The whole process takes forty days. This is as I remember it.

Hannah

Though Miriam and her neighbors were busy doing their part, silk production throughout *Syria* had already dropped off since she was a child. Mulberry trees had been attacked by locusts, silkworms by disease, and with the opening of new trade routes to the Far East, Europeans had gained access to silk as cheap as and finer than could be produced in Miriam's two-room house or reeled in Lebanon's silk factories. What was happening to the silk industry was happening, too, in other sectors of the economy. The transition from subsistence farming to cash crops (such as silk worms and the mulberry groves to feed them) had raised people's standard of living, but it had also made them vulnerable to economic forces over which they had no control.

At this critical moment, when aspirations raised by a generation or two of relative prosperity seemed likely to be frustrated, young people in Mount Lebanon (and soon other parts of *Syria*) came to believe that in some distant land lay the answer to their dreams. It was as if a door had suddenly swung open or been carelessly left ajar and through it people caught glimpses, highly colored as a postcard, of storybook places whose inhabitants led privileged lives and where they, though newcomers, could earn more money than they had ever seen.

In truth, that door had been opening gradually for over half a century, to make way for Westerners who had come on various errands to the Arab world. Poets and artists of the "Oriental" school had arrived seeking the exotic and, like other adventurers with harems on their mind, primed for sexual titillation. Merchants and diplomats had come too, peddling their several wares; pilgrims appeared (organized tours of Palestine began in the 1850s), as well as archaeologists and biblical scholars hoping to confirm the truth of holy scripture; and, not far behind them, entrepreneurs. The immigrant autobiographer Abraham Rihbany remembered that it was in the home of a French factory owner that he saw, for the first time in his life, a bedstead and wallpaper (105).

But in terms of their influence on emigration, the most important emissaries from the West were Presbyterian missionaries from New England. Not particularly successful as prosletyzers, they made their mark as physicians and, above all, as educators. But even in those secular roles, they were not universally welcome.[5] In the northern Lebanese village of Bishmizzeen, for instance, a mob of boys, egged on by the Orthodox bishop and their elders, drove the native Protestant teacher out of town and vandalized his one-room schoolhouse. Later, when the bishop refused to establish an Orthodox school in Bishmizzeen—education, he said, would only make the young unruly—the villagers invited the Protestants to return (Tannous, "Trends" 175–178). In Miriam's village, the Catholic priest was equally resentful of encroachment by Protestants and tried to prevent her from sending Elias to a mission school.

The priest said Elias had to go to a Catholic school because we were tenants then in a house that the church owned. My mother got very angry. So when I was born, she had the Protestants baptize me. Then I got sick, and my mother got worried. "Merciful *Allah*, I have only this one daughter," she said to herself. So she sent to ask a priest at the seminary if I should be rebaptized by the Catholics. He sent word back, "My daughter, whether your baby was baptized by the Protestants or the Catholics, so long as they said 'In the name of the Father, the Son, and the Holy Spirit,' all is well." So my mother was relieved.

Then when Naseeb was born, they baptized him in the Protestant church, too. I used to say, that was because I turned out so well.

Hannah

The missionaries' most celebrated legacy is the American University of Beirut (established in 1866 as the Syrian Protestant College); in time, they also founded a press that turned out Arabic Bibles, religious tracts, and textbooks. Together, the two institutions helped inspire, among an educated elite, a lively commerce of new ideas in politics and literature. So lively, in fact, that in 1880 it invited Ottoman censorship and persecution. (With the sultan's hand raised against them, a number of *Syrian* writers moved on to Egypt or the United States, from which outposts they spearheaded an Arab literary and journalistic renaissance.)

But of more significance to average families were the American elementary and secondary schools concentrated in Mount Lebanon, and the native-run schools fashioned after them.

In the old country, I went to Teacher Rasha—she was Protestant—who had a school in her home. Naseeb went with me. We used to walk to school every day, carrying our lunches and a book bag. In the morning we studied arithmetic and Arabic; in the afternoon we studied English. I was very good in arithmetic.

George S— and his older brother—you know them—were in my class at Teacher Rasha's. There were ten of us altogether, and we'd stand in a row to recite. If one didn't know his lesson, the next in line would be asked. If the second child could answer correctly, the teacher would say, "Pull [the first one's] ear and go stand in front of him." Oh, how often I pulled the ear of George's brother!

Hannah

The Protestants seemed to be everywhere, but they were not the only foreign missions with schools in *Syria*. By the 1890s, when my father was a boy, his home town of Zahle (the largest in Mount Lebanon) had foreign schools representing Roman Catholic, Russian Orthodox, British Anglican, and American Protestant churches, as well as a Jesuit college and two libraries, one run by Jesuits, the other by Americans (Naff 37).

Though the American missionaries seem not to have explicitly encouraged emigration ("Oh, mother of Rashid, how can you leave such a beautiful country?" one of them asked Miriam), in themselves and through their textbooks and curriculum they helped plant the United States in the imaginations of thousands of people throughout *Syria* and, at the same time, though perhaps inadvertently, began the process of acculturating them to American society.

With all the pieces in place—a reason to leave, a place to go, a fantasy to be realized—it took only a precipitating event to start the ball of emigration rolling, and that event seems, in retrospect, to have been the Centennial Exposition of 1876, held in Philadelphia. Among the exhibitors were *Syrian* and, more specifically, Palestinian merchants who found a ready market for the icons, rosaries, and crosses from the Holy Land that they had brought with them. Word of their success and of the opportunities available in America quickly spread from the merchant class in the cities to peasants in remote villages. By the 1880s, *Syrians*—hundreds and then thousands each year—began coming to America not only from mountain villages and market towns, but from Damascus, Beirut, and Jerusalem.

Most who came—90 percent or more—were Christian, a statistic that has been accounted for in various ways. Some have held that the bloodshed of 1860 had frayed the Christians' ties to home. Others, adopting an opposite tack, have argued that Christians, through mostly poor, were generally not so poor as Muslims and thus were better able to afford overseas passage. But the most widely credited explanation has been that Christians—simply by virtue of their religion—already felt or could easily cultivate some sense of kinship with the West and, in any case, were more likely to have come under the influence of American (and European) missionaries. Muslims, on the other hand, would probably think twice before casting their lot among people who did not share their faith, might be hostile, and, worst of all, might corrupt the hearts and minds of their children.[6]

Whether Muslim or Christian, the first adventurers to America had to improvise since there was no established mechanism in place to guide them. But by the 1890s, an impromptu network of *Syrian* steamship agents and translators, money-changers and money-lenders, hotel keepers, restaurateurs, and purveyors of other services—licit and illicit—stretched from mountain villages to Beirut and across the Mediterranean, helping to route traffic from the Near East and sometimes, if it meant greater profits, to misroute it. Jiryas was not the only one to set sail for the United States and make shore elsewhere.[7]

Like Jiryas, most of the first to arrive in America probably did not intend to stay. Their plan was to work for several years, accumulate a nest egg, and then return home to buy land or build a fine house, and generally lead a more comfortable life. Confidence in the feasibility of that plan was reinforced every time a neighbor or relative returned to *Syria* in Western dress, with money in hand, and an undisputed right to center stage. Letters from abroad, with remittances enclosed, were also powerful persuaders.[8] The reputed success of two or three brothers might trigger the wholesale departure of up to a hundred from a single village or town (Naff 91). The American adventure and the dividends it paid had become part of the everyday competition for status and wealth.

Into the early years of the twentieth century, a common toast among Arab Americans was "May your return home be soon," to which the proper response was "In your company." Before World War I, perhaps a quarter of those entering the States did return home as planned,[9] but not necessarily for good. Most of them—like Jiryas and Miriam—eventually settled in the West, sometimes after criss-crossing the ocean several times. The few who had come primarily in search of political freedom and stability probably knew from the start that they were emigrating permanently, as did those who came to escape service in the Ottoman army (from 1908 on, some Christians were subject for the first time to conscription). But finally, it was the war itself that put an end to the dream of return. The devastation it wrought—half the population of Mount Lebanon succumbed to starvation or disease—meant that home had become bitterly inhospitable, a place to flee. After the Armistice, *Syrian* immigration, which had been nearly extinguished by the war, surged again as newcomers arrived and families separated by the war were reunited. Soon it fell off again, discouraged first by new American laws limiting immigration and then, even more decisively, by the Great Depression. In the 1930s, immigration records show an average of only about 120 *Syrians* a year entering the United States.[10]

It had been a great adventure strung out over half a century. But its brief telling glosses over the unprecedented personal and family tensions it gave rise to and the casualties it created among those left behind: grandparents, afraid of dying alone, who held on fiercely to at least one grandchild (surety that the child's parents would return); village girls whose sweethearts disappeared and forgot to send for them; angry wives and husbands who were abandoned or to whom long loneliness felt like abandonment.

My father's son Assaf [from a previous marriage] had gone off to America. One day his wife brought their son and came from her village to ours. My mother welcomed her—*"Ahlan wa sahlan."* Then his wife said, "I've come to leave this boy with you. I can't raise him by myself." He was young, only about seven years old. My mother said, "Yes, leave him here." (I was listening to everything.) Assaf's wife stayed all day and then got up to go. She said to the boy, "Good-bye, I'm going to leave you here," and then she went as far as some high bushes and hid behind them to see what her son would do. She saw him crying, and she didn't have the heart to go. So she came back and said, "All right, come with me." That was the only time I saw him, and then we came to America.

Hannah

Other casualties of the "American fever" included those for whom emigration never quite worked; who, once uprooted, could never again find home.

After we were in America, my brother Alexander used to get restless. "What kind of place is this?" he'd say. "I'm going to our own country, Christ's country." (He was always reading the Bible.) So he saved his money, bought a ticket, and went home. Then a letter came: "As soon as the ship started on its way, my heart sank, and I said to myself, 'Why did I leave?' " After a while he came back. He did that three or four times, the last time just before World War II. He left then and never came back. Naseeb used to look after him, but he didn't try very hard to bring him over.

"Why should I," Naseeb would say, "when as soon as he gets here, he'll want to go back again?" So Naseeb sent him money care of our cousins, and we heard that once a month he'd come down from the village into Beirut to pick it up, just like a worker collecting his pay.

Hannah

4

WOMEN IMMIGRANTS

One day when Hannah was a little girl and sitting on the low stone wall outside her house, an old woman she barely knew came by and stopped to quiz her.

"Is your mother still in America, my love?"

"Yes, auntie, she is."

"And do you hear news of her, my soul? Do your brothers write?"

"Sometimes they do, auntie."

"And when is she coming back, joy of my eyes?"

"I don't know, auntie."

"Ah, poor child, has no one told you? Your mother has found a new husband, she has a new baby. She is never coming back."

Alone with her secret, too terrified to tell anyone what the woman had said or to ask if it was true, Hannah waited to see if Miriam would return.

(My mother told me that story when she was over ninety. I think it was the first time she had ever told it to anyone.)

If Miriam—who had come to America to visit her sons—was subject to such scandal-mongering (and Hannah to such cruelty), what must have been said of women who crossed the ocean on their own, without benefit of her excuse or an equally good one? In a society where male protection and patronage were essential guarantors of a woman's respectability, to go alone among strangers—especially for young, unmarried women—was a daring if not brazen act.

It is no surprise, then, that at first, *Syrian* emigration to America was the project of men, mostly young and single, and of a much smaller number of

women. But in a short time, the ratio of women to men began to climb. By
the turn of the century, one out of every three *Syrians* who entered the
United States was female, a figure that held steady until just before World
War I, when the percentage of men soared, swelled by those of draft age
who were bent on avoiding service in the Ottoman army.

The percentage of *Syrian* women arriving on American soil—higher than
in comparable ethnic groups[1]—has usually been accounted for with little
difficulty. The theory is that the first *Syrian* men here, out to make as much
money as they could as quickly as they could, soon realized that it made
sense to send for wives or sisters or daughters, whose earnings could sup-
plement their own and thus hasten the day of their return. The tendency to
send for women (or bring them along in the first place), it is said, only
accelerated as time went on and it became increasingly clear that the family's
future lay in America. Thus, after the Armistice, women immigrants actually
outnumbered men, as wives whom the war had stranded overseas were at
last able to join their husbands in the United States.

The major deficiency of these explanations, or of the terms in which they
are cast, is that they reinforce the idea of men as trail blazers, and women
as followers and dependents who came when summoned and not before.
Few writers acknowledge that even early on, a number of women, both
married and single, traveled westward on their own. Some may have done
so at the behest of husband or father (an "evil" commented upon in the
immigrant press[2]). But many others seem to have been acting on their own
initiative and for the same reasons as men. Above all, the siren call of riches.
True, they soon discovered that even in America gold was not to be had for
the gathering, but cash was indeed to be had for the earning if they were
willing to work hard. Then after several years away, a woman might return
home in triumph, as a certain "Aunt Mary" did one day in 1903. Her niece,
interviewed by historian Alixa Naff, remembers the figure Aunt Mary cut:

> My aunt had made a lot of money peddling [in America]. . . . Ho! She was dressed
> and fixed [up] . . . she was about twenty-four, twenty-five years old . . . she was in her
> prime and glory, . . . silk and ostrich feathers and diamonds and a watch pinned to
> her chest . . . she was dressed to the hilt. (N. Simon)

Flamboyant Aunt Mary must have planted ideas in the minds of more than
one young woman.

But I imagine it was not just money and the things it could buy that sent
them on their way. Women, like men, must have been tempted by the sheer
adventure of crossing the ocean and of seeing America with their own eyes.
They, too, had heard marvelous stories of the United States and, in some
cases, had come under the influence of American missionaries who had always targeted women and girls for special attention. It was at a mission
school in Sidon, for instance, that lecturer and writer Rahme Haidar first

learned about the United States. "I often pictured the beauties of the new land," she later wrote, "—not only a land of liberty, but a land of opportunity, and the desire to sail forth to its shores grew keener and keener. I had become enamoured with everything Occidental" (26).[3]

Saleemie Yazgie, born in 1868, was also educated in mission schools, including a teachers' training academy, after which she taught small children for two years or so before marrying and starting a family. According to her great-granddaughter Paula Hajar, "It had been Saleemie's dream, for years and years, to come to America, and she was always lobbying for that at home" (interview).

Her husband, a descendant of famous poets but, himself, a horse-trader, liked his life as it was and "would always say no." He relented only when a disaster—fire or theft—cost him his livelihood. Just after the turn of the century, a plan was laid whereby Saleemie, accompanied by her oldest daughter, would lead the way to Lawrence, Massachusetts (sometimes called "Immigrant City"), where an unmarried sister had preceded her. Five years later, after working all the while in textile mills, Saleemie and her daughter had saved enough money to reunite the family in America, but at Ellis Island her husband was diagnosed with trachoma and sent back. On the return trip he got as far as Naples, where he died.

Paula never knew her great-grandmother, but older relatives have passed on stories of how "forward-looking" she was and how she wanted to be the first in her circle to buy a car. Based on family lore, Paula concludes that "Saleemie's sense of adventure was stronger than her need to stay secure. Her first need, I think, was to get going. And to see what she could squeeze out of her world" (interview).

Saleemie's story tells about one woman's determination and daring. But it also suggests that even when couples emigrated together, it might not always be at the instigation of the husband. How much more reasonable to assume that *Syrian* women, too, could dream of faraway places and that, like women everywhere, often had their say and sometimes their way in important family decisions. At last, if not at first, Miriam was just as eager as Jiryas to emigrate, and she pushed for it.

Saleemie was not the typical immigrant woman. But in essentials, neither was she unique. Recently I happened to see an older cousin, and since such things were on my mind, I asked her if she knew when her husband's parents (natives of Zahle, Lebanon) had come to this country. It was in the 1890s, she said, that her mother-in-law had arrived. I asked about her father-in-law. No, my cousin said, he hadn't wanted to, so his wife came on her own and left the children at home with him; she'd heard there was "good money to be made" in America. And (according to my cousin) she made it, peddling linens and lingerie, and then, after three years or so, sent for her husband and her two daughters. Since there was no arguing with her success, they came.[4] Such anecdotes could be multiplied many times; wherever a com-

munity of Arab Americans is found, similar stories are told.[5] In fact, according to historian Afif Tannous, half the women who left his village took that
step independently. "Some of them were single," he says, "some were wid-
ows, and some left their husbands and children at home" ("Emigration" 72).

Tannous quotes from a pathetic letter sent by a woman whose child had
stayed behind—no mention is made of a husband—while she adventured to
America. To her kinsman in Bishmizzeen, the woman writes,

The news of my son's death has broken my heart and my life. . . . He was my only
child. I brought him up until he was married, and then prevented him from sailing
to America, as I did not want to expose him to any danger. I sailed away in his place,
and have been laboring for years to gather some money on which his children could
grow up comfortably. ("Emigration" 69)

There is no reason to question the reasons this woman gives for her sojourn
overseas, and who could doubt her grief? But is it farfetched to imagine that
her motives in coming to America were mixed and that she might have been
secretly glad of the chance to sail away, to be on her own, and to test her
mettle? Whatever the truth of that supposition, her letter does show how
traditional female values—in this case, self-sacrifice—could be invoked to
justify bold new undertakings by women.

In other cases, a young woman or her family might give out the story that
she was sailing to America to keep house for her brother or to earn money
on which her parents might live more comfortably. Promoting the welfare
of those to whom she owed duty and deference was a high female virtue.
But sometimes it concealed the unstated (shameful to state) truth that she
was looking for a husband. As the American fever intensified, many villages
in Mount Lebanon were being stripped of eligible men and turning, as one
historian has said, into "shelters for senior citizens" (Saliba 1983, 39). A
young woman might get tired of waiting for the right young man to return
and claim her or for a letter from America announcing a match arranged on
her behalf.

On the same ship with the girl hoping for a good marriage, might be a
woman trying to escape a bad one—someone like poet Kahlil Gibran's
mother, who brought her four children to Boston, leaving her ne'er-do-well
husband behind in Besharri, Mount Lebanon (Gibran 23). Or it might be
someone like the grandmother (in Vance Bourjaily's semifictional memoir)
who, at the age of twenty, ran away from the husband to whom she had
been married off at fourteen; hand in hand with her five-year-old son, she
"walked barefoot across mountains, . . . worked in Beirut to save passage
money," then sailed for America (236). Even when a woman left home with
her husband's blessing or in accordance with a scheme he had hatched, her
heart might harbor desires that he knew nothing about. As the immigrant
journalist Afifa Karam wrote in 1910, some women might go along with

their husbands' plans because they thought it their duty to obey, but others might agree only because they saw in those plans a route of escape from all husbandly commands. "In the second case," Karam warned the *Syrian* man, "[your wife embarks] not for your sake but to promote her own happiness and pleasure" ("Syrian Immigration" III). What seems clear is that to women dissatisfied in their marriages or restless and unhappy for whatever reason, America offered new options never before available; as my grandmother Katreen perceived, it was a land where one could begin again.

Of course, to say that women came on their own is not necessarily to imply that they were acting with total autonomy; usually they had their family's approval or acquiescence. Nor did their adventure amount to leaping off into a great unknown, with no one to catch them or break their fall. Most women, like most men, selected a destination where they could picture a familiar face, where someone—a distant cousin, an uncle's wife, a former neighbor—would take them in for a while or rent them a room and give them pointers about making it in America. But despite such support, removal to the United States could bring a lone woman more misery than she had bargained for—or so said Karam. What appalled her was not just the heavy responsibility borne by a woman alone or even her lonely longing for her children and kin, but rather the compromising moral position she occupied. "She suffers in resisting her critics and corrupters," Karam wrote. "She suffers in refuting the accusations of evil tongues. And if she is a beauty, her suffering increases manifold" ("Syrian Immigration" III).

When ocean separated husband and wife, gossips on either continent had a windfall to feast on. (Witness Miriam's case.) Sometimes the rumors bruited about were true. Karam spoke (more openly than some liked) about the sexual temptations assaulting those who suddenly found themselves far from home and its constraining influences. Even en route, an inexperienced woman might fall prey to a pimp, wrote Karam, and be led to "heinous deeds and vices." She cited horrific instances of women who "fell," as well as of one woman, "an example to her sex," who threw herself from a moving train rather than succumb to a would-be ravisher. But rape and prostitution aside, Karam believed that a married woman with no husband by her side to support her, share her struggles, and answer her sexual yearnings might well be susceptible to romantic seduction; "a woman is a human being . . . of flesh and blood," she warned husbands, "and has a beating heart" ("Syrian Immigration" III). These are sentiments and stories of a sort conspicuously absent from usual Arab American myth.

Despite Karam's alarmist editorializing, *Syrian* women who came to America on their own were always a minority. For each one of them, whether wayfarer or immigrant, many more waited at home for their husband's return or for a letter with a steamship ticket enclosed. Some waited in vain. (I have often wondered if Hassan, son of Jiryas, ever reappeared to comfort his wife and care for his child.)[6]

Sometimes broken promises were due to treachery, forgetfulness, or the seductiveness of new people and places. But not always. Political upheavals, which ordinary people could not foresee and over which they had no control, also intervened. With the onset of World War I and the disruption of civilian traffic across the Atlantic, separations perhaps meant to last only a couple of years stretched longer. Meanwhile, life for those left behind gradually became a nightmare. Once the Ottomans entered the war on the side of Germany, the Allied Powers imposed a death-dealing blockade along the *Syrian* coast, preventing the entry of food or medicine. The effect was most cruelly felt by *Syrian* villagers whose own crops were confiscated to feed Turkish soldiers or consumed by locusts. Survivors interviewed by Gregory Orfalea told of harvesting lemon and orange peels from garbage heaps, of gleaning hay from horse dung, of people murdering or being murdered for a piece of bread (1988, 66).

With so many able-bodied men overseas, women, children, the frail, and the elderly were often left to fend for themselves. Many did not make it. Disease joined with starvation to decimate the population. By some estimates, one-fourth of Lebanon's inhabitants—100,000 people—did not survive the war.

In his autobiography, the immigrant writer Salom Rizk (1909–1973) remembers that in the middle of the war, his grandmother and uncle set out on an expedition over the mountains to bring back wheat to their hungry neighbors. Weeks later, they returned, their mission accomplished. "Almost half the village ran down the hill to greet them. [My grandmother] we greeted with great shouts of joy, and smothered her feet in kisses. She was hailed as a Joseph bringing salvation to a starving village" (44–45).

Like Rizk's grandmother, many women in *Syria* took on responsibilities that they had never dreamed of. Often they alone bore the brunt of caring for their parents and their children. Mary Kfouri Malouf used to leave behind a single loaf of bread to sustain her children while she scouted miles around for food. During one of her absences, a son died; two weeks later, another. The tragedy was unremitting. One day Mary's daughter saw a woman dig a hole under a tree. "I was watching her. She go in the house; she take her son, put him in the hole, and cover him. Right in front of her house under the tree" (Orfalea 1988, 66–67).

Equally harrowing scenes occur in a recent family memoir by Elmaz Abinader, its principal chapters set in World War I. In 1914, Abinader's grandmother Mayme and her daughter were left behind in Lebanon when her debt-ridden husband sailed for America. In his absence, she gave birth to a second girl, tended her dying mother, and also cared for his parents in their last illness. She also lost almost everything she had to her husband's creditors and was reduced to living in the cellar of the fine house that she and her husband (the former village sheik) had once owned.

But Mayme had held back some jewels, and once a week she left her girls and traveled over rough mountain roads to Tripoli to barter an expensive bracelet or ring for "small bags of flour, a skin of oil, a handful of salt, lentils, and rice."

Behind the church Mayme wrapped the food in her bag and placed it under her skirts, between her legs, . . . She would be lucky if the Turkish soldiers didn't search her; she would be blessed if they didn't rape her. (151)

Human connections were tested during the war; in their extremity, neighbors hardened their hearts against one another. Worse yet, family members sometimes forgot the claims of blood kinship, or abandoned their posts in despair. Mayme's sister-in-law, whose husband was also in America, ran away, no one knew where, leaving her two daughters to shift for themselves. Within weeks, they both died of influenza. Out of terror at not being able to feed his own twelve children, Mayme's brother-in-law Rachid, the one who had not gone to America, turned on her. "Nothing is yours anymore," he told her (159).

Although Arab American historians have told and retold the story of *Syrian* immigration in the late nineteenth and early twentieth centuries, they have paid little specific attention to women immigrants of that era. Certainly, they have understated the initiative those women displayed, either in coming to this continent as independent agents or in helping shape the decisions that sent husbands, couples, and eventually families on their way. By the same token, though historians have briefly referred to the hardships that World War I brought to Syria and Lebanon, their purpose in doing so has usually been simply to explain the surge of emigration that followed the war. Orfalea has movingly detailed that suffering, but even he has not dwelled on its consequences for women, the hard lessons it taught them about survival and self-sufficiency, the new roles it forced on them. These were women many of whom would subsequently emigrate to America with memories that set them apart from those who had come before and with a sense of deliverance that many earlier immigrants had not felt. Mayme's first act when she reached her husband and her new home in Uniontown, Pennsylvania, was to kneel and kiss the ground.

Mayme's generation of women and those that came before her are worth remembering. For Arab Americans in particular, it matters that our history here began with women who knew more, felt more, and did more than has usually been acknowledged. Paula Hajar's response to her great-grandmother Saleemie provides a good example of why stories about our forerunners—in the family or in the ethnic community—are so important. Clearly, Paula delights in Saleemie, is proud of her, and is proud too that others see a similarity between her great-grandmother and herself. "Everybody's always talking about her and always saying, 'Paula, you would have loved her.' And this lets me know what they think of me." A professional woman, in her forties and unmarried, Paula does not conform to type in her extended family. She is, in her own words, "an oddball." But with Saleemie in mind, Paula's kin can place her—even those who have spent their lives about the second-generation task of fitting in and not over-reaching. More important, Paula can place herself in a tradition reaching back three generations. As maverick, she is Saleemie's legitimate heir.

In similar fashion, women of Arab ancestry in America want to feel ourselves, spiritually if not physically, a part of our ethnic community, but at the same time need role models from our collective past that will, implicitly, give us permission to be oddballs—to see what *we* can squeeze out of our world even if we have to break a few rules to do it.

5

PEDDLERS

"You can make money here"—that was the message America flashed across the seas to *Syria*. There were other messages—about technology, democracy, education—that stirred the imaginations of various people at various times. But drowning them out, almost always, was the no-nonsense promise of American dollars.

Often the message was distorted or incomplete, embroidered with tales of streets paved in gold, barely audible about the effort that would be a condition of survival in America. But those acting on the message were mostly peasants, used to long hours of labor, whose lives had never been easy; hard work might surprise, but it could not daunt. The important fact was that in America their labor could bear fruit. Even in sweatshops or factories, most were less conscious of being exploited than they were of the opportunity to save enough cash to return home in style. If they decided to stay, their frugality stood them in good stead.

It did not take very long for *Syrians* to realize that women, as well as men, could earn cash in America. Without that ability, there would have been no independent exodus by women, no ready escape from abusive husbands, and far fewer separations of mother and child.

Perhaps the opportunities for women were understood more quickly because *Syrian* men in America so often entered occupations that were also open to women: mill work, garment making, shopkeeping, and peddling. In Boston's Arab community, peddlers were a familiar sight.

Many of the women went peddling, carrying a big bag with lots of merchandise—laces, thread, stockings. They went from door to door carrying the bags on their shoulders and taking the streetcars wherever they went. They didn't know how to read the signs on the cars, so they went by the colors. This color car goes to Cambridge, this other color to Chelsea, another color to Winthrop. In the evening, they'd leave their bags in the dry goods store where they bought their merchandise.

Hannah

But it was not just Boston. At one point or another, many of the first
Syrians throughout America—some would say most—peddled for a living.[1]
It was an occupation that made sense for people in a hurry to make money
but with no special training (they could begin at once), no capital (they took
merchandise on consignment), and little English (their wares spoke for
themselves). It was also a business easy to liquidate whenever they decided
to return home. Since at first that was almost everyone's intention, an itin-
erant lifestyle in the meantime was no great evil.

My mother was familiar with urban peddlers, most of whom went out
each morning and returned home each evening. Others made longer excur-
sions that kept them on the road for days, weeks, or—in rural areas—even
months at a time. According to Alixa Naff, the prime authority on the subject, women out for the day would go in pairs or groups but on longer trips
would travel under the protection of men, "at least one of whom was a close
relative or family friend; in this way, their honor and self-respect were safe-
guarded" (178).

But there must have been exceptions to this pattern. Gregory Orfalea's
grandmother Nazera, her parents dead and her siblings moved away, was
part of an all-female interstate operation. According to Orfalea, "She hooked
up with a couple of other Arab immigrant girls ... hung a peddler's tray
from her neck stuffed with beads, cheap necklaces, toilet water, and yes, vials
of holy water, and the group was off making the circuit of the five boroughs
of New York" (Orfalea 1987, 177). Later, having added cigarettes, snuff, and
exotic perfumes to their wares, the troupe expanded their route throughout
the Northeast and as far west as Cleveland.

It is no surprise that Nazera's stock-in-trade included holy water. From
the very beginning, *Syrians* had been capitalizing on the one feature of their
background that was immediately both familiar and attractive to Americans,
their association with the Holy Land. Rihbany made much of it in his autobiography; Kahlil Gibran consciously cast himself in the role of prophet
from the East; and peddlers hawked crosses, icons, and rosaries, often produced in New York but always advertised as made in Jerusalem. As for Nazera's holy water, she blessed it herself.

Other merchandise carried by peddlers was more mundane. Housewives
relied on peddlers for notions (thread, combs, shoelaces, and such), needlework, and dry goods; farm families living in remote areas were happy to have
a selection of workshirts, aprons, and fabrics brought right to their door.
Wherever people had money for luxuries, there was a market for the more
up-scale items that the most ambitious peddlers eventually carried—laces,
imported linens, and even oriental rugs.

Peddlers roamed city and countryside from the Atlantic seaboard as far
west as the Dakotas and Montana and deep into the South. At first, they
traveled long distances on foot (following railroad tracks) or if more pros-

perous, by buggy, and spent the night in deserted train depots, in empty schoolhouses, or in the farmhouses and barns of their customers. Sometimes they had to fend off unfriendly animals or would-be robbers; always they had to cope with weather. Naff retells stories of "icicles forming on moustaches; of women's frozen long skirts slashing cold ankles; of men forced to sleep in their buggies, who froze to death" (182, 183). Urban peddlers out for the day had less to contend with, but even their rounds could be both physically and emotionally exhausting. Peddling was not for everyone.

In 1912, when Alice Nackley was twelve years old, she tried it and didn't like it. Her mother had died that year, and her father, who had been his wife's peddling partner, was uneasy about carrying on alone. "My mother spoke better English than my father," Alice told me. "She was the one that had the personality, she was the one that earned the bread and butter." So Alice and her father made their way to Cape Cod that summer and hired a horse and buggy to take them from village to village and house to house. While her father showed his handmade tablecloths, bedspreads, and dresser scarves to the lady of the house, Alice peddled handkerchiefs with pointed lace to the servants. Sixty-five years later, Alice still remembered the kindness of people like the young matron who invited her in for "a glass of milk and a nice piece of chocolate cake, just like fudge"; or the boardinghouse keeper, "a little, short, roly-poly, with the sunbonnet on and the gathered apron, like what you see on the margarine package," who gave Alice her own bed. But Alice was young, shy of strangers, and afraid of animals like the bull dog that came roaring at her one day, reducing her to howls and tears. "We sold our merchandise that summer," she recalled, "but I told dad I wouldn't go out again if I was to make a thousand dollars a day."

Still, other girls not much older than Alice took happily to the road. "Unmarried girls, they all did it," Alice told me, "and they did very well. I remember your Aunt Josephine way back in those days. She used to have a bag she'd carry to the subway to go sell merchandise all by herself. She was a worker!"

My Aunt Josephine, who reluctantly retired at the age of eighty, was one of an elite who took peddling (though she wouldn't call it that) about as far as it could go. Introduced to the road by her immigrant father, she made a career of selling fine linens, hand-detailed silk lingerie, and eventually designer dresses to wealthy New England women, usually in their homes, often at the summer spas they frequented, occasionally on their yachts, and—when I knew her—always by appointment. Her customers, she bragged, were "big people," "multi-multi-millionaires," but all the nicer for that, she said, and every mother's daughter of them was "the most beautiful girl you ever saw!"

Josephine's husband (my Uncle Shikri) who quit his job to keep her books, pack and tote her merchandise, and provide companionship on the road, generally seconded her accounts, but on occasion he could be subversive.

He liked to tell about the time a customer to whom they'd been showing their wares all morning asked them to wait while she had lunch, it apparently never occurring to her that they, too, might be hungry. Nor could they grab a bite nearby since this customer lived in splendid isolation on an island. Rich or poor (my uncle concluded), Americans were jackasses, twice over.

Setting up her appointments, going to New York for the spring showings, Aunt Josephine always struck me as a glamorous anachronism in an age of shopping malls and shop-by-phone. By 1910, when she was a teenager, the peddling culture in which she had her roots had reached its peak and was probably already in decline; after World War I, far fewer immigrants shouldered the peddler's heavy pack. Even housewives in remote areas now had other tastes and other ways to shop, whether in person or by mail, and *Syrians*, themselves, were settling down and turning to more "respectable" pursuits. As Naff has said, "At the same time the *Syrian* was outgrowing his trade, American society was outgrowing his services" (200).

But for three decades, peddling had done well by a significant number of *Syrians*, though just how well, it is difficult to say. Naff calculates that in the decade between 1899 and 1910, a peddler earned, on average, at least $1,000 annually (about four times as much as a farmer and one-and-a-half times as much as a miner, salesperson, or factory worker) (197). By the turn of the century, says Naff, *Syrian* peddlers as a group were grossing at least sixty million dollars a year (197).[2]

Whatever the sum, it is impossible to know how much of it was being taken in by women or even how many women peddled. For instance, a 1903 report said that peddling was still the most popular occupation of New York City's *Syrians* and that over a third of the peddlers were women (Miller 40). But even if reliable, this report does not necessarily tell us much about *Syrians* in other parts of the country.

Statistics aside, a consensus of those who have studied the trade and those who remember it holds that women who peddled (whatever their number) did as well as men and often better. Perhaps that was because homemakers felt more comfortable buying personal items or domestic notions from a woman or because a woman at the door was less threatening than a man or a more plausible object of sympathy.

Aunt Mary of the feathers and silks, however, seems to have relied less on sympathy than on her own daring. According to her niece, Aunt Mary even peddled to fancy women in Fort Wayne brothels "because there was so much profit in it." Other peddlers, "they don't dare go in." One way or another, Aunt Mary earned enough to bring over and support her niece, her nephew, and then their father, for whom she opened a grocery store, just as she later opened a pool hall for her niece's husband to run (N. Simon).

Aunt Mary had a good head for business. So did James Ansara's grandmother, who was peddling at about the same time in Lowell, Massachusetts. Illiterate, widowed, with a large brood of children and stepchildren to care for, she did so well, Mr. Ansara told me, that she came to own substantial property in the city. His wife (not of Arab descent) told me about her first woman-to-woman talk with this formidable in-law.

When we first met, after Jim and I were married, she called me into her bedroom, and the first thing she said was, "You know, Jimmy give you twenty dollar a week for the house. You put five dollar"—and she pointed to the pocket of her apron—"you put five dollar away, but you do not tell Jimmy, you do not tell. You save it up, you buy a tenement. You save up some more, you buy another tenement." Which was an indication to me of how she had painfully, painstakingly acquired her property and was able to take care of all her children. As she peddled away, she must have tithed herself.

Meanwhile, in the neighboring town of Lawrence, novelist Vance Bourjaily's grandmother was also peddling, making enough money to put her son through private school. Monte Bourjaily grew up to be a well-known journalist and the ghostwriter of Eleanor Roosevelt's daily column, "My Day" (Orfalea 1988, 132). As it happens, William Peter Blatty, author of the _Exorcist_, also has a peddler in his past. His mother Mary, a _Syrian_ immigrant with a personality so overbearing that it drove her husband from home, supported her child by peddling quince jams and jellies on the streets of New York. Once, says Blatty, when FDR was in town to open the Queens Midtown Tunnel, Mary broke through the crowd to force a jar of "homemake jelly for when you have company" on the astonished president (10).[3]

The guardians of public morality in America would not have been amused by Blatty's mother, much less impressed. To their mind, peddling was morally suspect and implicitly un-American. In his 1903 report on the New York community, for instance, Lucius Miller put the case this way:

By its very nature [peddling] tends to irregular habits of life. The returns are irregular, often in the nature of a lottery, and this lessens perseverance and increases dependence upon fortuity. On rainy days and in the winter season, work of this sort is, of course, out of the question, which means idleness and all its attendant ills. The work itself encourages overreaching and deceit. (41)

Of all the charges compressed into that short paragraph, the claim that peddlers, male and female, were deceitful may have been the most common. It is found, for instance, in an 1899 report of the Associated Charities of Boston, warning tender-hearted American housewives not to be taken in by the pathetic fictions of _Syrian_ peddlers.

Some peddlers may well have been actors and con artists; there is nothing surprising in that. And no doubt few had scruples about charging what the market would bear. But the Boston complaint that _Syrians_ "always find an excuse for refusing work, even when offered them, as long as they can earn more by peddling" (Associated Charities of Boston, 59) is hardly damning.

Who could blame them? This was, more or less, the response of Louise Houghton who in 1911 made a detailed study of *Syrians* in America. In her opinion, the *Syrian* preference for peddling was neither astonishing nor deplorable.

The peddler is a free man—more often, no doubt, a free woman. Why should she give up the open air, the broad sky, the song of birds, and the smile of flowers, the right to work or to rest at her own pleasure, [in order] to immure herself within four noisy walls and be subject to the strict regime of the clock? Why should she who has been a whole person, and her own person, become a mere "hand," and that the hand of another?[4] (648)

To Houghton, the peddler was a romantic figure traveling the open road. To the author of the Boston report, the peddler was a parasite feeding off honest folk who worked for a living. But what irritated the Boston author as much as anything was the gender of the peddlers.

Who has not seen these dark-complexioned women, with black kerchiefs over their heads and baskets under their arms, getting in or out of the electric cars? . . . . They sometimes take their babies with them, but more often leave them behind, to be looked after by their idle husbands. . . . It is not the custom in this country to let the women work and have the men remain idle at home. (57–58)

Perhaps some women were being exploited by their husbands. (Afifa Karam certainly thought so, though she had in mind husbands who stayed in *Syria* while sending their wives overseas in their stead.) But perhaps, too, some families had figured out that it made sense for the person, of either sex, who could earn the most to set about doing it. Perhaps the writers had their facts wrong to begin with. One might put more stock in their reports were it not for the unabashed racism with which they write. The peddling women in Boston are guilty, among other things, of being "dark-complexioned"; the seclusion of the *Syrian* colony is bad, we are told, because it encourages *Syrians* "to live their life, not ours" (58). And Miller instructs us that "the Oriental [i.e., the *Syrian*] . . . is especially apt to confuse liberty with license" (50).

Still, these remarks are temperate when compared to a report issued by the federal government in 1901, which described *Syrian* peddling as an enterprise of "merchants (so-called) whose cupidity and indolence reinforced by exaggerated patriarchal authority, enables them to make use of the pleasing appearance, glib tongues and insinuating manner of their women" (in Kayal and Kayal, 92). In one feverish sentence, this writer manages a double-pronged indictment of the Oriental woman as both victim of male domination and dangerous seductress. After him, one turns with relief to Houghton's calm rhetoric.

In general it is the women who peddle, because women can more easily find entrance into houses than men; but in the majority of cases a woman peddler is not the drudge of an idle husband who lives upon her hard earnings. . . . The husband too was a peddler until their joint economies enabled him to open a little store somewhere. The wife goes on with her peddling, but she is at once the partner and the agent of her husband.[5] (650)

Syrians themselves, it should be added, also had misgivings about peddling, but their concerns centered on the impropriety of a woman's leaving the protection of her home to walk the streets and have commerce with strangers. In 1899, the issue was troubling enough to be tackled in the pages of *Al-Huda*, the leading Arabic newspaper in America. Though granting that "women who take up peddling are exposed to all kinds of trials and dangers," one author suggested that a woman's honor would only shine the brighter for being tested, that idleness was a more likely source of mischief than was labor, and finally that "honest work never demeans women" ("Syrian Woman" 17, 16). In another issue of the same paper, Layyah Barakat, an educated and socially active woman, urged her sister immigrants to "find elevating work to do because the more self-reliant [a woman] is, the more people respect her." But it was not peddling she had in mind.

By work I do not mean knocking on doors bearing bags and cases because that is not considered honorable work. In fact it is often dangerous for good, simple-hearted, naïve girls who have been exposed to evil and whoredom as a result of knocking on doors. I have heard painful stories in this regard which I cannot repeat on the pages of a newspaper.

What did she suggest in place of peddling?

I advise the *Syrian* girl to leave the business of selling and to work, if she is needy, as a maid in Christian households, serving good people who belong to the cream of society. There . . . she will learn virtue and housekeeping, becoming fit to manage her own home and children in the right manner and becoming an object of pride to the members of her sex. (Barakat 1911, 19)

But housework in someone's else home appealed to very few *Syrian* women. And for many of them, peddling was too lucrative a calling to turn one's back on. The earnings it yielded enabled uneducated, untrained women who were on their own to support themselves and their children. More commonly, it enabled wives and daughters to contribute to the family project of earning enough to return home on or else to survive on in this country. With such tangible benefits to be gained and such impeccable motives to be appealed to, qualms about propriety or female modesty were quieted if not always quelled. Furthermore, peddling was a job particularly compatible with family responsibilities. A peddler could stay home with her sick child far more easily than could a mill worker or factory hand; if need be, the peddler could even take a child with her on her rounds.

Perhaps the largest claim made for peddling is that it hastened the acculturation of *Syrian* immigrants, especially of the women among them. Daily intercourse with Americans improved their English, and entering American homes familiarized them with the details and tone of domestic culture in the United States. Naff, the most energetic proponent of this theory, claims that "the most fundamental factor in the assimilation of *Syrians* in America was pack peddling" (128).

If she is right, peddling may have carried the seeds of its own destruction since, ironically, one of the lessons some peddlers learned may finally have been a disdain for their own undertaking. In 1911, Houghton hypothesized that "when the [*Syrian*] woman yields and abandons peddling for less congenial (and usually less profitable) work, she yields not to argument, but to a subtle and keen consciousness that her social standing among these incomprehensible Americans will somehow be thereby improved" (648).

When I was a child, I thought that my social standing among "Americans" would be improved if my mother quit her job (though she was not a peddler). Good mothers stayed home with their children. I knew that from my Dick-and-Jane readers and from Miss Young, my fifth-grade teacher, who never passed up a chance to moralize. (In her later years she would marry a preacher.) Working mothers, Miss Young told us, just didn't know any better. It was a reproof directed against the *Syrian* children in her class or rather against our mothers, many of whom—as she knew—were stitchers in Boston's garment factories. Already uncomfortable about my foreign family, I tried not to let on that mine was one of those negligent mothers who went to work each day. It had been her habit for as long as I could remember and, though I didn't know it then, for decades before I was born.

6

MILL GIRLS, FACTORY HANDS, AND ENTREPRENEURS

By the time I was in the fifth grade, it was her own business that Hannah went off to each day, a small sportswear factory within walking distance of home that she had started shortly after World War II, when she was fifty. The shop was Hannah's baby, her dream, her destination. It was to her what America had been to Jiryas, and like him she'd made more than one stab at getting there.

Thirty years earlier, she and Naseeb had opened a small apron factory in the East Boston neighborhood where they lived. It was Hannah's idea, prompted by worry about her brother's future. He'd shown no interest in becoming a barber, her first suggestion. Nor did he seem to be settling down to anything else. But when she suggested the apron business, he agreed.

They took over a front room in Rashid's house, and while Naseeb started in cutting fabric, Hannah stationed herself at her machine and began stitching. Wherever Elias went on his regular sales route, mostly down through West Virginia and Kentucky, he drummed up customers, many of them *Syrian* shopkeepers and dry goods merchants. Business became so good that a cousin, a sister-in-law, and several neighbors now helped Hannah sew smocks, children's dresses, and aprons of every style. Sabbagh Brothers, Inc. ("Sister" would have sounded odd) was a going concern. But soon their modest success went to their head. A "real" factory, they decided, should be in the heart of the city, not on its periphery. Elias tried to talk his sister and brother out of that notion, but they wouldn't listen. In downtown Boston, rent was steep and expenses skyrocketed. It was the beginning of the end of their venture.

This time, Hannah was determined, would be different. She began with half a dozen sewing machines in a suburban storefront, then added a family of new machines to fell hems, pink or overlock seams, tack on buttons or make buttonholes, and taught herself to run them. Her oldest nephew worked the new pressing machine.

With orders coming in regularly now, Hannah expanded into the storefront next door, installed more machines, and recruited more stitchers, mostly neighborhood women for whom her shop was tailor made. They could walk to work (instead of riding the cars downtown); if they had small children in school, Hannah let them go home when school let out; if they needed money, she lent them small sums, interest-free. Every day at noon, Hannah and her workers pulled out their brown bags, put on the coffee, and crowded around the heavy oak table that had once filled her dining room at home. Between bites of hard boiled egg, pickled turnips, and Syrian bread, Hannah—star performer—would hold forth. When she told funny stories, her laugh was always the loudest.

But factory work was no joke. By the end of the day, the women's backs would ache, and their eyesight would blur. In summer, fuzz from the wool they were working on—they were always one season ahead—would coat their sweaty faces and arms. Sometimes tempers got testy. One woman with an enormous chest and prodigious hot flashes commandeered a machine by the outer door, which she opened and closed according to her private climate. What right did *she* have?! Words passed, and feelings were hurt. The women squabbled with Hannah, too, sometimes about who got the fattest bundles to sew, but mostly just about pay. For each new style, a new price would have to be negotiated.[1]

Hannah was not good at negotiation. Never one to jolly people along or sweet talk them, she mistrusted every form of blandishment and those who resorted to it; in her eyes, even tact was next door to hypocrisy. And so, especially as she grew older, she just spoke her mind, never understanding when the workers didn't see things her way.

At home, Hannah did the payroll—it took her two evenings a week—and hung out her laundry by the light of the moon. Once in a while, she got a midnight call from the cop on the beat, telling her she'd left the shop door unlocked. Each time, when she hurried back, she found garments missing— slacks or robes that she knew the cop had taken for his wife.

Hannah never made a lot of money (though she made more than her husband Wadie, who ran a one-man printing press). But she loved the shop. She loved to work and could never understand people who retired before they had to, any more than she could understand a suicide. To her, life and work were the same. Neither was easy; both were good.

When Hannah finally surrendered the shop at seventy-one, she began expending her surplus energy around the house, keeping a vegetable garden—flowers were also beyond her ken—and baking banana bread to salvage blackening fruit in the pantry. Sometimes, coming to visit, I'd find fresh baked hermits too, and remember the cookies and lemonade my best friend's mother had always had waiting for her after school.

Hannah had never had time in her day for tea parties, just as she'd never had room in her head for my teachers' names. As long as the good grades kept rolling in, school personnel could be left to their own devices. Miss Young meant just nothing to her.

As an entrepreneur, my mother was true to an immigrant tradition, but one usually associated with men. In 1911, for instance, Louise Houghton claimed that nearly all the *Syrian* men in Albany and in Cincinnati owned stores, as well as 75 percent of those in Minneapolis and Toledo, and 50 percent of those in Pittsburgh and Boston (652–653). Although her figures are probably exaggerated,[2] it is true that wherever *Syrians* lived together in any number, their own coffee shops, restaurants (my Uncle Rashid had a string of them), and groceries sprang up, as did bakeries and confectionery shops. Dry goods stores were ubiquitous—Houghton counted fifteen in Portland, Maine, alone. Often doubling as peddling depots, they were the hub from which peddlers took off and to which they returned after a day, a week, or months on the road. To map their sites (as Alixa Naff has done) is to trace the expansion of the *Syrian* population into small towns across America.

Some *Syrian* merchants went big time. In New York, import houses shipped dry goods, notions, and "oriental" goods to traders throughout the country as well as in the West Indies and South America, where there were prosperous Arab communities. *Syrians* also made a good living by manufacturing a range of products from mirrors to tools to suspenders. They owned several lucrative cigarette factories, were prominent players in the silk industry (familiar to them from home) and dominated the manufacture of kimonos.

As capitalists, large or small, *Syrians* seem to have won respect, sometimes from the very people who maligned the pack peddler. Lucius Miller, for instance, reported that "careful inquiry" had "failed to discover anything but high esteem for the *Syrian* business man" (43). A writer for the Massachusetts Department of Education passed on this back-handed compliment: "Allowing for their oriental cunning, [the *Syrians*] are thoroughly honest" (W. Cole, n.p.).

By and large, *Syrian* businesses were owned and run by men. Most of the big success stories, like Haggar slacks, are tales of male achievement. Still, I know of a woman in Fall River, Massachusetts, who made a small fortune buying boxcars of damaged goods and selling them at discount prices. And it is well known (or used to be) that in New York, a number of successful women shopkeepers made linens and lingerie their stock-in-trade. In a similar venture, Makanna's Incorporated, once celebrated as "the trousseau house of Boston" (with branches in up-scale Wellesley and Hyannis) was the creation of a mother and her daughters from my father's hometown of Zahle; years of peddling had provided the seed money for their enterprise. On a less grand scale, many of the little businesses in the *Syrian* community were mom-and-pop affairs, to which women contributed labor and imagination.

But in the first half of this century, the best-known Arab American entrepreneur, male or female, may have been the jewelry designer Marie Azeez El-Khoury, whose place of business once stood on Park Avenue in New York and before that on Fifth Avenue, just across from Tiffany's. Born in 1882, El-Khoury was just five when her family emigrated from Mount Lebanon to the United States. In time, her father established a jewelry store on the boardwalk at Atlantic City. She was sent to private school and then to Washington University, becoming (it is said) the first *Syrian* girl to graduate from an American college.

After a flirtation with journalism and marriage to a journalist, El-Khoury inherited the family business, moved it to Manhattan, and turned The Little Shop of T. Azeez (renamed after her father) into what the *New York Times* later called "a rendezvous for New York society women seeking jewelry of the finest design" ("Marie El-Khoury" 17). Away from work, she cultivated artists and writers, some of whom she subsidized, as well as journalists and individuals prominent in the Arab American community. The celebrated Arab American writer Ameen Rihani was a member of her salon, as was the poet Kahlil Gibran, with whom she was once rumored to have had an affair. (When Gibran died, it was she who arranged for the taking of his death mask.) As a hostess, her taste was all for the sumptuous. The dinners she gave in her penthouse were spectacular performances, each keyed to the color of a particular gem (on one menu, every course was emerald green) or inspired by the epicureanism of the *Arabian Nights* (she might serve "a calf stuffed with a turkey, inside of which was a chicken, inside of which was a squab, inside which was a little nightingale").[3]

When she died, one Arab American newspaper called Marie El-Khoury "the most colorful personality ever to live in our community."[4]

In Arab American folklore, stories about immigrant entrepreneurs are second in popularity only to stories about immigrant peddlers. We have liked to think of our forebears as independent businessmen who disdained to work for others and had the courage, against all odds, to strike out on their own. It's in the genes, we say, nodding in the direction of our "Phoenician ancestors" or commenting sagely about the rugged mountain stock from which our grandparents came. Many or most of the very earliest immigrants may, indeed, have peddled or kept shop, but in focusing on them, we have tended to forget the many *Syrian* immigrants who were wage-dependent members of the American proletariat.

In the Northeast, for instance, many *Syrians*, both male and female, worked in the textile industry, though their participation in that labor force has been largely ignored by historians of the Arab American experience.[5]

In my mother's family, two brothers were the first to enter the mills, almost as soon as the family set foot on American soil. Alexander and Litfallah learned to run looms on the job in Waltham (outside of Boston), to which the family had moved within a few months of being reunited in America. My mother and Uncle Naseeb, too young to work, entered the public schools. But the opportunities for steady work in Waltham were not what the family had hoped, and Waltham was a lonely place. Within a year, the family was back to Boston, and then within another year, on to Fall River, Massachusetts, where jobs were plentiful and the living promised to be cheaper. They would stay there for the next five years.

When we moved to Fall River, I didn't go to school any more. I had to work. My mother and father weren't working. Rashid had gotten married and left us. Elias was working as a salesman in the South. Alexander had learned to weave, but he didn't work much. Litfallah had learned, too, and when we went to Fall River he taught me. I was fourteen then. After three or four weeks, when he saw I could handle the job, he quit. He gave me his job and left. Then he got married and moved back to Boston. So I had to make money for the rest of us to live on. At first, I made about seven or eight dollars a week.

I worked in the biggest textile mill in Fall River. We made gingham. I learned how to operate the looms, six big looms, just like a man. I did it very well. The looms ran by themselves, but when one stopped, I'd go and examine it to see what was wrong. If a thread was broken, I'd rethread it. If the spool was empty, I'd replace it. Some days luck was bad, the machines would keep breaking down, the threads would keep snapping, and you had to undo the damaged sections. Other days everything went smoothly.

But it was hard work. When I first started, we used to work twelve hours a day, from six in the morning til six at night. And on Saturdays, til twelve.

Hannah

The first women to work in the textile mills of New England had been Yankee farm girls whose labor was no longer needed at home. To reassure their parents about the respectability of mill work, owners had set up boarding houses for the young women, with matrons, curfews, and rules compelling church attendance. Despite these middle-class flourishes, working in the mills had never been easy or particularly safe. Ailments and accidents were part of the job, as were the incessant roar of the machinery, the lint-clogged air (windows were nailed shut), and the deliberately high humidity intended to discourage thread from snapping. (Until late in the nineteenth century, hot steam was injected directly into the weaving room.)

By the middle of the century, as jobs were "speeded up" and each operative given more looms or spindles to work, farm girls began withdrawing from the mills, to be replaced by immigrants. These newcomers were, of necessity, willing to work longer hours under worse conditions, for less money. In short, they had many of the same characteristics that had first induced mill owners to prefer hiring women rather than men.[6]

In part because mill overseers played one immigrant group against another, it took a long time for the workers to recognize their collective strength and act on it. A major turning point was the famous Bread and Roses strike of 1912, which shut down the textile mills in Lawrence, Massachusetts. Prompted by an unannounced reduction in wages, the strike lasted two months, drew national and international attention, and led to dramatic Congressional hearings that focused on the exploitation of children.[7]

At the time, there were 2,700 *Syrians* in Lawrence, many of them employed in the mills. We know that *Syrian* women joined in the strike, singing Arabic songs, and that they ran soup kitchens for the workers, dishing out *Syrian* bread and plates of lamb, rice, burghul, and yogurt (Menconi n.p.).

Two months after the strike began, it ended in victory for the workers. In summarizing the roles played by various nationalities in the job action, Donald Cole wrote that the longer established groups—Yankees, Irish, and even French-Canadian workers—were least supportive of the action, while more recent immigrant groups, especially the Italians and Franco-Belgians, were the most ardent. "In a lesser way" he reported, *Syrians* also contributed. "Though generally peaceful, [they] did help stop the machines" (189).

At the time of the Bread and Roses strike, my mother and her family had already moved to Fall River, a city that produced more cotton fabric than any other place in the United States. There they had joined a community of somewhat fewer than 500 *Syrians*, most of whom—like themselves—had been in the United States for less than five years.[8] The 1910 federal census of Fall River reflects emigration patterns typical of a *Syrian*-American community in its early stages. There were, for instance, twice as many men as women and substantially more single men than married; and even of those who were married, a significant number had left their wives behind in *Syria*.

Among the women, too, those who were single seem to have emigrated in larger numbers, usually with or to join their kin. But given the oversupply of young men in Fall River, a number of these eligible girls had since wed, meaning that by 1910 married women were actually in the majority. Though just a teenager, my mother might have joined their ranks.

There were a lot of Arab young men in Fall River, more than girls. Anyone who had a good opinion of himself would try to get someone, either my friend or my sister-in-law, to convince me to talk to him. Sometimes the young man's sister would approach me. I'd say, "No." And my mother—whenever she heard of anything like this—would say, "No, what do you want with this business?" She'd always say, "Later, later, she's too young." She had five sons, you know, but I was the only daughter.

Hannah

The 1910 census also shows that nearly every unwed *Syrian* female in Fall River (fourteen years of age or older) had a paying job, almost always in one of the city's cotton mills and usually—like my mother—as a weaver.[9] This going off to work among strangers was a departure from patterns prevalent in *Greater Syria*, although *Syrian* women had always contributed in other ways to their family's economic survival. In the pre-industrial culture from which the immigrants came, the line between workplace and home was not so clearly articulated as in America. Peasant women in Mount Lebanon, for instance, cooked, kept house, sewed their family's clothing, and preserved food for the winter; they also raised silkworms, kept chickens and a cow or sheep, cultivated a garden, and often helped harvest crops. Sometimes they also supplemented family income by selling their needlework or handcrafts. In these stay-at-home tasks, women were assisted by their daughters, who were thereby groomed for the wifely roles they would later assume.

But in America, as production of goods and accumulation of cash was increasingly centered outside the home, wage earning became the province of those who could most easily leave the house each day. Wives and mothers, who had primary responsibility for domestic chores and especially for child rearing, were usually not so well positioned for venturing out as were their husbands and older children—thus, the widespread practice of unmarried girls joining the labor force at an early age.

One imagines that these young women who went into the mills did so with some trepidation. And that their parents must have been at least as concerned about letting the girls out of their sight and away from their protection as Yankee farmers were about giving freer rein to their daughters. One way of understanding the parents' feelings is to recall what happened in the village of Bishmizzeen, Mount Lebanon, where—between 1880 and 1895—five silk factories were established. At first, says Afif Tannous, the workers were all male, as careful parents kept their daughters safely at home. To do otherwise was "dangerous and its consequences uncertain." It might also suggest that the girl "was in need and that her people could not take care of her" ("Trends" 158–159).

Within a few years, however, the expanding factories needed more labor than could by supplied by men alone. Girls were hired (at lower wages and not in supervisory positions). As feared, the consequences were sometimes unhappy.

Occasional scandals began to take place, involving love affairs, undertaken independently, and of which the parents did not approve. Village gossip enlarged upon these affairs and the families concerned were bitterly hurt by it. However, they had to put up with it, for the work of the girl at the factory meant cash for the family, and cash had already become a highly significant value. ("Trends" 159)

In America, cash was a necessity, and the need for girls to work was more urgent, sometimes in mills or often—as with Jews and Italians—in the needle industry, specifically that branch of it devoted to producing ladies' garments. A few women went on to run their own small factories. My mother, of course, reversed the usual procedure, starting out as a boss. But between her two stints as an entrepreneur, she put in twenty years stitching for others.

When Naseeb and I went out of business, I began working as a stitcher in a big Boston factory. That was about 1925. I worked in a union shop, we paid 10 cents a week dues.

Once they called a big union meeting of people from all the shops. We met in a big hall and listened to speeches. One man was a very skillful speaker. "A man works his whole life away! He shouldn't have to kill himself! He should get a good living!" So we went out on strike. I thought we could just stay home. But no, we had to go in every day and walk in the picket line. I was very embarrassed. How could I walk in a picket line! There was a very spirited woman I worked with. "Well," she said to me, "do you want someone else to fight your fight for you?" We lost that time, and I lost my job.

Another time there was a big strike in front of 35 [75] Kneeland Street.[10] Police came on horseback and held the strikers back so the strike-breakers could go in. Sometimes the strikers would stop them as they left work and talk to them. "Why are you doing this? This is our bread and butter we're fighting for!" Sometimes they would beat up the strike-breakers.

The union was very good in some ways. If a girl had worked in a place for a long time and decided to go to the old country, let's say for a year, when she came back, the boss had to give her back her old machine. Sometimes the girl who had taken over the machine would want to keep it, but if the old girl insisted, the boss had to give it to her. And when you first started a job, if the boss didn't like your work, he could fire you. But if you worked several weeks, then he couldn't fire you no matter what. I remember one woman who worked with us. She was a bad stitcher, and she used to spoil dresses sometimes, but she'd been there a long time. The boss used to say, "I'd give $25 out of my own pocket if only she'd leave." So you were sure of your job.

Hannah

In the mid-twenties, when my mother resumed working for others, a sewing machine operator made about $20 a week; if she was paid by the piece and worked fast, she might make a little more. Still, that was better than the $5 a week she would have earned in a turn-of-the-century sweatshop or hunched over her sewing machine at home. Not just pay but the conditions of work had improved even in the few years since 1911, when the Triangle Shirtwaist fire in New York took the lives of 146 workers (mostly young women between 16 and 23), who either perished in the fire or leapt—sometimes holding one another's hands—to sure death on the pavement below.[11]

The Triangle fire intensified efforts at unionizing the garment industry and, like the Bread and Roses strike the following year, prompted new legislation protecting women workers. But whatever laws were passed, enforcement remained a problem. And even under the best conditions, working in a garment factory was still laborious and uncomfortable and required a good wash-up at the end of the day.

Into the fifties, as I saw the stitchers in my mother's shop pause work to wipe their damp faces or, at the end of the day, clean oily grime from their machines and go out the door with threads clinging to their skirts and lint dulling their hair, I promised myself I would never work in a factory and hoped my mother didn't expect me to follow in her footsteps. But I remember, too, winter afternoons after school, when I helped out at the least skilled jobs, turning belts right side out or snipping long threads left hanging from hems and seams. On those gray days, the hiss of the steam press, the buzz of the sewing machines in lively conversation, their jabbing spindles, each in its small pool of light, transformed the shop into a home and made family of the middle-aged ladies with calm faces and deft fingers who kept track of one another's lives and listened to my chatter.

7

STUDENTS AND TEACHERS

For some reason—failure of nerve or of imagination—I never asked my mother how she felt about dropping out of school at fourteen to become her family's most reliable source of income. The decision may have been casual, a simple matter of someone—parent, neighbor, or brother—being the first to say, "And Hannah is old enough to work, too." In the face of family consensus, she would not have argued the point. But as she pictured herself entering the mill yard, she would have been scared (after that, she always was scared and couldn't get down her breakfast when starting a new job for a new boss). And seventy-five years later, her astonishment at Litfallah's cunning had not been put to rest—"He gave me his job and left!"

Apparently a girl's ability to generate income in America was a double-edged sword. On the one hand, it could raise her stock in the family and pave the way to greater autonomy in her personal life. "My parents never told me what to do," my mother once said. "After all, I was going out and earning money to support the family." On the other hand, a girl's newfound usefulness could tempt others to take advantage of her. My mother's tone, if not her words, told me she felt betrayed by Litfallah, the brother immediately her senior and the one to whom—until he shrugged his responsibilities onto her shoulders—she had felt the closest.

Still, exploitation (to the extent it existed) was not necessarily limited to girls. In 1903, Lucius Miller complained that the education of some *Syrian* children in New York, presumably both sons and daughters, was "interfered with more or less by the selfish demands of parents upon their children's earning capacity" (48) though he conceded that, in general, *Syrians* in America "are as keenly anxious for the education of their children . . . as any race which comes to our shores" (46). On the latter point, Louise Houghton was equally vehement, claiming that *Syrian* immigrants "greatly covet education for their children, and make real sacrifices to keep them in school" (34).

The difference was that where Miller saw greed, Houghton saw only need. "In many cases," she wrote, "poverty compels parents to withdraw [their children] from school at the earliest legal age, that they may go to work" (788).

When that step was their only recourse, parents might regret it, but they could remind themselves that by village standards, a child who could read and write and do arithmetic was educated. And mothers, most of whom were illiterate, could recall that at fourteen or a little older, they had been deemed ready to assume the responsibilities of marriage.

The decision to take a child out of school must have been easier when the son or daughter was unhappy there or seemed not to be learning. Usually the older the age at which the child had emigrated, the higher the level of frustration. Miller pointed, for instance, to the problem of placement. An older child's ignorance of English, he wrote, "unfits him for a place in the grade to which he would naturally belong on the basis of age," and yet it was "unpractical or unwise to put him in the kindergarten or primary" (46). Back in the village, my mother had learned to read English. But she'd had little practice speaking it, and so was one of those older children for whom there were only awkward solutions:

They put me at first with the little kids in the first grade, and I was older, about twelve. When anyone talked to me in English, I couldn't understand them very well. But when they put an arithmetic problem on the blackboard, I'd look at it, and fast, fast, I'd figure it out in Arabic and put down the answer in English. In five minutes, I'd be done, and my answers were always right. The teacher looked at them, and then she went and talked to someone. They moved me into another grade, and after a while into another and then another.

Hannah

Within a year, though, the family was back in Boston, with my mother and my Uncle Naseeb enrolled in new schools; a few months later they were in Fall River, and my mother's school days were over. Perhaps if she (or her parents) had been younger, or if the family hadn't moved around so much those first two years in America, or if her older brothers had been of a different mind, she might have made it to the higher grades. But I think it was not in her nature to repine. Besides, she took satisfaction in providing for her family; she was proud of being literate in two languages; and she never doubted she was smart.

As the first decade of the twentieth century gave way to the second and then the third, more Arab American children finished high school, and some went on to trade school or college. Of course, among *Syrians*, as among others, the belief persisted that it was more important for a boy to get an education than for a girl. So when hard times, especially during the Depression years, continued to force children out of school prematurely, it was girls who were the first to drop out.[1] In fact, a boy's education was often financed, at least in part, by his sister's earnings. Some sisters never thought to question a system that sent them to the end of the line, especially since such discrimination was endemic in the mainstream society as well. But other Arab American girls protested. In 1926 a second-generation Mississippi girl wrote an indignant letter to the *Syrian World*, complaining about "narrow-minded parents" who "neglect . . . the proper education of their daughters, although [they] put forth a great deal of effort to educate their boys to the full extent" (Ferguson 56).

The gradual extension of schooling, the higher priority placed on boys' education, the expectation that girls would devote themselves to their brothers' advancement—none of this surprises. Nor is it astonishing that from the beginning, *Syrian* immigrants included a handful of university-educated men. Less predictable and usually forgotten is the fact that also included were a scattering of *Syrian* girls and women who had studied (and sometimes taught) at excellent mission schools, were accomplished enough to speak several languages, devoted themselves to social causes, gave public lectures, and even wrote for Arab American newspapers or magazines.

Beginning in 1892, the *Syrian* American community produced a large crop of Arabic periodicals, most of them short lived, a few more durable.[2] At their worst, these publications exploited and exacerbated religious and political divisions within the community. But at their best, they educated, providing information and counsel that helped their readers cope with a new land and an unfamiliar society.[3]

By and large, the Arab American press was a man's game. But women were sometimes allowed to play. Implicitly (as role models) and explicitly (in the content of their writing), female columnists provided guidance to the immigrant woman, whom writer Layyah Barakat[4] described as "occupying difficult ground between her countrymen, on the one hand, and, on the other, the foreigners with whom she mingles and from whom she acquires new ideas" (1911, 17). According to several writers, certain new ideas—those that inspired the *Syrian* woman to pursue an education, to cultivate gentle manners, or to join in charitable causes—were noble. But others—those that encouraged licentious behavior, bad habits (smoking, drinking, and cursing), and vain indulgence in fine clothes and jewelry—were corrupting and degrading. "Like a caring mother," wrote Barakat, "I advise you, oh pure *Syrian* girl . . . not to make the freedom which you enjoy in this country the way to evil" (20).[5]

A young woman's route to genuine freedom, most columnists agreed, was through education. "I call on you, *Syrians*, to educate your daughters," wrote the immigrant Philomena Yusuf al-Barid.[6] "Do not think that knowledge will harm them and corrupt their manners" (174). Nor should *Syrians* fear, she said, that education would lead women to neglect their housewifely duties. On the contrary, the uneducated woman was more apt to gad about, spreading false gossip wherever she went. "But an educated woman," said al-Barid, "never leaves her home except when necessary" or "to assist in reforming society and promoting humanitarian causes" (172).

Perhaps the boldest advocate for women was Afifa Karam (1883–1925), the best-known woman journalist of her day, and a person of fiery style and absolute conviction. Karam, a native of Mount Lebanon, had married at thirteen and then immigrated to the United States accompanied by her husband and her mother. Eager to pursue her studies of the Arabic language and with never any children of her own to claim her time and energies, she was eventually fortunate enough to come to the attention of Naoum Mokarzel, owner and editor of *Al-Huda* (*Guidance*), the most successful Arabic newspaper in America. Mokarzel took Karam under his wing, suggesting books for her to read, critiquing her writing, and eventually making her the first female journalist on his staff. In fact, he thought so highly of her that when he had to be out of the country for six months in 1911, he placed her in charge of the paper. In the same year, encouraged perhaps by that editorial experience, she began a magazine of her own, *The Syrian Woman*; it gave way in 1913 to *The New World for Women*, which Karam operated for several years.

In thinking to start a women's magazine, Karam was almost certainly inspired by the literary scene in Egypt, where feminism was on the rise among a segment of the intelligentsia and where several women's journals had been established just before and just after the turn of the century. In an early issue of the *New World*, Karam specifically pays tribute to women's magazines in Cairo as well as in Beirut and Damascus, casting her own publication as their "child." Other material in the same issue gives further evidence of Karam's agenda. Women's achievements are celebrated through profiles of such disparate figures as Abraham Lincoln's mother, Isabella of Spain, and an eighty-year-old American artist. One feature article focuses on the education of Egyptian girls; another, on the unthinking choice of marriage partners among *Syrians*—her subtext being that educated girls make the best wives.

The emphasis on education was no anomaly. Like other female writers, Karam consistently identified ignorance as the major disability under which *Syrian* women labored. Her article "Between Two Men" is a typical example. It was ignorance, she argued, that facilitated a woman's exploitation by her father (who might marry her off to the man with whom he could strike the most financially advantageous bargain), her husband (who might expect his comfort and pleasure to be her only concern),[7] and, in youth, by her would-be seducer (who would find her easy prey to his advances). To guard against the last danger, Karam urged elsewhere that parents explain the "secret facts of life" to their children. Otherwise, girls who reached an age when "they [felt] things without knowing the cause" might be "led to perdition" ("Girls" 62, 63).

In speaking openly of sex, Karam expected, as she said, that she would become "a target for the barbs of pens, eyes, eyebrows, and tongues" ("Girls"

60). But even her more general advocacy of advanced schooling for girls, as spelled out in another *Al-Huda* article, did not pass unchallenged. In a subsequent issue of the same paper, a woman named Hannah Shakir Salim responded to Karam by bringing up the tired argument that "God created man first and then created woman as a helpmate to him, and so she should be educated only insofar as required for that role." Furthermore, a woman's capacities were limited; she was weaker than man both physically and mentally (4).

This was an argument that Karam—when her turn came round again—dismissed with dispatch, pointing to the achievements of both Western women and women in the immigrant community. Then, never shy about attributing selfish motives to men, she claimed that the *Syrian* man was perfectly happy to have a woman work with her hands, for the sake of the money she could make him, but wanted to reserve for himself all intellectual, scientific, and artistic endeavors, as well as the privileges of writing in newspapers,[8] founding societies, and speaking in public. Weary of protestation by fathers that they loved their daughters as much as their sons, Karam called for deeds, not words. She wanted to see daughters treated equally and their education encouraged. And to those (presumably like Shakir Salim) who claimed that higher education "does not befit woman," Karam bitingly retorted, "Is education vile or virtuous? The answer, no doubt, is virtuous. Then, what sin have women committed to be deprived of it? And for what reasons? And according to what law?" ("Reply" 4).

When I wanted to go to college, my mother raised no objection, though neither was she convinced of the need for it. My father, it emerged, was harboring fantasies of a daughter at Bryn Mawr, for him the pinnacle of classiness. It wasn't just snob appeal. Compared to my mother, he had greater faith in the virtue of learning—all his aspirations took that turn, as did his vanity. When he died, he was still carrying in his pocket my third-grade report card with its unbroken ranks of straight A's and his five signatures (one for each term) in penmanship that curled like Arabic script.

I never applied to Bryn Mawr, and my father settled for his second choice, Wellesley. My mother was glad because it was only twenty minutes from home. She was growing old, she said, and waited for the implications to sink in. I lived on campus, anyway.

Though, like most Arabs, Hannah loved poetry, aphorism, and elegant turns of phrase, she had little inclination toward learning in the abstract. Her deepest admiration was reserved for people who could do useful things—tailor a jacket, hang wallpaper, unjam a window, change a flat. She was handy, herself. Standing watch over six looms had taught her the pirouettes of cogs and wheels and pulleys. When one of her sewing machines acted up, she could often set it to rights with screwdriver, pliers, and bits of old curtain rod. At least she could try. It was as defeatist (and extravagant) to send for a repairman at the first sign of trouble as to call a doctor for every ache or fever.

Once, up on a chair to examine a light fixture, she fell and fractured her ankle, then hobbled around for twenty-four hours before letting me drive her to the doctor's office. Aspirin, she thought, could cure anything. And in her case, she was nearly right. At ninety, she took one tiny pill a day for borderline hypertension, and that was it, except for a single Bayer on days when she felt "blue."

When she felt the lump in her breast, she kept it a secret, like her childhood terror that Miriam would never return, tracking its growth to the size of a fist. She must have told herself that nothing could be very wrong since she was not in pain and she was being a good girl now, seeing her doctor every three months—humoring him. He'd take her blood pressure, listen to her heart, but never bothered to schedule a mammogram. "At her age, she'll never get breast cancer," he explained, "and even if she does, it won't grow." Sixteen lymph nodes tested positive.

There were things Hannah could never understand: how to read a map, why I wanted my own apartment, that a poem doesn't have to rhyme, that cancer doesn't have to hurt. But she read the *Christian Science Monitor* every day and could tell you what was happening in remote parts of the world. She watched the Sunday morning talk shows, too, though she was skeptical of the media in the way Arab Americans often are. Her politics were mostly liberal, influenced probably by Wadie, who in the last decade of his life supported Red China's bid for a UN seat and thought Truman was right to fire MacArthur. In religion, Hannah followed a middle road, not counting on eternity but never starting a journey or ending a day without asking God's blessing. In the morning, she was full of projects and plans she had cooked up during the night, not just for herself but for everyone she cared about. She could not let well enough alone.

I wanted peace; she wanted action, and she wanted it now. It set her teeth on edge to find me deep in a novel on a Saturday morning, the very time she and God had set aside for decent people to clean house. When I finally bestirred myself to help, I was still a sorry spectacle. Hannah would almost rather see me back in bed than plopped down on a dining-room chair, twisting myself every which way to dust it.

Years later, when I was a Ph.D. student in literature, she'd see me with a book and ask what I was reading. "Stories," I'd tell her. "It's for school," I'd add, cutting the ground out from under her. It sounded crazy, but she couldn't be sure, and so I had her at a disadvantage—until the summer day she caught me on the front porch with Chaucer. "What are you reading?" "Stories. Would you like to hear them?" And out spilled my giggly versions of the Miller's and the Reeve's tales. Now she was truly shocked and no mistake. Not so much by the arse-kissing and the pissing—her own sense of humor was too earthy for that—but that this was the stuff of my higher education. When she considered, too, the stories I told her about my classmates and professors, their affairs, divorces, and drug dealing, her disappointment was complete. "We used to respect educated people," she told me. "Oh, we thought they were high above us. But now my eyes are open. Your schooling has taught me a good lesson."

8

CLUBWOMEN

On Thursday nights, I sensed that Hannah was stepping out on important business and mustn't be delayed by any nonsense. As she sped through the supper dishes (no task for a man), she'd squeeze in a quick consultation with Wadie on that evening's agenda. The message I got, lingering at the kitchen table, was that the claims of the Ladies' Aid Society were sacred. Hannah showed up in church about twice a year, but only a seriously ill child could keep her home on club night.

Illiterate or college educated, Arab immigrants found ways to reach beyond the daily tasks of life and participate in the larger life of the community. Church or mosque beckoned many from home, but so did other institutions; from the beginning, Arab Americans were joiners. Some organizations brought together people from the same hometown. Others were built around a particular purpose, sometimes merely social, often educational or charitable, occasionally political. They ranged from New York City's *Al-Rabitat el-Qalamiyya* or Pen League (made up of emigré writers whose work helped revolutionize Arabic poetry) to drop-in coffee houses where men smoked, played cards, and told stories.

Women, too, had their clubs and community activities, some sponsored by settlement houses or urban missions. Designed as instruments of assimilation, such clubs offered classes in American cooking, or in nutrition, infant care, and civics. In Lansing, Michigan, in the mid-1920s, the Syrian Mothers Club at the Y ran programs on "Our Health," "Our Homes," "Our Community," and "Our Flower Gardens." A middle-class agenda was asserting itself.

A generation earlier, settlement houses in major American cities were already serving the needs of *Syrian* immigrants. Among the best was Boston's Denison House, planted in the heart of the *Syrian* community and staffed by women who seem to have had the knack of providing help without giving offense. By 1910, the House was deeply involved in work with the community, sponsoring at least half a dozen *Syrian* clubs, offering *Syrians* classes in English, encouraging their young people to put on plays and hold dances, and opening its rooms to neighborhood meetings. It had also established an ethnically mixed workroom where women could earn money by sewing simple garments or making lace. The House's 1915 report on the workroom is remarkable for the respectful attention it pays to the circumstances of the women's lives.

Some [women who came to work this year] were victims of irregular, seasonal industries, work was "slack" in the factory where they or their husbands were employed. Some were the wives of small merchants, who felt the pinch of other people's hard times, giving unlimited credit until they themselves faced ruin; some were the wives of peddlers, unable to find even back-door customers; some were braving a strike on infinitesimal strike benefits; some were deserted wives. Some were obviously unemployable,—incompetent through lack of education and early training, incompetent through physical disability, incompetent through old age. (Denison House 1915, 4)

The following year, in explaining again why women sought work at the House, the report probed more deeply.

They come to us for many different reasons. The husband may be sick or out of a job. Perhaps the husband has a good salary, but the wife may have no money that she can call her own. It may not be money that she needs, but friends who will relieve her loneliness in a strange land; or she may be in a nervous condition that will be cured by doing beautiful work that will be well praised and paid for. (Denison House 1916, 29)

It is easy to see why immigrant women might have grown attached to the House and wanted to please a staff who seemed to understand them so well. Perhaps that desire—as much as any incipient feminism—was the reason they turned out in numbers when social workers invited women of the workroom to march with them in a parade supporting female suffrage. According to the Denison House report that year, "Women from Lebanon, Sicily, Tripoli [Syria], Damascus, Albania, and Germany marched with the 'Americans' " (Denison House 1916, 30).

Denison House, and agencies like it, provided facilities and services that the immigrant community could not easily provide for itself and fostered clubs that made a difference in the lives of many people. But even more important may have been the community's homegrown organizations, many affiliated with churches and mosques. When it came to matters ecclesiastical, women may not have set the agenda or even been given a voice, but without their hard work, many houses of worship would never have been built and, once built, would never have prospered.[1] In the late 1920s, for instance, women in Cedar Rapids, North Dakota, took the initiative in raising money for a mosque, forming a society for that purpose and urging men to do the same (Naff 287). At about the same time, in the Orthodox parish of Worcester, Massachusetts, the ladies' society rolled enough grape leaves and baked enough sweets to pay off a $15,000 mortgage on their church building (Saliba 1992, 48).

Of nonsectarian clubs, one of the earliest must have been the Syrian Women's Union of New York, started in 1896 by educated immigrant women from well-established families, who had the time, means, and desire to help those still struggling to survive. At their weekly sewing circle, Union members made clothes for poor children and did fancy needlework that they auctioned off to benefit the poor. Their most ambitious project was a day nursery for small children whose mothers worked in factories or peddled, as the *New York Times* said, "carrying a child on one arm and a basket on the other" (March 19, 1899). The nursery, with its flowered wallpaper, white and brass beds, and tiny rockers, got off to a good start, the *Times* reported (May 21, 1899), but how long it operated is unclear, as is how long the Union, itself, survived.

About a decade later, in 1907, twelve New York women of the same class and background as the Union membership, formed the Syrian Ladies' Aid Society, its primary purpose to provide "financial, medical, and moral aid" to *Syrian* women and girls arriving at Ellis Island. In a short time, the Society had placed a matron on the island and was helping the immigrants find work, housing, or the relatives they had come to join (Houghton 794).[2]

One successful ladies' aid spawned others, the best documented being the Syrian Ladies' Aid Society of Boston,[3] to which my mother belonged. Founded in 1917 and originally intended to help people in *Syria* whose lives were being devastated by war and famine, it brought its mission closer to home once the Armistice was signed. To immigrant families in greater Boston, it distributed coal, food staples, milk for children, and monthly cash stipends. Sometimes, too, members accompanied immigrants with little or no English to doctors' offices or to courtrooms; helped them secure government assistance; or arranged passage for the old, sick, or discouraged who wanted to return home.

To finance these activities, the club staged one fund-raising event after another: suppers, bazaars, picnics, rummage sales, whist parties, and Halloween and New Year's Eve parties, as well as grand *haflis* featuring prominent speakers, local folk poets, and New York musicians. By 1925 a report of the International Institute of Boston had identified the Ladies' Aid Society, 400 members strong, as the "most active organization in the city's *Syrian* community." Four years later, even as the stock market was crashing, the club consolidated its position by purchasing an elegant townhouse that would be its home for the next three decades and would also serve as the community's busiest meeting place. In its rooms, clubs would convene, dignitaries be received, weddings celebrated, and the dead waked.

When they first came together, the Society's founding members could not have foreseen that their enterprise would enjoy such success. In fact, theirs was a risky venture, an exercise in public and, therefore, potentially unwomanly behavior. But from the start, they enjoyed widespread community support. Had they banded together for another purpose, their reception might have been cooler, but during World War I, the need back home was so urgent that it justified even female boldness. It helped, too, that serving others was a traditional female virtue and thus a legitimate sphere for organized female action. "Charity," a visiting bishop told members, "is the most beautiful jewelry a woman can wear."

Backed by men, supported by the community at large, the Ladies' Aid afforded immigrant women (many of whom were illiterate) exciting and relatively guilt-free opportunities for exercising their powers and developing their talents, for leading rather than following, for being public as well as private people.[4] "We looked forward to a meeting," one woman told me, "as if it were a wedding!" But a residue of anxiety still surfaced when the club attempted anything new or particularly exciting, like their first big *hafli*.

It was a musical evening. We had a violinist from Egypt and a *Syrian* Jew with a lovely voice. But we were so nervous. We were afraid men would come, bring bottles, drink, and get drunk. And then people would say, "A ladies' club! And they have such goings on!" No, we were worried. We hired a policeman to stand at the door, and our men friends stood at the back of each aisle, just in case. But all went very well, very smoothly. We made eleven hundred dollars."

Hannah

Then, there was the troublesome matter of the plays. To understand the women's feelings about appearing on stage, one need only turn to Afif Tannous's account of his native village of Bishmizzeen. There, shortly after the turn of the century, a newly built schoolhouse made possible new kinds of village events, such as lectures, concerts, poetry readings, and—most popular of all—stage productions. At first, only young men performed.

The villagers [wrote Tannous] had a strong taboo against acting by girls. Acting involved the parading of the girl on the stage in front of the crowd including young men and strangers. Remarks might be made about the girl, causing trouble between her family and those who made the remarks. Such parading had the further implication that the parents were eager to present their girl for marriage. That went against the custom which demanded that the girl should wait at home until her suitor came for her. The strongest objection was that the people had always associated regular actresses with "bad morals" ("Missionary" 341).

After a while, young women also began staging plays, but quite separately from young men. According to Tannous, "The village could not go beyond that and allow boys and girls to act together" (341).

These were the attitudes that many village people carried with them to America, which is why the first Ladies' Aid plays had all-female casts. And why, even so, there was plenty of room for embarrassment.[5]

In one play, a Russian one—I forget the name—I took the leading part. I played a man and shot a gun. My brother Elias used to be out on the road selling, for several weeks at a time. And while he was away, I accepted this role. But then I began to worry. How was I going to wear men's clothing and go up on a stage and everyone looking at me. I was so embarrassed. Probably it was shameful and I oughtn't to do it. But still I was going to the rehearsals. When Elias came back, I had this thing on my mind. I respected Elias more than anyone else I knew. I said to him, "You know what?" He said, "What?" I said, "I'm going to wear men's clothing in this play. Is that proper? I'm going to wear men's clothing and be on a stage with everyone looking at me." I thought he'd say, "No, how could you agree to do such a thing?" But what he said was, "Ah, it's all right, it's all right. As long as you make money for the club."

Hannah

Hannah was a charter member of the Ladies' Aid and for many years, because her Arabic was good, its recording secretary. As long as she was single—that is, for fifteen years into the life of the club—custom prevented her from moving up to the presidency. But the moment she married, she was elected to that office, as if it had been reserved for her all along.

By then, admirable stage presence and a voice that carried without a microphone had made Hannah the club's chief orator. In later years, she loved to tell about the evening she spoke, as always in Arabic, at the burning of the club's mortgage, while seated behind her on stage was James Michael ("Vote early! Vote often!") Curley, the rascal mayor of Boston. As she turned from the podium, Curley—that master of ethnic politics—took her hand, congratulated her on her speech, told her he'd understood every word. "Wasn't he silly!" she'd laugh happily, recalling that bright moment, and it would bother me every time that he had charmed her so easily.

The last time Hannah took the stage was at the club's seventieth anniversary celebration, when she was ninety-two. She recited from memory a long, light-hearted poem on uppity clubwomen that Litfallah had written half a century earlier in immigrant-speak, a comic mix of colloquial Arabic and broken English. Midway through the 200 lines or so, her hands and arms and shoulders began to tremble, but her voice was strong to the end, and her recall perfect.

Hannah's five brothers were long dead by then, and the glory days of the club long over. But years before, Naseeb had carefully labeled and stored away a record of those days—over thirty years of club minutes, most of them in Hannah's own hand. For many months, she and I had been reviewing them—usually after supper on as many evenings as I could manage. She read, translated, reminisced; I asked questions and took notes. It wasn't always harmonious—sometimes I'd prod and push for answers she didn't have; she'd get fed up or tired and threaten to quit. But mostly it was companionable. For once, our enthusiasms had come together—I wanting to know about the past, she wanting to relive it, both of us determined to see the task through to its end. Two days after her mastectomy, Hannah was propped up in a hospital bed, minutes again in hand, concentrating, and I—feet resting on the foot of her bed—was still taking notes. It was not a bad way to heal.

9

MAKING A MATCH

"God grant I may dance at your wedding!" That (in loose translation) was my thank-you whenever I served coffee to my parents' guests or passed around a tray of sweets. And when I was introduced to any older person, it was the polite greeting I almost always received.

I have a lot to answer for. All those good people looking forward to a party, and I have never produced a groom. If only I'd been born fifty years earlier and to a family that stayed put in Mount Lebanon, I would almost certainly have done right and would probably be a grandmother at this age. Somebody else—my father's mother, my mother's sister—would have found the man and arranged the match, then sent me off on my wedding night without a clue to what would follow. The initiation into sex would likely have been a horror, but I'm not prepared to say the old ways were all bad, much less to argue that computers come up with wiser matches than those the elders put together.[1]

Although my mother's marriage was not arranged and she never tried, as far as I know, to arrange one for me (or even to push me into one of my own choosing), she could be a warm advocate for a system she remembered from her youth.

Yes, in the old days girls did as their parents wished. They didn't keep going out with this one, then that one. It was better then. The girls themselves were happier.

And the parents knew [what was best]. For instance, if you were going to marry someone, wouldn't I be able to see whether you'll have a good life together? I can tell if he'll suit you or not. Through experience. Parents know better than the children. We know. We can tell.

Hannah

My mother would have had me believe that the only goal of an arranged marriage was to promote compatibility. The corollary was that mutual attraction is a treacherous basis on which to build a life together.

Afif Tannous is more romantic. He has written lyrically of young love in Bishmizzeen, as it played itself out in the generations before emigration and access to cash undermined the integrity of the village culture and subverted the biblical simplicity of its daily life.

It is at the village well, when the girl comes for water, or among the trees of the orchard, when she is picking the fruit, or at the threshing floors, when she takes lunch to her father and uncles that her boy meets her and love starts between them. They do not meet each other often, they do not speak much to each other, but they know they love each other and they know they must get married. ("Trends" 53)

Although Tannous concedes that when it came to marriage, "the word of the family and its welfare [were] paramount," he leaves the impression that, in most cases, adult arrangements merely sanctioned the desires of a young couple already in love, and that if one or another set of parents proved recalcitrant, intercession by a respected third party usually brought them around. When all else failed, the young couple's final recourse might be elopement, what the villagers called "stealing the bride." Here is how it worked in Bishmizzeen.

[The boy] meets [the girl] secretly and agrees with her about the time and place of elopement. At the appointed time, usually late at night, he appears at the place, with a strong gang of his friends and relatives. . . . In a short while, the girl appears, trembling with tears in her eyes, for she cannot easily detach herself from her loyalty to her family group. But she is thrilled at the adventure; she knows she loves her boy. Horses are ready, the gang mount, and soon they are swallowed by the dark night. ("Trends" 56)[2]

Most couples who resorted to elopement were eventually received back into the community, but there could be a sordid side to such shenanigans. My mother's old friend Mary told this bitter tale. It seems that Hassan, a young man, came one day to her village to live with his uncle, and Mary, who was only thirteen, soon caught his eye. He learned that she was unhappy at home (her widowed mother suspected her of flirting and used to beat her) and persuaded her to run away to her aunt in another town. He would help her do it. Instead, abetted by a female accomplice, he arranged for her to be led to his own village, where she had no choice but to spend the night.

Though, all along, Mary's mother had despised Hassan ("that shit!"), she considered their marriage a *fait accompli* since neighbors would assume the worst of any girl who had been away from home overnight. "To bring me home and have people say I was returned after being taken—it would be shameful." Within a month, Mary and Hassan were married.

Still, in the tug of wills between generations, parents more typically kept the upper hand, especially when it came to disposing of daughters.[3] Sons probably had greater say, but even they were expected finally to obey. The general idea seems to have been that marriage was too serious a matter to be left up to inexperienced youngsters. But even that may be the wrong way of putting it. To Arab villagers, the whole family had as much of a stake in the marriage as did the bride and groom. Pride played a part. A good match—wealth, status, and kinship were major criteria—would enhance family honor; a poor one would diminish it. But there were more down-to-earth considerations, too. In a society where several generations "lived together" (whether in the same house or not) parents had a legitimate concern about whom their son might be bringing home to stay or about the household to which they were entrusting their young daughter. And she might be very young, indeed.

Girls were sometimes married off even before their first menstrual period, in order to forestall any possibility of scandal. On the wedding night, custom sometimes required young men of the families involved to stand outside the house where the newly married couple were bedded, waiting for the groom to fire a pistol, signal that his bride was a virgin. In other villages, the bed sheets, honorably stained with blood, might be displayed in the morning from a window of the bridal chamber. The ultimate horror, a premarital pregnancy, could result in social ostracism for a girl's entire family. In such a cultural atmosphere, a girl unmaidenly enough to encourage on her own the advances of a suitor ran the risk not only of compromising her reputation but of dishonoring forever all her kin. Even in this country, my mother remembered being cross-examined by Litfallah (though not by her other brothers) whenever she had been out of the house.

Litfallah always wanted to know "Where have you been?" "Who were you with?" "Who did you speak to?" "Who spoke to you?" And he used to tell me, "Don't even respond to a hello from a man. He'll think you're not a good girl."

Hannah

With the stakes so high, it was better to be safe than sorry. Thus, the arranged marriage.[4]

But what if the girl wasn't ready to marry or didn't care for her parents' choice? According to Tannous, she might be "threatened" or "maltreated," and if she persisted in her refusal to marry, she might be disinherited. Still, most parents probably didn't resort to such extremes. There were other ways.

Take Asma, who had studied in Beirut to be a kindergarten teacher. In 1911, just after graduating and three months before she would have started her first job, her parents introduced her to a man fifteen years her senior. "I didn't want it," she told me. "I resented it from the beginning. They didn't force me, but . . . well, you know the old custom. The uncles and the cousins and the priest all came and said, 'Oh, please, why don't you marry him? He's a good man.' " She did marry him a couple of months later, and one week after the wedding, the two of them sailed for the United States. Her husband *was* a good man, she said, a quiet man, a handsome man, but the sudden uprooting had broken her heart, she told me, and demolished her own plans for the future. Over seventy years later, she still cried at the memory.

From first meeting to marriage, Asma's courtship lasted only weeks; her suitor, an emigré back in *Syria* on a visit, had no time to waste. His case was not unusual. In the early years, when there were not enough immigrant girls to go around, a number of men in America sent home for brides their parents had chosen (or approved of) or else went back to see for themselves who was available. In the rush to return to America (or to go there in the first place), the pace of courtship quickened and its rhythms syncopated. If the couple had not known each other before, there was little time to get acquainted now.

Feminist Afifa Karam thought it a bad system leading to unhappy marriages. Writing in 1913, she marveled at the way a young man

entrusts his business to someone and rushes off to the home country to fetch a bride as if she were a piece of cloth sold by the yard. He limits the time he must spend—a month or two—in choosing a bride who has never before set eyes on him in her life, nor he on her. . . . They marry without having exchanged as much as ten words, having spent the brief time they had together preparing for the wedding. . . . What results may be expected of this? . . . Endless misery and regret. ("Marriage" 328, 329)

According to Karam, young men who looked about for a bride on this side of the Atlantic were equally reckless.

Similarly, a girl might arrive from the home country, and the suitors flock around her as if she were an exotic new fruit, each desiring to beat the others to her and competing to ask for her hand . . . and any girl will do, as if the purpose of marriage is for people to congratulate the young man on his wedding, with no consideration of the long life which this word implies. ("Marriage" 329)

"Any girl will do." It is a comment that brings to mind my Uncle Litfallah, a man in a hurry to gain a wife. This is my mother's version of the story;

While we were still living in Fall River, my brother Litfallah [twenty years old at the time] came to visit Rashid [the oldest brother], who had stayed behind in Boston. Litfallah told Rashid, "I've come to get married."

"What do you mean?" asked Rashid. "Do our mother and father know?"

"Everyone knows," said Litfallah. "They want me to get married. Who can I marry?"

"Well, there's Tifaha," said Rashid, "and Saleemy. We'll ask Saleemy. She won't say 'no.' " We all knew Saleemy because when we first came from the old country and lived on Tyler Street [in Boston], she and her father had the flat above us. So Rashid and his wife Munnee talked to Saleemy's father, and he said, "Yes, all right, just as you wish." Then right away they got married without even telling us, as if Fall River were as far away as Lebanon.

After a few days, Rashid and Munnee came to visit us. I remember they came up the stairs, Munnee carrying her little boy and crying out, "Yes, we married your son for you!"

"What son?" said my mother.

"Litfallah."

"God punish you, Munnee. How could you do such a thing!"

"Didn't you send him to be married?" asked Munnee.

"No!"

"Well, he said he had your blessings."

"Who did you take for him?"

"We took Saleemy."

"Oooooooooooohhhhhhhhhhh!"

Poor Munnee, she'd been so proud of herself, thinking she'd done something important. And then to discover they disapproved! My father, as soon as he heard, was very upset. He began to cry and went to his room. I went into another room and sat down and I wouldn't open the door. How could he do it! We were very close, him and me, more than I was with the others. How could he get married without telling me! When Litfallah arrived, we wouldn't talk to him.[5]

Five years later, when Elias (age thirty-one) was ready to marry, he chose his own bride but postponed the ceremony long enough to observe the basic courtesies.

One day Elias said to me, "There's a girl I want to introduce you to." He took me to Mr. Moosa Batrooney's house on Hudson Street in Boston. Adele was still at church. After church she came to meet me. She was wearing a light blue dress. Moosa's wife wanted us to get acquainted so she brought out a deck of cards and said, "Here, enjoy yourselves." Then she went into the kitchen. But I felt so shy.

Hannah

By that time—1914—my mother herself had had several offers of marriage, beginning with the family's relocation to Fall River, where there was an oversupply of *Syrian* young men. But it was not until she was almost thirty-seven that my mother married:

I knew your father for a long time. Then one time he asked me if I'd go out with him to the movies. I said no, I had a date with my girlfriend. "Next week?" he said. I agreed. All that week I kept thinking about it. Should I go? Not go? I'd never been out on a date before. At last I said all right. We went to the movies near Scollay

Square. Afterwards he said, "What about next week?" "Oh, next week? So soon?" "Yes," he said, "not just next week but maybe every week." I said, "We'll see."

Within a couple of months, he had proposed and she had accepted.

Then I told Elias. Later we told my mother. [Jiryas was dead by then.] It was important that Elias know first; we respected him a lot.

Hannah

When my Uncle Elias told my mother about Adele, he was keeping her informed, being gracious, and laying the groundwork for a good sisterly relationship between the two women. But when my mother told Elias about my father, she was—even at her age—implicitly asking not just his blessing but his advice. Unlike Naseeb, he would have a say, and if he'd wanted to, perhaps he could have scotched the budding romance.

Still, unlike Mary or Asma or even Saleemy, she had chosen her husband for herself. In America, the old courtship patterns could not persist, nor could the ideal of the modest, bashful girl, ready to do her parents' will and afraid to look a man in the eye for fear of what people would say. For one thing, the intimate network of relationships that had made the old system possible was permanently disrupted by emigration. For another, the impact of American culture, with its emphasis on romantic love and individualism, could not be avoided even by those living in an ethnic enclave. Crucial, too, was the fact that daughters could now earn their own way. It meant that they married later (though seldom as late as my mother) and for that reason alone perhaps, exercised more discretion and initiative in their choice of a husband and in all their social behavior. Holding down a job, in itself, encouraged self-respect and deference from others and might sometimes make it easier for a woman to know what she wanted and to feel she had a right to say so.

Still, change came hard, and pockets of resistance survived, sometimes for decades. As late as 1926, a correspondent wrote the *Syrian World*, complaining of "our *Syrian* system of betrothal," in which boys and girls are married "against their wishes," as illustrated in this fictional dialogue:

Father: Now daughter, you are seventeen years old, and it is time that you thought of marriage. If you wait too long people will begin to talk about it. But now they have no chance. There is your cousin so and so, he ought to make a fine husband for you. He is rich and has a good reputation, and you will be able to live with him like a princess. You cannot get a better one, and any girl will be glad to have him. . . .

Daughter: But father, I have never had a chance to know him, and do not feel that I like him enough to marry him.

Father: Listen to me my daughter, for I know what is best for you. Besides, you will have a chance to see him tomorrow, and I am sure you will like him. His parents are coming to talk matters over and have everything settled. (J. Simon)

Two years later, again in the *Syrian World*, editor Salloum Mokarzel (under the pen name A. Hakim) deplored the number of matches still arranged between *Syrian* couples where the daughter was "treated like so much chattel, totally subservient to the will of her father and mother" (3.5:28).

But if women I have interviewed from that era are any indication, such total subservience was not the rule. Almost all felt that they had married the man of their choice and that the initiative had lain with the couple rather than with their parents. But like most of their *Syrian*-American contemporaries, they had followed an etiquette of courtship that modified rather than revolutionized the Old World system. Though by the 1930s, most *Syrian* American marriages (except in insulated communities) were probably not arranged, introductions frequently were and parental approval usually remained all important. "I never would have married a man my father wouldn't give his blessings to," one woman told me. Of course, the accepted suitor was almost inevitably Arab, his family commonly from the same village or a neighboring one, and of the same religion. More often than not, *Syrian* women in America married the men they would have married back home.

Even in America, girls did not date though they might go out with boys in mixed groups or gather at someone's home. Progressive parents might let the young people roll up the rug, put on the victrola, and tango. A young man seriously interested in courtship was expected to call on the girl and her family, thus alerting them to his intentions and allowing them opportunity to inquire into his family background and his worldly prospects. Sophie, a second-generation girl, born in 1910, told me that she entertained her young man at home for three years until the day his parents formally called on hers to ask for her hand. Only then did the young couple go out alone.

Though twenty years younger than Sophie, Lucille told a similar story:

My father taught me this way. "Home courtship is the cleanest." That means having the young man call at home to be in a family setting. I never did go out alone on a date in my whole life. Except the only time was after my father's death, and it was a young man that proposed before I went out. And he talked to my mother before I consented to go with him. Now I was in my thirties [and a successful businesswoman] then.

This parlor courtship worked well for girls who accepted it, as most probably did. But some rebelled, in word more often perhaps than in deed. In 1929, a debate erupted in the *Syrian World*, precipitated by a three-part series, "The Marriage Problem Among Syrians," written by Salloum Mokarzel, owner and editor of the magazine, who was the father of five children, all of them girls. Mokarzel advocated "the modern method of personal choice [of a mate], with the sanction and approval of the parents" (Hakim, 3.5:28), pretty much the system that Sophie, Lucille, and many other girls were governed by. It was not a radical proposal. But it prompted an outpouring of letters. One American-born girl actually defended the custom of arranged marriages.

I would say that [in] the marriages in which the parents did the selecting, the results seem to have been very successful and encouraging. . . . They generally use good judgment. (Absi 48)

To girls who complained that they were not allowed to date but their brothers were, she replied,

Our parents impose restrictions mainly for [our] protection; . . . so, girls, let's not complain about not being allowed privileges as are the Syrian boys because our prudent parents know exactly what they are doing. (Absi 47)

The other side was represented by the following letter from Mishawaka, Indiana:

Girls everywhere are beginning to awaken. They want more freedom. They are going to demand it—and will get it. Every time a bunch of girls get together all they can talk about is why they can't have the same freedom as the rest of girls, and why should the boys have all the freedom, and they none.
    It is not fair. (Soloman 3.7:48)

Writing again two months later, she warned that rather than abiding by their parents' rules, "many girls will step out secretly" (3.9:46).
    Some certainly did. One second-generation girl, born in 1906, told me this story:

One time I was supposed to have gone over to my friend Alexandra's house, but instead the two of us went with her sister to a christening. What a time we had! In the bathroom, they had scoured the bathtub, and there was this pig all roasted in the bathtub. They had caterers, and the liquor was flowing. So Alexandra met a fellow and I met a fellow. He wanted my name, and the other took hers. We were going to double date. But somebody got whiff of it, and I couldn't go out for a whole week, even to Alexandra's.

The double standard applied to sons and daughters troubled girls, not just because it seemed unfair, but because of its practical consequence, the loss of potential husbands. The editor of the *Syrian World* saw the same danger. In 1928, he remarked on the increasing number of *Syrian* boys marrying girls of other nationalities and offered this explanation:

Boys are naturally more adventurous and enjoy among us much more freedom than do the girls. Our boys go the way of their American chums and encounter no restrictions in courting and taking their girl friends to dances and parties and theatres, the natural result being proposal and marriage.

These same boys may know *Syrian* girls for whom they might have developed preference as wives if it were but possible for them to meet oftener under favorable circumstances. (Hakim, 3.6:23)

But meetings between *Syrian* boys and girls were exactly what community gossips fed on. Or, as one young man in Detroit complained,

It still seems the unchanging rule among the old folks that a young man cannot speak to a young lady unless he contemplates marriage, and that once a girl is seen talking to a boy it necessarily follows that they are engaged or otherwise people will begin to question the character of the girl as to why did So-and-so stop his calls on her. This is carrying the point a little too far and stands in the way of our girls finding mates. (Aboud 47)

The upshot of the matter, said another Arab American newspaper, was that

Syrian and Lebanese young women in America are placed at a disadvantage. They are hidden pearls whose beauty is not permitted to be brought to light by proper social contact. Due to this deplorable condition, the number of unmarried girls among us is steadily mounting. ("Breach" 46)

All this is a bit overstated. The vast majority of *Syrian* girls did marry. Still, running over in my mind the women of that time and generation that I have known, I have been surprised at the number who remained single despite growing up in an ethnic community where marriage was considered every woman's natural and inevitable fate. Most of the women I broached the subject with, whether married or single, laid the responsibility for involuntary spinsterhood squarely on the shoulders of the parents. "I had plenty of admirers," Alice told me, "and they were all nice, respectable men; but any time one of them would come to the house, my father would put on a long face and say, 'You'll have no luck here.'" Why did her father act this way, I asked. "He didn't want to lose me," she answered. "My mother was dead, I was the oldest, I did everything. He was lame and couldn't work. Without me where was the bread and butter going to come from? If a daughter was valuable at home," she added, "the fathers did not let loose."

It is only fair to say that no other woman I talked to identified parental greed as a reason why girls did not marry. "Oh, no," said one when I asked her about it. "I don't think they would want me not to get married just for the few dollars they were getting from me. I think they wanted someone real nice who could give me a good living and came from a good family."

But she, too, blamed her parents for overprotective behavior, like her father's meeting her every day after work to escort her home and so scare off any young man who might happen by. Another woman put it this way:

You know, if the Prince of Wales came and asked for me, my father would say, "No, you can't have her." He didn't want to part with me. Poor fellow, he was the dearest man that ever lived.

A woman who married late in life spoke more bitterly.

Whenever anyone came around, my mother and father said he wasn't good enough for me. It's fine to please your parents, but too much is too much. Everyone should look out for their own future. But when we were young, we didn't think like that. Now we know better.

This woman regretted not having defied her parents as girls sometimes did. "Elopement was the only way a lot of girls got married in those days," one told me. "When the parents found out, they were mad for a little while, but they got over it."

Emigration brought new opportunities to *Syrian* women and their daughters; in America they could achieve economic independence and, partly in consequence, a greater degree of self-direction in their personal lives. Parental authority, however kindly meant, was undermined; in choosing a mate, the burden of responsibility gradually shifted from parents to children. But at that point where parents felt less responsibility, less need, and sometimes less desire to marry off their daughters, and where daughters were still constrained, even if unconsciously, by Old-World notions of female decorum and filial piety, the price was paid. If fewer daughters were cajoled or pressured into matches neither of their choosing nor to their liking, others were prevented from marrying at all and so from having children—in short, from achieving what their culture had taught them to believe were women's proper goals and their only avenue to dignity and happiness.

My first admirer was Robert Hope, the class showoff who swallowed ants, flies, and anything else the other kids fed him and whose lips were always blue from sucking on inky scraps of composition paper. He'd yank my thick pigtails when I wasn't looking and chase me home from school each day, careful never to catch me because what would he do with me then? Once, though, in a fit of malice, he got close enough to swipe at my arm and made me spill a stack of Christmas cards our teacher, Mr. Karp, had given me to mail. Envelopes upside down in the snow, white on white, I couldn't be sure I'd retrieved them all. Mr. Karp would be very angry, and he would blame me. When I tried to tell him about it the next day, I was so nervous I couldn't think of the word "I." "Me dropped your letters," I said.

When I reached the fifth grade, Ernest Donaruma, who lived in a fancy brick house on the West Roxbury Parkway, said would I go to the movies with him, then pinned me against a lamp post outside the schoolyard and pushed his face in close to kiss me. When I hollered and scratched him, he backed off in a hurry. After that, I wasn't sure the invitation was still open, but I liked Ernest, so I thought I'd just mention it to my mother. She kept saying, "What! What!" and that my father'd better not hear about this.

She hadn't taken that well, I thought. So I never told her about Edward Dunn, the new boy in class that my best friend Ruth and I tailed home one day, not knowing what else to do when we liked a boy. Ruth's parents were sober-faced Methodists, her father superintendent of the Sunday School; mine were Arabs who sent me out of the room whenever adult conversation threatened to take an interesting turn. Prissy and smug, Ruth and I made the mistake of hanging out with each other, instead of with the C+ run of girls, who were busily piecing together the facts of life.

When I finally got wind of how things were, I wanted to be sure. And I was mad. Why should everyone know but me? I found my mother upstairs in my bedroom, putting new white sheets on my bed. "I want you to tell me where babies come from," I screamed. And I made her do it. In two clipped sentences, which was all she could manage, she diagrammed the mechanics of sex. So it was true. It was awful. "You just have to put up with it," she said smoothing out the last wrinkle, "it doesn't take long."

And yet when I got my first period, she was all smiles, only astonished that I didn't know what was happening to me. Hadn't I heard girls talk? And no dire warning about boys. No curfews ever, or rules about where I could go or friends I could go with. No dates either, of course. I didn't much care except maybe when I missed my senior prom. But, since I went to an all-girls school, I would have had to do the asking, and though I fantasized all the time about boys, there was no flesh and blood specimen I could think of to be seen with. So my high school years passed without our ever having it out.

Once I got away to college, my parents couldn't stop me from dating— the little bit that I did date. They just looked the other way and trusted that once I put my mind to it, I would meet some honorable young man from a good Arab family and marry him. But no hurry about that.

Meanwhile, there was Steve, the handsome WASP I dated for most of my junior year. ("How did you land *him*!" asked a friend I never forgave.) Once when I was home for the weekend, he picked me up and drove me back to campus. And then, a couple of times, he dropped by the house when I wasn't there, thinking he could charm my parents into liking him. They were always polite—would not have known how to be otherwise. But they must have wondered who was this blond outlander and what did he want from them? Surely, not their daughter.

That spring break, Steve came by the house again, and we went out and came back late, parked the old VW bug down the street, and made out for an hour. At one point, the neighborhood cop, walking his beat, stopped to peer into the car, but when he saw it was only me, he smiled and moved on. My mother met me at the door, beside herself with fury and, I suppose, with panic. Where had I been? Wretch that I was, what had I been doing? She would not let me go to bed until I told. There was so little to tell, but even that little would have been too much for her. It had been a late party, I said. What was the problem?

She scared me that night. I'd been pretending to myself that I could go and come as I pleased; I'd forgotten what she could never forget, the village culture in her bones, the dread of being shamed, never able to marry off your children or visit your neighbor, the misery of having everyone look through you as if you had ceased to exist or were less than the dirt under their feet. Born in the nineteenth century and into another world, old enough to be my grandmother, she did her best. And I learned to do my part, lying and leading a double life, anything rather than rouse again that killing rage.

PART II

From Second Generation to Third

10

FIGHTING "POLITICAL RACISM"

In his stirring address to the 1984 Democratic National Convention, Jesse Jackson did something no candidate for president had ever done before from such a platform. He spoke of Arab Americans. And he did so in sympathetic terms. "Arab Americans, too," he said, "know the pain and hurt of racial and religious rejection. They must not continue to be made pariahs." As Jackson was well aware, the rejection experienced by Arab Americans in recent decades has had much to do not just with race and religion but with international politics, specifically the Middle East conflict between Arabs and Israelis. More than any other circumstance, that conflict has influenced the way in which Americans have come to view Arabs and, even more important, the way in which Arab Americans have come to view themselves.

In the months leading up to the convention, Jackson had drawn heavy fire whenever he deviated from the strictly pro-Israeli position to which presidential candidates had always adhered. Now in his convention speech, he again reminded his audience that there were twenty-two nations (not just one) in the Middle East, a statement that encapsulated his advocacy of closer ties with the Arab world and his criticism of American policies in that part of the world. That such a position should be considered so beyond the pale of legitimate political discourse explains why Arab Americans have often felt alone and frustrated in their attempts to influence American public policy. This kind of blackballing, in which a group of people with an unpopular point of view are vilified or ignored or intimidated into silence, constitutes a special genre of ethnic prejudice, one that has been labeled "political racism" (Samhan 11).

Not that Arab Americans have been immune to the more garden varieties of prejudice regularly visited upon immigrants and their children. Earlier in the century *Syrians*, too, were victims of the nativist hysteria that blamed

America's social and political ills on the millions of southern and eastern Europeans streaming into the country. According to the pseudo-science of the day, these "new" immigrants—Italians, Jews, Poles, Greeks, and others— were a different breed from the peoples who had built the United States. Racially inferior, genetically incapable of understanding America's institutions or operating within its laws, the newcomers and their progeny—so the theory went—could never be "Americanized."

The Chinese, although not really "new" immigrants—they had arrived on the West Coast at the same time the Irish were arriving in the East,— were the first to be identified as unassimilable, and by 1882, the country had shut its doors to virtually all of them. Soon the same charges leveled at the Chinese—that they were intellectually retarded, morally debased, yet about to overrun the country—were also brought against the so-called Alpine and Mediterranean races. In 1916, Madison Grant, an anthropologist at the American Museum of Natural History, explained how the hordes would take over. Real Americans, he warned, unwilling to subject their children to a society rife with imposter Americans, would simply refuse to procreate.

The native American of Nordic stock will not bring children into the world to compete in the labor market with the Slovak, the Italian, the *Syrian*, and the Jew. He is too proud to mix socially with them and is gradually withdrawing from the scene and abandoning to these aliens the land which he conquered and developed. . . . These immigrants adopt the language of the native American, they wear his clothes, they steal his name, and they are beginning to take his women, but they seldom adopt his religion or understand his ideals. (359)

Within a decade, Congress passed legislation intended, as its proponents openly admitted, not so much to limit the total volume of immigration as to all but eliminate the entrance of lesser "races." As President Calvin Coolidge said in signing the bill, "America must be kept American."

It was in this charged atmosphere that the Reverend A. W. Mansur, a regular contributor to the *Syrian World*, declared, "I know the meaning, suffering, and consequence of race prejudice. I have seen my crucifiers plan my crucifixion, prepare the cross, and with hammer and nails crucify me on that cross" (9). His calling must excuse his rhetoric. The fact of the matter is that *Syrians*, as a group, did not bear the brunt of nativist prejudice. Their numbers, relatively speaking, were so few (and therefore so unthreatening) that *Syrians* were usually just lumped in with other undesirables and did not attract the widespread hostility directed specifically against Jews, for instance, or before that, against the Irish.

Still, as non-Europeans, *Syrians* occupied a vulnerable no man's land between West and East and, when noticed at all, were often seen as even more alien and degenerate than other Mediterranean peoples. One need only recall the Boston social worker who wrote that "next to the Chinese, who can never be in any real sense Americans, the *Syrians* are the most foreign of all our foreigners, . . . and out of all the nationalities would be distinguished for nothing whatever excepting as curiosities" (Woods 46). Thus it was that the *Syrians* saw their right to citizenship—previously unchallenged—suddenly called into question in the second decade of this century. Did they belong in the same family with Europeans or with their fellow "Orientals" to whom citizenship had long been denied? That question was debated in a series of court cases running over fifteen or more years before being laid to rest, the *Syrian* finally being deemed "white" enough for naturalization.

To millions of Americans, the darker pigmentation of many new immigrants proved their inferiority. In Birmingham, Alabama, where *Syrian* merchants were doing well, a candidate for coroner distributed handbills that read,

They have disqualified the negro, an American citizen, from voting in the white primary. The Greek and *Syrian* should also be disqualified. I DON'T WANT THEIR VOTE. If I can't be elected by white men, I don't want the office. (Hitti 89)

In that same city, older *Syrians* recall being turned away from "whites only" restaurants and other public facilities (Conklin and Faires 77). In Arkansas, even in the early fifties, a Palestinian I know, traveling through the South for the first time, stood for long minutes staring uncertainly at a gas station's two rest rooms, one for "whites" and the other for "coloreds," bitterly conscious, as he never had been before, of his brown skin and black hair.

In all this, there was little to set *Syrians* apart from other "new" immigrants. Likewise, children of all the "new" immigrants knew pretty much the same pain: humiliation at the myriad details of food, religious observance, and household ritual that marked their family as foreign. (I would not take *Syrian* bread to school. And Miss Young refused to believe that at home her *Syrian* pupils ate a mix of bulghur and onion, ground with raw lamb. "*Rare* lamb, children," she kept correcting us.) Then, too, there was embarrassment at the accent of most parents and at the illiteracy of some; "This too we remember"—writes an Italian American historian—"that America has taught children to be ashamed of their parents" (Vecoli 120–121). For the daughters of "new" immigrants, there was also despair at ever looking American pretty no matter what we did with make-up, clothes, and unruly hair, or how often we used depilatory.

Still, many in the second-generation persisted in trying to melt down into all-American blandness. Signs of that effort were evident even in little things, such as the dinner menus of *Syrian*-American clubs in Lansing, Michigan. Year after year, immigrant women raised funds by serving meals of stuffed

grape leaves, Arab-style roast chicken, hummus, and baklawa; the organizations their sons and daughters formed also gave dinners, but theirs started
with fruit cup, moved on to steak, and ended with lemon meringue pie. The
push toward Americanization also dictated what the groups called themselves. Straightforward names like Syrian Women's Club or Syrian Mothers
Club were good enough for the immigrant generation. Their children
adopted exotic monikers like the Phoenicians or (in Boston) the Caravaneers,
and logos featuring sand dunes and oases that had nothing to do with Lebanon, a land of mountains, seacoast, and fertile plain.

It was partly high spirits and the desire for a catchy name, one that would
conjure up a romantic storybook picture. But in exoticizing themselves, these
young people were seeing themselves through the eyes of others, having
already become half other themselves. Their stunted ethnicity, increasingly
restricted to home, was allowed out only when it was safe, for instance when
Syrians were offered a table at an ethnic fair or invited to participate in an
ethnic fashion show. On those occasions, their *Syrianness*—or some tamed
version of it—was paraded before the American public, like a well-groomed
house cat out on a leash that could be relied on not to scratch or hiss.

The second generation married and had children of their own. Born in
the boom days of World War II or shortly thereafter, the third generation
were given things many of their parents had wanted but often missed out
on: dance classes, summer camp, college, license to date. More outlandishly,
they were allowed to bicycle across America or to backpack in Europe. Many,
children of their time, fell away from organized religion; others, taking their
cue from their parents, found they were more comfortable in Episcopal,
Methodist, or Roman Catholic churches than in Eastern-rite churches or
mosques. Though generally conservative and more wedded than they knew
to home values, a few let it all hang out in the sixties—flirting with drugs,
free love, and one protest movement or another. *Syrian* Americans, their
own historians repeatedly said, were one of the best acculturated ethnic
groups in America.

Still, there were frequent pinpricks and sometimes deeper wounds re-
minding even the American-born of their heritage. Middle East politics
would not go away. Many *Syrian* Americans distanced themselves from the
overseas trauma, denying that it had anything to do with them. But whether
they liked it or not, the conflict between Arabs and Jews was gradually becoming inseparable from their sense of themselves. As was probably inevitable, given the persistence with which the United States was involving itself
in the Middle East and given, too, the public discourse that followed from
and was used to justify that involvement.

Already by midcentury, the tension between Middle Eastern Arabs and
transplanted European Jews had been reduced to a morality play in which
the forces of good, represented by "little Israel," confronted the forces of
evil, represented by the millions of Arabs in whose midst Israel had been

established. In the 1960s, a Jewish friend told me she had never in her life heard anyone criticize Israel, the implication clear that she was not about to begin listening to such nonsense now. But it was not just Jews or even the American public at large who heard the same drumbeat on any station of the dial they tuned to. The David and Goliath script was so much the currency of the time (and the horrors inflicted on Jews in World War II still so raw in people's memories) that even Arab Americans—especially of the second generation—sometimes bought into it. Quincy (Vance Bourjaily's fictional stand-in) recalls that in youth, his political leanings were, if anything, "vaguely Zionist" (247).

For those Arabs born in this country who did not subscribe to a Zionist reading of history, the incessant celebration of Israel in the press (as if oranges had never grown in Jaffa until the Jewish state commanded them to) and the corresponding denigration of Arabs (as if they had not created grand civilizations) might enrage, but it did not surprise. Arab Americans had grown up with this script, read it in schoolbooks, heard their friends parrot it, listened as it was preached from the pulpits of progressive American churches. But for newcomers from the Arab world, especially those predisposed in favor of the United States and believing in its noblest ideals, the anti-Arab mind set they ran up against was a body blow.

In the late 1950s, Jean Said Makdisi, a young Palestinian born in Jerusalem, educated at British schools in Cairo (and later to become dean of the Beirut College for Women), enrolled as a freshman at Vassar. Thanks largely to her father, who had once lived in the United States and still celebrated Thanksgiving and the Fourth of July, Makdisi arrived in Poughkeepsie, New York, already steeped in the mythology of America as the "land of opportunity, freedom, equality, and justice for all" (117).

Early in her career at Vassar, Makdisi was invited to participate in a panel on women in the Arab world. After delivering a lighthearted talk about her own upbringing and that of her schoolmates back home, she was bombarded with hostile questions that had nothing to do with her topic. "Why do you hate Jews?" "Why do you want to throw all the Jews into the sea?" "Why should you deprive Jews of their right to their ancestral land?" (Never mind that her own family's home had been confiscated by Jews in 1948.) The audience's response was, she says, "a bitter experience" and a "turning point" in her own consciousness. From that day on, she learned to be on the defensive, always ready to parry an attack (123–126).

But there was worse to come. Makdisi stayed on in the United States for ten years, so she was still here in 1967 when Israel launched a deadly attack against Egypt, followed by punishing incursions against Syria and Jordan. The Six-Day War left Arabs everywhere stunned and humiliated by the ease with which Israel, supported by the United States, was able to crush the strongest armies in the Arab world. In this country, Egyptian president Gamal Abdul Nasser (already perceived as a demon) was blamed for provoking the war. Anti-Arab sentiment reached a frenzied pitch, what Makdisi calls "an outburst of cultural hatred, unprecedented in my experience." She remembers how Arabs became a target for television comedians and talk-show hosts and the subject of cruel caricatures by political cartoonists. She says that

[even] those backing the civil rights and [Vietnam] antiwar movements . . . often seemed oblivious to the parallel Arab demands for justice. . . . The story of Palestine, of the unjust dispossession of its people was entirely ignored. . . . This was a declaration of war on an entire culture and I was stunned by it. (128–129)

If it was a declaration of war, there were those ready to engage. In retrospect, the Six-Day War had one unlooked-for result; more than any other incident since the establishment of Israel (with the possible exception of that country's later invasion of Lebanon in 1982), the 1967 war galvanized the energy of Arab Americans and stirred them to action.

Even then, their response might have been more sluggish had it not been for two decades of renewed traffic between the United States and the Middle East. A fraction of that traffic was made up of Arab Americans touring Crusader castles, taking courses at the American University of Beirut, or searching for the particular house they or their people had once lived in. But most of those taking off across the Atlantic were traveling west. After World War II, young people began heading to the United States to attend college or get advanced training in their fields; many—succumbing to the brain drain phenomenon—decided to stay, often after marrying American wives. In some cases, it was socialist revolution in Egypt and Syria, threatening to penalize the privileged, that discouraged them from returning. Other newcomers had no homes to return to; since 1948, Palestinian refugees of every social class had begun making their way to America.

In fact, war and upheaval in the Middle East have generally meant an influx of Arabs in the United States. Which is why since mid-century Palestinians have made up one of the largest groups of Arab immigrants to the United States, as have the Lebanese and the Egyptians. Tens of thousands have also arrived from Iraq, Syria, and Jordan (many of the last, displaced Palestinians) as well as smaller contingents from the Maghreb and the Arabian peninsula. In comparison to the pioneer generation of immigrants, these newcomers (usually thought to be about 60 percent Muslim and 40 percent Christian[1]) have often been not only better educated and more affluent, but also more politically aware. Many, too, have harbored a deeper sense of grievance, sometimes against their own governments or fellow Arabs, but most commonly against Israel and its chief ally, the United States.

Although for a long while, the new and old immigrant communities led largely separate lives—one side suspected of being too Arab, the other too American—they sometimes crossed paths in church or mosque or on college campuses. There, in the 1940s and 1950s, second-and third-generation *Syrian* Americans helped newcomers improve their understanding of American culture. In return, American-born students got a crash course in Middle Eastern politics.

It was a slow process, this infusing of new blood and ideas into the established *Syrian*-American community, reviving its sense of connection with the Arab world and inspiring a sense of responsibility toward it. Even today, large numbers of the original community are indifferent to, ashamed of, or frightened by the Old World and its problems, about which they usually know very little. Still, through the 1950s and into the 1960s, a groundwork for large-scale political action was being laid. When the time was ripe, Arab scholars and teachers (yesterday's students) would lead the way, in cooperation with a few American-born colleagues of *Syrian* descent.

One such colleague was Elaine Hagopian, professor of sociology, whose parents were born in Damascus, Syria. Elaine's political education started at home, where her first teacher was her immigrant father, a grocer who could read and write neither in English nor in Arabic, but who nevertheless had a lively interest in world affairs. To pursue that interest, she told me, he subscribed to newspapers from around the world and sent young men to the library to borrow books on history, politics, and law. Friends or family would read to him from the books and newspapers; he would listen and draw his own conclusions.

I remember, as a youngster [said Elaine], the Palestinian problem was heating up, and my father said to me, "You know, Palestine's going to be lost. And if Palestine is lost, it will reflect on and have an impact on anyone who is of Arab origin. . . . It will be a real test of the ability of the Arab people to remain dignified and to have their rights."

Elaine was her father's best audience, the one child always interested in what he had to say. "I knew," she says, "that somehow he was giving me a message about what I should do with my life." But it took some years for that message to come clear. In 1962, with her Ph.D. in hand (her father did not live to see it) and an appointment to the faculty of Smith College, Elaine began to network with Arab-born colleagues. Under their influence, her attention was again directed to the Middle East, and she began remembering her father's words—"Dignity." "Don't forget Palestine."

Then in 1967, just as Elaine moved on to Simmons College, the Six-Day War broke out. For Elaine, as for Jean Makdisi, the American public's delight at Arab defeat was devastating. In response, she and a group of colleagues originally from Egypt, Syria, Lebanon, and Palestine (all but two were foreign born) decided it was time to reach as many Americans as they could and tell them a different story. They organized the American-Arab

University Graduates (AAUG) and set about publishing books on the Middle East, holding public forums, and sponsoring seminars.

These activities made Elaine's first year at Simmons difficult; not only was she learning the ropes of a new job, she was also speaking out publicly on the Middle East, thus drawing the attention of those who opposed her politics. A letter writing campaign was launched—she believes by Zionist organizations—urging the college president to fire her. When she came home after classes, she would find the Zionist slogan, "Never again," scrawled on her door; at night, anonymous callers would telephone her, breathe heavily, and tell her she was going to die. When AAUG opened an office, heads of dead animals—cats and dogs—began showing up on the doorstep, and once, someone fired gunshots through the window.

Over the years, Arab American activists have continued to face harassment, occasionally violent or potentially so. In 1985, for instance, a Palestinian man, the regional director of a national Arab American organization, was killed when a bomb exploded as he opened his office door. In the wake of that murder, then FBI director William Webster warned that "Arab individuals or those supporting Arab points of view have come within the zone of danger, targeted by a group . . . yet to be fully identified and brought to justice" (in Samhan 17).

Members of the extremist Jewish Defense League, which expressed satisfaction at the bombing, are generally believed to have planted the explosive. Mainstream Jewish organizations do not, of course, resort to such measures. But some of them (most ironically the Anti-Defamation League of Bnai Brith [ADL]) have attempted to silence Arab American activists by branding them as terrorists or terrorist sympathizers and developing strategies to prevent them from speaking on college campuses.[2] In 1993, in a major West Coast scandal, it was revealed that the ADL and police departments in several California cities had been illegally sharing secret files on dozens of Arab American organizations (as well as on groups listed under the headings "ANC"—for African National Congress—and "Pinko.")

Sometimes, too, the United States government, itself, has spied on Arab immigrants and students, its actions usually justified on the basis of national security. In 1972, for instance, after Israeli athletes were killed in Munich, the Nixon administration launched Operation Boulder, a campaign of intimidation against Arabs in this country, commissioning the FBI to investigate their political views and the people they associated with and deporting some for minor visa infractions.

Some things (like intermittent FBI bullying) stay the same, but others change. Five years later, Elaine was part of a delegation of Arab Americans (at least one of whom had been targeted in Operation Boulder) whom Jimmy Carter invited to the White House for consultation on the Middle East. These days Elaine is even invited to speak at Jewish synagogues. She has been impressed by those Jews in her audience who are "really, really interested in trying to understand the issues." At the same time, she criticizes both Jewish and Arab Americans who turn a blind eye to the misdeeds of their favorite Middle East nation, whichever one it may be. Ethnic chauvinism is a trap she tries to guard against.

If the members of the community over there [in the Arab world] are wrong or their leadership is wrong, say it. Because you're of Arab origin doesn't mean you have to be biased. But it does mean you have an obligation to bring some moral understanding to [Middle Eastern] issues. It's not your exclusive duty; I'm as interested in South Africa as I am in the Middle East. But you have a particular duty towards [the Middle East] because your origins are there.

Those who try to ignore their ethnic roots, she warns, may be in for a rude awakening.

Someone some day will come to them and say, "You are Lebanese," or "You are Syrian," or "You are Palestinian," and I've watched many of them stand there and say, "Yes, but I'm not that kind," or "I'm a Christian [not a Muslim]." They're always trying to differentiate themselves, or they become Uncle Toms, or they say, "I'm American." Well, we are all Americans, that's not the issue.

When Mary Rose Oakar, the former congresswoman from Ohio, first stood for national office, she was not trying to run and hide from her Arab ethnicity, nor was she flaunting it. But she did attend the annual conference of a national Arab American organization at which members donated a total of approximately $900 to her campaign. Other contributions, rival camps pointed out, had also come from people with Arabic-sounding names.[3] Though, as a matter of course, American politicians turn to their ethnic communities for financial support, the modest sums Mary Rose raised in this way were made to seem ominous. "Somehow," she says, "there's a stigma attached when you're Arab American."

In an extension of that stigma, money donated by Arab Americans, even to candidates outside their community, is also suspect. So much so that several politicians have refused to accept such support. In one well-known instance, the campaign of Representative Joseph Kennedy of Massachusetts returned a $100 donation from former Senator James Abourezk of South Dakota (then national chairman of ADC), even though Abourezk had been a supporter of both Kennedy's father Robert and his uncle John F. Kennedy and had campaigned on their behalf.[4] "What is wrong with our contributions?" asks Oakar. "Are we less American?"

Politics, we're told, is a dirty business. But even apolitical Arab Americans are sometimes broadsided by anti-Arab hysteria. One young woman I know (half Lebanese and half Irish), returning from a visit to her fiancé in Florida, was quietly reading a book while she waited for her flight to take off. Suddenly, an airline official appeared at her seat, escorted her off the plane, and—joined now by other airline personnel—asked to see what she was reading. After flipping through her book, he handed it back and instructed her to put it away because it was making another passenger nervous. Perhaps that passenger knew that the book was critical of Israel; more likely, all he knew or needed to know was that the title contained the word "Palestine." When the attorney general of Massachusetts wrote the airline a letter complaining about the infringement of the young woman's civil rights, the carrier refused to concede any wrongdoing. "The airline has no apology to make," a spokesperson told journalist Nat Hentoff. "What happened to that young woman could happen again" (A23).

Two years ago, I was at a party where most of the other guests turned out to be Jewish emigrés from the Soviet Union. They had not had an easy time under Communist rule; one man, in particular, had been jailed for a number of years on some flimsy political pretext.

I was standing in a small group with this recently released prisoner, listening earnestly to his story, when it made a sudden detour into Middle Eastern politics. When he was in Israel, he told us, his friends there had asked his opinion of Meyer Kahan (a member of the Israeli Knesset, since murdered, who advocated the immediate expulsion of all Arabs from territories under Israeli occupation).

"I told my friends," the emigré said, "that they should not openly support Kahan, but neither should they stand in his way. You know, you have to strike fear into their [the Arabs'] hearts." His American-born wife (who had earlier characterized herself as an unrehabilitated flower child of the 1960s) volunteered that, unfortunately, violence was "the only language Arabs understand."

A few months later I saw in the paper that the husband—this closet supporter of ethnic cleansing—had been appointed to a human rights committee at one of our country's leading universities.

Israel invaded Lebanon in 1982, killing thousands of civilians, bombing Beirut day after day with American-made war planes and American-made bombs. The fighting had barely stopped when I went to a party one evening and ran into a colleague, a Jewish woman with whom I'd always been friendly and who taught in another department of my college.

It was a time when the war was still very much on people's minds; the TV pictures of the devastation in Beirut had been shocking, though the massacre of Palestinians in the Sabra and Shatila refugee camps had yet to come.

My colleague, too, was concerned about the fighting. "It's too bad about this war," she told me. "Israel's gotten so much bad publicity, it will make it tough for Jewish politicians to get elected this year." I understood that she was asking me to commiserate with her at the unfairness of things. I said nothing.

1982 again. Another party, this time dinner at another colleague's house. Feminism, the topic. The women around the table were spirited advocates; they fought the good fight; they set everyone straight.

The conversation veered to politics. Our congressman, up for re-election, was praised. I said, "Yes, but he's defended the invasion of Lebanon." At first, my comment was ignored. Then one of the men said resentfully, "You're assuming we don't support the war. But I do." "Anyway," said another man, "it's been a good opportunity to test out American weapons, see how they do in actual combat." Why am I always taken by surprise? I tried to argue the point, no one helped—the women were silent.

PAULA

"The message I got at Radcliffe was 'Cut this part out, it's of no use to you here. In fact, it gives us all a headache!' "

Although Paula Hajar grew up in my home community, West Roxbury, Massachusetts, a streetcar suburb of Boston, and went to the same public schools I did, we did not meet until sometime in the mid-1980s. By then, Paula had already had a successful career as a teacher and administrator in a private school and was about to begin a doctoral program at Harvard's School of Education. She has since completed her degree (after writing a dissertation on tensions between parents and teachers of Arab American children), and is now on the faculty of the Teachers' College of Columbia University.

In the narrative that follows, Paula focuses on the tricky business of making her Arab American identity part of her public persona. The problem Paula seems to pose is this: what to do with an ethnicity the very mention of which makes others uncomfortable?

You know, at one point it became so clear to me that the Arab world was a source of headache for so many people in the United States, that to induce that headache on command seemed very anti-social. And so I did that classic accommodation of getting to know someone first so that they would like me so that then when I told them I was Lebanese, they would have something to fall back on. This was from the mid-1960s on. Before that, everything about being Lebanese was still a source of pleasure.

In fact, I chose to go to Radcliffe partly because they offered courses in Arabic. I have a long history of trying to learn that language. When I was seven I got my *jiddo* [grandfather] to teach me. He also used to talk about Douma [his hometown]. He had this picture of Douma, one of those long browning photographs, kind of cracking at the edges. I would look at it and look at him, and he would say, "It's like paradise. Paradise!" And then he would tell tales about the fruit and the mountains and the snow and the sea. When I went there in 1968, Douma was exactly the way he had described it.

Anyway, this *jiddo* used to spend a lot of nice time with me. He used to take me on little walks to Grove St. [a small shopping area] to buy candy, and as we would pass, people would be tending their gardens. They all knew him, and they would all say to me, "I'm your aunt so-and-so" and cut zinnias from the garden and give them to me. This is what it means to grow up in an ethnic enclave. Everybody that I could see was Lebanese.

I actually grew up with the idea that there were two kinds of people—*us*, the Syrian-Lebanese, and *them*, which was everybody else—and that we were really at the center of things and everybody else would love to get on the inside where we were.

Later, when I would tell someone [outside the community] that I was Lebanese, a smile would break over their faces, and they would immediately launch into some story like "I had a Lebanese friend once. I went to his kid's wedding, it was fantastic." It would always be a very pleasant association. Then, the summer I graduated from high school, I was a nursing aide at the Deaconess Hospital. I wore a little button with my name. "Hajar?" someone would say, "what's that?" And I would tell them. The same beatific smile would spread over their faces, and they would launch into the food-weddings rap. I began to realize that being Lebanese, by itself, was a bit of a card that I could use to cheer people up. Invariably, it made them happy.

[Even so, there were inklings of trouble ahead.]
When I was thirteen, I remember reading *Exodus* [a novel by Leon Uris, demonizing Arabs] and being swept along like everybody else, but then hearing a cousin discuss it in terms that were rather pejorative. I'm not sure what he said, but it made me understand that this was a story that was presented in a certain way to make one side look very bad. That was the opening to realizing that this was going to be our story for a while, we were going to be made to look very bad.

Then I got to the tenth grade, and in World History we were learning about the Middle East, and they were giving the usual textbook Zionist rap about little Israel coming into the world. I remember one of my best friends, who was much more of a provocateur than I was, stood up and gave a whole different side. I think that was my first awareness that it was going to be quite a struggle for me to buck prevailing winds. My most familiar position would be to sit there, listen to it, and then go complain to somebody offstage. It would be a tremendous struggle for me to risk ridicule or being wrong or being unpopular or being in a minority.

All this is a lead-up to an event in college when the girls found out that

I was not studying Arabic just to be cool. Within a week of my arriving at Radcliffe and beginning my study of Arabic, one girl asked me what a certain word meant. Her boyfriend had spent some time in the Peace Corps in Morocco, and every time they sat down to eat, he would propose this toast in Arabic, but he wouldn't tell her what it meant. She asked me to find out. Well, I looked in a dictionary, but my skills were really poor at that point, and I couldn't find anything. So I asked my mother and, blessedly, she didn't know because it was really a filthy word.

Anyway we were sitting at lunch in the dining room about a week later, and the same girl asked me did I find out what that word is. The table was full, and the head residents were sitting there, too. I said, "No, sorry, I looked in the dictionary, I couldn't find it, I even asked my mother and she didn't know." And then the lights started going on, and one girl who lived across the hall from me said, "What? Your mother knows Arabic, too?" And I said, "Yeah." She said, "Wait a minute. Are you . . . ? Are you really . . . ? But you don't look. . . ." She couldn't finish any sentence she began, she was stunned. She kept gulping air, and then she put all her silverware on her plate, on her tray, and pushed her chair back, and just got up and left. And every other girl got up and did the same thing, left. So suddenly I was sitting at an empty table except for the two head residents.

Had the head residents not been there, my first reaction would have been to deny what happened. You know, when you are assaulted you try to blot it from your memory. But the head residents seemed so upset, I thought they were going to cry. They immediately started pressing me. They said, "Has this happened before?" I said, "No, this never happened before," but I had a lump in my throat.

I'd had all this kind of positive identity and pleasure from being an Arab, being Lebanese, and suddenly these girls were dropping like flies, they couldn't take it. That wasn't the end of it. Within the next week or two, people would come up to me and say things. For example, the sister of one of the girls who was at the table came up when I was brushing my teeth and said, "Is it really true?" I said, "Is what really true?" She said, "Are you *really* an Arab?" I said, "Well, my grandparents came from the Middle East." She said, "Well, what country?" And I said, "Lebanon." She said, "Well, that's not so bad."

I remember calling my mother up, but I couldn't tell her what had happened because there was nothing my parents had ever said to me that had prepared me for this. So I just said, "This is a very strange place and there are some pretty strange people here." I was afraid that my parents wouldn't know what to say to me. I *knew* they wouldn't know what to say to me.

I never brought it up with any of those [girls at Radcliffe], I became very good friends with at least one of them, actually the one who did the main questioning. I figured she needed a month to cool out. She did cool out. By the end of the year, we were doing photography together, she was teaching

me yoga. But she and I never talked about that episode or what she had
been feeling or what effect it had on me. The effect, I think, was what I said
before. I decided that since accommodation and making people comfortable
was such a big part of our [Arab] culture, then that meant you didn't bring
this [being Arab] up, just like you didn't bring up politics or religion if you
thought it was a hot topic. But my ethnicity was such a central part of me
that to avoid talking about it became a kind of mental or emotional gym-
nastics. It stripped me of a basic tool that I used to measure the world. It's
where I stood to experience the rest of everything else. In other words, the
message I got at Radcliffe was "Cut this part out, it's of no use to you here.
In fact, it really gives us all a headache."

Nowadays you'd think, "How could you give them so much power over
you? How could you let that happen?" But I was just a child. Nowadays I
would see it, but I couldn't see it then.

*[In 1967, when Paula was a sophomore at Radcliffe, the Six-Day War swept
through the Middle East like a hurricane.]*
It was a bitter experience, the 1967 war. I was working with some college
friends at a state hospital doing mental health research. Every day we used
to watch the UN debates [about the war] on TV while we were working.
Every time an Arab delegate would get up to speak, these friends would scoff
or they would start talking over him. I said nothing, but I felt *great* distress,
like I'd stepped into another universe and I was all alone in that universe.

So I decided that what I really wanted to do was to go to the Middle East.
I had had training as a nursing aide, so I spent the whole summer of 1968
in Jordan, taking temperatures and weighing babies. This was a year after
the occupation had begun on the West Bank.

That trip really politicized me—it just created a kind of gut level understanding of the Palestinian situation. But also I suddenly came face-to-face
with the reality of how badly portrayed Arabs are in the United States. Even
I had bought this picture that Arabs [in the Middle East] were really not
quite full people, not really human. So when I met them and found them
to be really loveable, I was shocked.

*[By 1973, Paula had graduated from Radcliffe, joined the faculty of a private
school in New York, and begun a rapid rise from teacher to department head. The
October 1973 War began as Egypt launched an attack on Israel.]*
I remember in 1973 living in a household full of roommates and during
that war they were doing the same thing [my Radcliffe friends] had done
during the 1967 war, which was to mock the Arab side and to cheer on Israel
and to cheer on the starvation of ten thousand Egyptian soldiers in the Sinai
Desert. My roommates *knew* I was Lebanese. That was what was so astonishing to me. I mean, I'd been cooking Arab food for them for years. In my
room, all the pictures of the Palestinian people that I had met in 1968 were

displayed. Yeah, they knew. But when it came down to it, it was as if I was invisible, or as if that side of me was feather light. I feel a little ashamed that I didn't pound the table and say, "Stop this. There's another side to it."

[In 1982, Paula resigned her job, just as war broke out again.]
I kept thinking, "Lots of people could do what I'm doing in the classroom, but I think there's something else that I need to be doing that only I can do." So I wrote my last report card and went out to get a newspaper and there on the news stand [was the headline] "Israel Invades Lebanon." It was so dramatic, almost as if one train left and the other came into the station. Just within minutes of each other.

Our little embryonic chapter of ADC [American-Arab Anti-Discrimination Committee] swung into action. We would mobilize people, giving them addresses and phone numbers of people to call to protest this, that, and the other thing, and then got all sorts of people out on the street all the time, at strategic locations, gathered card tables and chairs, delivered leaflets. We were going great guns all summer.

I can remember furious long [telephone] talks with the aides to my United States congressman. One aide said, "The congressman is not interested in this [Arab American] point of view." "Well," I said, "if 500 of us showed up at his doorstep, his headquarters in Manhattan, would he change his mind?" And he said, "No."

[As the 1980s wore on and the Palestinian intifada *erupted, Paula made other visits to the Middle East and continued her political education, both on those trips and in leftist political circles in New York. But political debate was not her forte. Teaching was. Soon she began planning ways to bring together the two worlds in which she felt most comfortable: the schools and the Arab community. One idea (now on hold) was to start an Arabic school. To do that, she decided, she would need a doctorate, and so in 1984, she entered the Harvard Graduate School of Education. There, at the university where she had once been silenced, Paula began to answer back.]*
It sounds obsessive, but in paper after paper, I found a way of illuminating the Arab American experience. For one course, I did an ethnography of an Arab school in Cambridge, which was put on library reserve forever; anyone who took the basic course in ethnography knew that study before they knew me. For another course, I did a case study of what happened [in a school near Boston] when a Palestinian student made the request to hang the Palestinian flag in the school cafeteria, along with the sixty-plus flags representing other students' national origins. That paper is still used in a Harvard ethics course.[5]

It would be an exaggeration to say that the things I've done are all a response to that Radcliffe incident. Jesus, a few people get up from the table and it changes the course of my life?! I suspect if that hadn't happened, something like it would have happened. In fact, later, if I would say something like "I went to an Arab American conference," there were people who would say to me, "My God, you really call yourself that!" Which was a gentler way of pushing away from the table. They thought of the very word *Arab* as a slur.

So my activism has had kind of an educative intention, letting people know what they're missing by not knowing Arabs. That's why I do projects—like interviewing Arab American people, trying to put things into print about the community or about what people's lives have been like. Because what I felt in that moment at Radcliffe was "Being Arab has been the source of so much for me, and here are these people who have utterly no sense of that possibility . . . they're missing it, they're missing it!"

POSTSCRIPT

[In the first flush of optimism created by the signing of the preliminary Israeli-Palestinian pact at the White House and the Rabin-Arafat handshake, Paula and I spoke again. She told me what she was feeling.]

This is a funny fallout, but since this peace agreement thing has gone through, I actually feel more positive about working in the Arab community. Which makes me realize that all the haranguing [against Arabs] had its effect on me. But now, with the cessation of some of the hostilities [in the Middle East], somehow I think Arabs are just going to be de-demonized. They're just not going to have to be sucking in their breath every time they say they're Arab.

11

RECONNECTING

Helen Hatab Samhan, born just a year after Paula, is also the granddaughter of Lebanese immigrants, but the ethnic grounding she received in her childhood could hardly have been more different. Although Helen's grandfather, the founder and editor of the *Syrian World*, was deeply involved in the Arab American community and had a working relationship with political leaders in Lebanon, his daughter (Helen's mother) was content to live a more retired domestic life, far removed, in nearly every sense, from the *Syrian* community. Consequently, her children were similarly removed, leading lives almost totally devoid of the things that usually build a sense of ethnic identity. Instead of attending an Eastern church, they were raised as Roman Catholics; instead of living in an ethnic enclave, they were the only Arab Americans in their suburban neighborhood. Not even her father's active participation in the Syrian Orthodox church impinged much on the children's lives. "We only saw it from a distance," Helen explains. "It was all very foreign to us." It's true that Helen's extended family maintained close ties and that her mother continued to cook *Syrian* food. But that was it. "I grew up not knowing Arabic music, not knowing Arabic dancing—I never knew how to do the *dabke* [a folk dance], never saw it done. None of the stuff that even assimilated families tend to continue."

Yet after college—for reasons she cannot explain—Helen began circling back to her family's beginnings. Her first step was to enroll in a graduate program at the American University of Beirut (AUB). For the first time in her life, she found herself in a country where people looked like her and where everybody could pronounce her name. "I felt so much at home," she says, "that it occurred to me that I must have felt a little alienated in my suburban, middle-class, very comfortable, very stable home environment. There must have been a sense of always being slightly different." At AUB, Helen majored in Middle Eastern Studies and wrote her master's thesis on the *Syrian World*. In her words, "it was like a discovery of a whole side of myself that I never knew existed."

While working on her thesis, Helen met Elaine Hagopian, who was then a visiting professor at AUB. When Helen returned to the States, Elaine, who had just been elected the first woman president of AAUG, invited her to join the organization. A few years later, at an AAUG convention, Helen met her future husband, a Muslim Palestinian now living in the United States. She had come full circle and then some.

I would not claim that such conversions are commonplace. Helen, for instance, was the only one among her brothers and sisters who ever grew beyond what she calls "kitchen Arabic culture." But rediscovery of roots *was* typical, in one way or another, of many third-generation Arab Americans who went on to become community activists and even of many who did not. If nothing else, large numbers of that generation developed a friendly curiosity about their grandparents' culture and less tolerance for hearing it maligned.

Some were rocked by the Six-Day War, which coincided more or less with their coming of age, and by the violent flood of Arab-phobia it released. Others were taken by the new fashions in American society that worked against ethnic amnesia. Inspired by the black civil rights movement of the previous decades, spurred on by Bicentennial fever, the so-called New Ethnicity of the 1970s sent young Americans of every background scurrying to trace their family trees, tape their grandparents' recollections, and make general boast—via T shirts and bumper stickers—of just who (ethnically speaking) they were. It felt like turning an old garment inside out, exposing the unfaded but long forgotten colors of the past.

These activities might have amounted to nothing more than an orgy of nostalgia except that there was also Vietnam. The Six-Day War struck just as anti-war sentiment on college campuses was about to drive Lyndon Johnson from office. If American foreign policy in Vietnam could be challenged, why not in the Middle East? Secure in their American identity, the third generation understood political protest as an acting out of American values, especially protest in the service of a liberation movement. And whereas they had once thought of themselves as Syrian or Lebanese, they now—like the activists of Elaine Hagopian's generation—tried on the more politically charged label "Arab," a statement about where their sympathies and conscience lay.

Several years after returning to the States, Helen Samhan began making a full-time career out of political advocacy. In 1980, she went to work for the newly formed American-Arab Anti-Discrimination Committee (ADC), which battles bigotry against Arab Americans and defends their civil rights. Five years later, she helped found the Arab American Institute, its goal to strengthen the political clout of Arab Americans by encouraging them to participate in party politics and by forming alliances with a wide range of groups outside the community.

Helen's career summarizes the political coming-of-age of the Arab American community and, to an extent, the women in the community. Earlier in the century, when American cells of Arab political parties got together to promote the liberation of *Syria* from Ottoman rule or the establishment of an independent Lebanon, any woman in the room was an anomaly. Politics as well as philosophy and literature—anything hard-nosed or intellectual—was generally assumed to be the province of men. Women who had a bent toward community service looked closer to home, meeting the immediate needs of the immigrant community; charity was their sphere.

Today things are different. Political activism is broader based to begin with, and women—many of them second, third, or even fourth generation—play a more prominent and occasionally a dominant role.

LINDA

"She asked me a question, but I was stuck on what she had just said— 'You're an Arab.' "

Linda Simon, daughter of a Lebanese father and a mother of mostly Irish ancestry, has been a journalist in Lebanon, in the Israeli-occupied territories of the West Bank and Gaza Strip, and for four years in Morocco. In the United States, she works as an independent paralegal, copy editor, and translator, while pursuing her mostly unpaid vocation as an activist on behalf of Arab American political causes.

In 1911, when he was four, Linda's father came to the United States with his mother and older brother to join his father, who had emigrated earlier. Then, sometime after World War I, the whole family went back to Lebanon, where the boys, teenagers by then, were enrolled in secondary school. That done, Linda's grandmother returned on her own to the United States, where she worked as a stitcher to support herself and pay for her sons' schooling. Her husband remained in Lebanon. They never saw each other again.

For Linda, her grandmother stands as an inspiring family icon, a model of what a principled and daring woman can do.

From what I know of her, I do identify with her. Everybody tells me she was loud, pushy, and fun. Everyone says she was difficult. But they also say that she was a go-getter, she was a catalyst in the community, and she would do whatever was necessary to make things happen. If she had to cajole or shame somebody into giving money or doing something [for a cause], she would do it. They probably cringed when they saw her coming.

And she was not only a factory worker, a stitcher, but she was active in the International Ladies' Garment Workers' Union. My mother says she was always right up front in the union, that she would help to barricade the doors if they were out on strike and probably caught a few rocks.

In my own case, I think from high school on there must have been some inclination toward public service although to even put a label on it defines it more clearly than it really was at the time. But my teachers were always telling me I had leadership abilities. Then in college I began taking a leading role in things that related to the women's movement: women's health, birth control counseling, and abortion rights.

[Up to this point in her life, Linda's Arab background was not a very important part of her identity. But it would soon become so, thanks to a fellow student.]

Miranda was a lovely young woman—she was beautiful, with cornflower blue eyes and silken hair. And she was always trying to get other people organized to do things; she would have political discussions; she was trying to be true to her political ideals.

One day I walked into a college sandwich shop, and Miranda was sitting there with people discussing something. It must have been right after an Israeli invasion somewhere. She said to me, "Linda, come here. You're an Arab, you tell me what. . . ." And she asked me a question. But I was stuck on what she had just said—"You're an Arab."

Well, I had barely heard the word *Arab* before, and I had never thought of myself as an Arab. Here she was asking me questions [about the Middle East], and she knew a lot more about it than I did, and so did all the other people sitting there hammering out the world situation. I forget how I got out of that spot, but afterwards I thought, "Gee, I'd better learn about this." So I took a course in Middle Eastern history.

At the time, I had been to Lebanon two or three times, but just to visit cousins, as a college student on vacation, and my cousins weren't involved politically. They were living nice middle-class lives in Lebanon and trying not to get into trouble. So I didn't learn much [about Middle Eastern politics] from them, just as I hadn't learned much from my father. He wanted us to be American. I asked him once to teach me the Arabic alphabet. He said, "What do you want to learn that grease-ball language for? You'll never need it."

Anyway, when I was in college, I began reading about the Middle East and realizing how much of a passive Zionist I was. I think a lot of America, without realizing it, is Zionist. They think of Israel, or the land of Palestine, as a place that the Bible gave to the Jews, that after World War II the Jews actually went home, as if they were the same biblical Jews. I was really ignorant about a lot of things.

But I was very fortunate at the beginning of my interest in Middle Eastern studies to have a couple of people who were very clear thinkers on this issue. One of them was an American Jew who was trying to get people interested in lobbying [on behalf of Palestinians] even before the Arab American organizations did it. Once I started learning and reading and talking to people who had either lived in the Middle East or knew about it, I felt I had to make up for all the years of ignorance.

Through that Jewish fellow and through churches, I met other people who were becoming interested in American-style activism on this issue. So by the 1970s, I certainly wasn't in the front line of any organizing, but I was working with organizations that were doing mailings and getting people to come to speaking events and organizing small dinners and speeches and an occasional demonstration.

[Inevitably, Linda's activism led her back to the Middle East, this time not to Lebanon but to the Occupied Territories of the West Bank and Gaza Strip.]

I wanted to be on the scene. I learned so much more when I was on the scene, I felt more authoritative, I felt I could help. So when I went to Palestine [Israeli-occupied territories] in 1988, I went with my journalism credentials, and I wanted to write stories about individual people, small incidents, things that were indicative of the larger picture but that didn't get enough exposure.

For instance, the *intifada* had been going on for a year, and people showed me gardens they were planting that they had never planted before. There was a guy who was a botanist who was giving people seeds and showing them how to start community gardens. And people in the refugee camps were interested in cottage industries, raising their own chickens and rabbits and things. The welfare institutions that the Palestinians were running were encouraging more of this. Even the middle-class women were planting little gardens. They always had beautiful fruit trees, but now they were planting their tomatoes. One woman said, "I never got my hands dirty in the soil before, but look at my cucumbers!" She was so proud of them. Her fingernails were painted, but she bent down and picked me a cucumber.

[In the six months Linda spent in the Occupied Territories, she managed to move from place to place with relative ease, either hitching a ride with a human rights worker or a doctor, or hopping into one of the taxis that ferry people between villages.]

I would find the most heartbreaking things. Once there was a boy, fourteen or fifteen—every bone had been broken. The boy was in a body cast. He was at home, but he had a cast on both legs and a cast on both arms, and he had cuts, and he could barely talk. His mother was sitting beside him with a hand on her son's shoulder. She didn't send her son out there to get beaten up. But the soldiers had a free hand, they could do anything they wanted. Rabin [defense minister, at the time] had recently announced that the way to deal with Palestinians was to break their bones.

I really have to emphasize that when you're occupied by an army, rights are suspended. You can't predict what might happen to you. People are walking around constantly nervous, but their determination is stronger than their nerves. At least, when they're young. You know, all youngsters think they're going to live forever. This is where the real courage [comes], maybe to the point of foolhardiness, but also this is where you see the mettle of a people, in the risks that their young people will take. I was just amazed.

They were always good to me. I don't know, maybe I looked like their mothers. But I'd go up [to the young guys] and tell them I wanted to talk to them. Or I would make friends with a teenage girl in the town. The girls were lookouts, they would throw stones, they would take care of the kids who got hurt, too. Some man said to me, "You know, in this place, after your children are five years old, they're not your children any more." He didn't elaborate, but you could see what he meant. I mean when there's a war going on in the street, the parent [can't say], "Stay inside and take a bath!" I mean it's irrelevant, and even a child can see it, so they go do their own thing.

[One of Linda's most haunting stories is about a Palestinian town that is no more.]

There once was a town called Ma'loul on the side of a hill in Nazareth, which is in Israel proper now. I heard about it when I was visiting a priest who lived on the outskirts of Nazareth. I told him I was interested in learning all I could [about Palestine] and meeting as many people as I could, and he said, "How about people from my village, which now no longer exists?" I said, "Fine." So the priest made his rounds talking to his parishioners, and he went to visit the most interesting ones that day—the ones who had stories to tell, the old people who remembered Ma'loul. I have such a notebook full of information from those oldsters, who all told me about how they had been terrorized out of their homes [in the 1948 war] and had refugeed to the outskirts of Nazareth. At the time, they just squatted on the land, but eventually they had to move in with relatives.

What happened was that after the people were driven out, the Israelis moved in, demolished the houses in this town, right down to the foundations, and then planted a pine forest on the site of the village. As you're driving along the highway, you just see a hill covered with pine trees, but if you go into the forest, the foundations of the houses are still there, and two churches and a mosque are still standing. They're standing, but they're pitted with marks of rocks and maybe bullets—I couldn't quite tell. There's graffiti scrawled all over what remains of the walls. Some of it says, "We love Ma'loul." "We will always remember Ma'loul." "Never forget Ma'loul." But other things are obscenities that, apparently, Israelis have written. Obscenities about Arab women and about the people of the town.

[While in the Occupied Territories, Linda was seldom afraid she says, although she apparently did not shy away from danger or hardship.]

Well, I was caught in demonstrations a lot. I mean *[laughing]* I would go looking for them. I felt that my contribution to this struggle was going to be to observe and to write about it. I felt like I had to take some risk, too.

I hit tear gas a few times. It scared me the first time because I thought, "Oh, my God, I'm going to be blind forever." It's like someone took a whole bag of pepper and rubbed it into your eyes, I mean *rubbed* it in. I was blinded, I had to be led away. I was real scared, but after about twenty minutes, when I saw the results were really going away, it didn't scare me any more.

[By the time Linda left the Middle East, she was full of anger.]
    I also felt I had a better reason [than before] for being angry. I had seen it [the situation], I wasn't making it up. It wasn't just that someone had told me something, and maybe I doubted their credibility.

[For instance] this kid in a hospital. They brought this little, little boy in. And he was struggling to . . . his eyes were moving, he was still alive, and he was looking up at all these adults who were *trying* to do something for him. He died a few minutes later, he just died, you know, with these big eyes looking at everybody, looking at everybody, then he closed his eyes, and he died. This bullet that had entered him, once it entered him it had exploded. I mean, he was dead inside before his eyes even knew it.

There was one guy—I don't know what they had shot him with or what the bullets had done. It was like almost his whole foot was open; there was an open sore on his foot that went up his leg, and he had another one up on his crotch. His friends were there in the hospital, and I told them, "Well, I won't take the sheet off." They said, "No, you take the sheet off and you take a picture of his groin, you go ahead." They covered his face and let me take a picture of his crotch.

So yes, there were plenty of things that hit you in the gut. Those things are horrendous enough, and they're affecting enough. But there's other things about this struggle for fairness in the larger, global context. You know, I'm concentrating on [the Middle East] because of my heritage, because this is where my intellectual interests led me, because of friends, relatives, but it's all part of something larger, something greater. Everybody will choose their corner of this greater struggle and work on it.

[Years earlier in Morocco, Linda had been the victim of personal violence that, in retrospect, helped her understand the physical and psychological circumstances in which Palestinians find themselves.]
    I had just moved from a suburb of Rabat, the capital city, to a part closer to the center of town. It was near some fancy shops and the flower market and near some embassies and schools, and I had no sense that it would be at all a dangerous neighborhood.

It was the day I was moving in, ten o'clock at night, and I decided to go out and get a bottle of mineral water. The store was one street away from [the apartment of] another American woman I knew who worked for Catholic Relief Services. I walked to her building and her lights were on; I was going to say, "Hey, how are you doing? We're neighbors now." But as I walked into the building, these three guys behind me walked in also, and they jumped me. They pulled my clothes off. They had a knife to my throat, and this one guy said, "If you scream, I'll kill you." He was hitting me with the butt end of the knife and with his fists on my head and back of my neck. I was cut, I still have a scar on my lip. I was also wearing a very pretty little gold amulet that my cousin in Lebanon had given me, and he tore it off my neck. Everything this fellow did, he was doing it deliberately to appear mean and aggressive. Like when he pulled the chain off my neck, he did it very roughly and glared into my eyes as he did it. He was playing a psychological game to keep me cowed. I felt like even if I wanted to do something, what can I do against three guys with a knife?

But as the guy kept beating me up, I finally decided that I was going to turn on him, and I made my move. I reached up and grabbed. I got his wrist and I was able to hold back his arm for maybe three seconds—like Indian wrestling—and then I felt he was gaining, he was going to win in just a second. So I took a deep breath and screamed. The moment I screamed, they all ran away.

Well, an incident like that, it made for a lot of introspection. I grew some from it, I understood more about violence against women. I will not let anyone be bullyish or violent with me. The man I was dating in Morocco was very gentle. He was not an athletic or in any way forceful guy. But at some point, he did something playful, kind of pushing me. I drew myself up, and I said, "You cannot touch me like that. You can't play with me that way." He was laughing. He said, "You consider yourself beaten?" I said, "It's just not a good game to get into. I don't respond well to it, so don't do it." So he never did. I would rather live alone and live without love than have anyone lay a hand on me.

To relate it to the political, I saw people in Palestine who had been pushed around, pushed and pulled and beaten by soldiers, who seemed to be using the same techniques as these muggers had against me—bully, push, pull, go in very aggressively, you've got the weapon, they don't, use all psychological modi at your disposal to accomplish whatever your goal is. With any occupying army, to keep a people under occupation means you have to keep them scared. Why else would they put up with it? What little things can you threaten them with every day, every minute, that will keep them worried enough to allow themselves to remain occupied?

Palestinians are living with daily, hourly threats against their lives, the lives of their children and families, their lives as a community, as a nation. If you do something unwitting such as change shirts and forget to change your identity card from one shirt to a new one, you run a major risk. You can be stopped any time by any Israeli, they can arrest you.

But to bring it back to when I was mugged. I don't blame myself in the political sense for having been mugged, but I can see where my submitting to it at first and cowering and hoping that they would go away only made it worse for me and made them feel more powerful. I think of scenes in movies where somebody is all tied up, there's like five guys holding on to him, and an interrogator, a general or somebody, walks over to him and says, "Well, now we have you." And the guy spits in his eye. It's futile! In terms of liberating the guy, it's futile. But it probably made him feel so much better. We may think that's foolhardy, but maybe it was more important for the fellow to show some defiance. It was more important for himself. I think Palestinians are showing this. Anybody I've read about or heard about who has been oppressed and has lived as a slave has said they would rather take any other hardship on than to do that. Although, I do want to be very clear about my own *strong* preference—not just lip-service preference—for non-violence and for negotiated solutions.

So I give abundantly more time to this community activity [on the Middle East] than I do to any others. I might support various women's organizations and issues, but it's not my central purpose any more. It was a wonderful issue to cut my teeth on. It was personal, it was also political. But [whether women or the Middle East], it's all the same issue really. Human rights and human dignity and self-respect and—maybe because I'm an American—also individual freedoms are all part of the same struggle. It's very easy to shift from one to the other because the principles remain the same.

12

WOMEN FOR WOMEN

It may be, as Linda Simon says, that there is no contradiction between being feminist and being Arab, that working for women's rights and working for Arab rights are two expressions of the same battle for human dignity. Nevertheless, Arab American women have not always found it comfortable or easy to be both feminist and ethnic. Take, for instance, Carol Haddad, another granddaughter of Lebanese (and Syrian) immigrants. "As an Arab American feminist," she has said, "I am caught between two worlds—worlds that should be easily integrated, but often are light years apart."

That lament came in 1984 as Carol addressed the annual convention of the American-Arab Anti-Discrimination Committee. To her ADC audience, some skeptical, some cheering her on, she argued the urgency of feminist issues and challenged her listeners to "look inward" at the position of women in Arab American families, churches, and organizations. Were women still doing the "dirty work"? she asked. Was male privilege still the rule?

Two years earlier and, as it happened, just a week after Israel's massive invasion of Lebanon, Carol had brought a corresponding message to members of the National Women's Studies Association meeting in California. Just as she would later urge Arab Americans to pay attention to the complaints of their women, so she now called on feminists to heed the concerns of Arab Americans in their midst. Instead of doing so, Carol charged, American feminists had generally followed (and sometimes led) the crowd who believe that all Arab women are victims of genital mutilation and forced marriage and that all Arab men are oil sheiks, terrorists, or religious fanatics. Such racist assumptions explained, she said, why "past Israeli bombings and the current [Israeli] genocide of the Palestinians in Lebanon [had] generated little public outcry."

Carol was not alone in her indignation. The conference's Third World Caucus sponsored a resolution condemning the Israeli invasion of Lebanon and calling for immediate withdrawal of Israeli forces. The resolution failed. Later, as if to rub salt in the wound, the feminist periodical *Off Our Backs*, in reporting on the conference, singled out Carol's presentation for criticism (Barkey 3).[1]

She decided to take further action. Within a year, Carol had launched the Feminist Arab Network (FAN) into which she eventually recruited about 100 women from across the country, about a third of them immigrants, the rest born in the United States. The members circulated a newsletter, organized panels, and wrote articles for feminist journals and newspapers. Today, many of FAN's members continue their activism on behalf of Arab and feminist causes, but within a few years of its founding, FAN itself was pretty much out of business, done in by the unwieldy dispersal of its members across the country. Despite its short life, FAN served two important functions. First, it introduced Arab American feminists to one another; people who had thought they were oddities found others of their background who shared their beliefs. The effect was to strengthen their resolve. Second, FAN introduced its constituency to the feminist community at large, letting them know, as Carol told me, "that you could be Arab and still identify yourself as a feminist."

The twin desires of Arab American women to join together and to be heard by others did not die out with FAN's demise. Organizations for women of Arab heritage continue to sprout, and their members continue to work with other feminists—often Jewish, Asian, Latina, or native American. Recently, too, an anthology, *Food for Our Grandmothers*, was published by South End Press, made up of essays by Arab American and Arab Canadian feminists.

In reviewing these efforts, it becomes clear that Arab American women of the second and third generation have usually been less intent on calling attention to themselves or to sexism in their community than on encouraging Americans to reappraise their attitudes toward the Arab-Israeli conflict and take a second, less condescending look at women in the Arab world. Whether through their efforts or not, those goals have been partially realized, as measured, for instance, in the pages of the new *MS* magazine, which since 1990, has run pieces on feminism in Arab countries, life in occupied Palestine, a Palestinian perspective on the Israel-PLO peace agreement, and an interview with Hanan Ashrawi, spokesperson for the Palestinian negotiating team. Ashrawi, a particularly engaging figure, was also a featured speaker at the 1992 conference of the National Organization for Women (NOW).

As for Arab American organizations, most are still male dominated but are gradually showing signs of change. For the first time in its history, for instance, both the chairperson and the president of ADC are female. At various national conferences, panels on women or on issues of concern to women, though still few and often tame, occur with some regularity. In a particularly daring move, ADC invited Patricia Ireland, president of NOW, to speak at its 1994 convention.

In her speech, Ireland worked carefully to establish common ground between feminists and Arab American activists, saying "we must strengthen our ties." Both women and Arabs, she reminded her audience, have been victims of malicious stereotyping, media insensitivity, and physical violence. Explicitly drawing a connection between the murder of a doctor at an abortion clinic in the United States and the massacre of worshippers at a West Bank mosque (an act carried out by a Jewish settler), she mocked the commonly heard argument that such violence can be explained away as the work of a lone, crazed individual. Behind those individuals, she said, are "the kingpins, the ones who may never dirty their hands pulling the trigger or lighting the match but who are equally culpable morally and legally, whether we're talking about the anti-abortion violence or the violence in Hebron." Given the fact that American feminism's obsession with abortion rights does not sit well with many Arab women, it was a daring analogy.[2]

Ireland's appearance at the ADC convention, a decade after Carol Haddad was there, was a marker of progress but also a reminder that relations between the Arab American and feminist communities have a way to go before achieving mutual understanding. On the one hand, her decision to address the group sparked controversy within NOW's ranks. On the other, her speech, although frequently interrupted by applause, "raised some eyebrows," reported the ADC newsletter, "and inspired a certain amount of throat clearing around the room." The newsletter attributed that response to her remarks on abortion and domestic violence ("NOW's Approach"). But Ireland's advocacy of gay and lesbian rights must also have made many members of her audience uneasy.

Many Arab American feminists feel caught between two worlds, but for Arab American lesbians the issues may be more intense and the risks greater, although some women have an easier time of it than others. Happy Hyder, founder and director of Lesbian Visual Artists (San Francisco), has found that her feminist circle—including Jewish women who work in solidarity with Palestinians—is by no means hostile to Arabs or Arab causes. Happy was also part of the Arab Lesbian Network, which (while it lasted) offered important support. "One of the things that was really wonderful about the group," she told me, "is that we could talk about what it was like to come out to our parents." When she came out, she met with a mixed reaction. After fourteen years, her father still struggles to come to terms with her disclosure, but her mother's bottom line, says Happy, is "if that's how God made you, then that's how God wants you to be." In token of that acceptance, stoic though it may be, a photo of Happy and her partner is mounted on her mother's refrigerator—"We're up there with the rest of the family."

Before Catherine, a divorced mother in Michigan, came out to her parents, she had already decided they were "expendable," which meant, she says, that "they could either accept my lesbianism or do without my friendship." Cutting family ties, she concedes, "would probably have been the most difficult thing I ever did." But she didn't think she'd have to. "I knew they'd come through," she explains. And so they have, she told me, except that they still find her "strange" on many counts—not just sexual preference but giving up a lucrative job in order to go back to school at age thirty-five.

Still, she says of her family that "even with all of their scrutinizing, they don't watch as closely as some of my feminist lesbian friends." It has been difficult for Catherine to come out as an Arab to these friends; she has not had the same faith that they would come through for her. The reason, she says, is that in the lesbian feminist community, "there is a lot of effort not to be anti-Semitic" and so "you have to be very, very careful about what you say about Jews." Yet, Catherine clearly has a lot of anger at Israel and its American Jewish supporters. In one of her college classes, for instance, she saw footage of the 1982 Israeli invasion of Lebanon as it made its way through the city of Sidon, her grandmother's home town. "I had to leave the room," she says, "I just couldn't take it."

On the other hand, the risks of speaking out against such aggression have seemed unacceptably high. "If I'm in a very safe environment among people who know me," she says, "then I will say something. But in general, I am silent." This is an especially frustrating stance for someone openly lesbian who has spent a lot of her life "learning how to not be quiet." So Catherine has begun searching for other Arab lesbians ("So far I've found five") with whom she can be less circumspect, and looks forward to the day when her discomfort at being silent in the face of injustice will drive her to "say more."

CHERYL QAMAR

"My heart's with the lesbian community, but my soul's with the Arab community."

Cheryl Qamar, the granddaughter of Lebanese immigrants to America, is a psychotherapist, whose clients are mostly lesbian. Cheryl herself has been "out" for many years. In her story below, she reflects on the two competing communities, Lebanese and lesbian, to which she belongs, how they compete for her allegiance, and what they share.

My parents always had a very strong ethnic identity. Their main friends then and even now were Lebanese, and their life centered around the [Lebanese] Church, which is one big extended family-friendship network and community. But in my growing-up years, assimilation was the thing. The whiter you were, the better you were. My notion of beauty was the Breck girl on the back cover of the magazines. I was pretty ashamed of the fact that we were different, that I was dark, that my hair was curly, that I had a big nose. And a lot of the kids that I grew up with were Baptists, so my church was considered very weird: incense and icons and men wearing robes. That was another source of embarrassment.

Yet, I enjoyed the community. I loved who the people were. They were louder and more fun than a lot of my [non-Lebanese] friends' parents. They would hug and kiss you and show a genuine interest in you. It was like another world.

[But as Cheryl moved on to college and became increasingly unconventional in the way that children of the 1960s often were, her ties with the church community, in effect the ethnic community, became weaker and her attitude toward it more critical.]

In college I stopped shaving my legs and stopped wearing a bra and stopped straightening my hair, which was long and very frizzed out; I was a hippie feminist. And as I was becoming more politically aware and very involved in civil rights in college, I began to notice the real racism and hypocrisy in my church.

Once when I was home from college—and I don't remember what triggered this—I became so angry sitting in a service, I just could barely contain it. So I snuck out of church, went into the Sunday School, and wrote this long diatribe on the adult Sunday School chalk board about why weren't there blacks in our church, why weren't there people of other cultures and ethnic groups in our church? Who did we think we were? And then I went back into church [and sat down]. That sort of signaled my good-bye to the Orthodox Church.

[Still, the church had been a formative influence. Even in thinking back to the roots of her lesbianism, Cheryl focuses on scenes at church.]

As I look back, the culture I grew up in was so segregated socially. I remember being at parties or church events, with all the women in one room and all the men in the other. I remember going back and forth to both rooms, and I always thought it was pretty neat that I could do that. The men were talking about the world of politics, the world of business or philosophy or religion, things that really intrigued me and that I wanted to know about. And yet I always found myself being drawn back to the room full of women, where there was more laughter, more gaiety, more affection and vitality. That's where it seemed the real love was and the closeness and the intimacy. But everything was so segregated, male/female, inner world/ outer world. There was a conflict in me and constant pulling. I wanted both, and there was nobody that had both, nobody that said you could have both.

[Not long after completing her bachelor's degree, Cheryl moved east to enroll in a graduate school of social work. After coming out to new friends there, she began the slow process of coming out to her family back home.]

That's a long, sordid story. Oh God, it's a horrible story. I went home after I'd just broken up with my lover of two years, who was a woman and black. She was my first lesbian relationship. At the same time, my sister had just broken up with a man that she had thought she was going to marry.

So I came home to find my sister very depressed, literally walking from room to room crying, and my mother supporting her, wiping her tears, following her around, catering to her constantly. I'm there and I'm observing this. My sister's getting all of this love and attention for her trauma, and I've had a loss that's as deep and profound for me, and I can't talk about it. But I couldn't hide it either. So my mother, being the intuitive person that she is, sensed something and kept saying, "What's wrong? What's wrong?"

By the third day, she said to me, "Please Cheryl, tell me, I know something's wrong. You must know that whatever you say I will never forsake you." Well, that's all I needed to hear. I so desperately wanted to talk to someone. She said, "Tell me, is he Jewish?" This *[laughing]* is the worst thing she could think of. I said, "No." So then she thought of the next worst thing. She said, "Well, is he black?" And I thought, "Gee, maybe I can tell a half truth here." But I didn't. I said, "It's a woman and I was involved with her for two years, and we recently broke up."

Well, no sooner had I gotten the words out of my mouth, than my sister came in the room, crying again. But right before she did, my mother said, "I thought so, but I never in my wildest dreams wanted it to be true." So then my sister came in, provided the diversion, and I left the room. I remember feeling a tremendous relief, it was out, I had done it. In my own naiveness I expected things would be all right once I'd told. So I was feeling good and positive.

The next day my father and sister went off to work, and I was left there with my mother, who then proceeded to light every icon in the house and pulled out her Bible and started lighting in to me about the horribleness of my behavior, how it was against God and against her. She was pretty hysterical. She told me that I was not wanted as a child, that she hated me. I don't think I've ever been through anything that hurt that much. I was so afraid that she was going crazy, I didn't know what to do. I just sort of sat there and took it. So this would go on for hours each day until my father and sister would come home from work.

She insisted that we not tell my father or sister so when they came home we had to pretend that we'd had this nice little day together and nothing was wrong. I agreed to it because I thought, "God, if she's having this reaction, I don't want to go through this with them."

My mother and I maintained that secret for about three years, not telling my father or my sister, during which time she would send me all kinds of Christian literature. My family was becoming more and more not just Orthodox religious but Bible Belt religious. So she would send me all this anti-gay literature, and she would call me up at work and just be screaming over the phone, "I hate you, I hate you. When are you going to change?" So I then decided, with the help of my feminist friends here, that I didn't have to take that abuse, and I began to withdraw from my family. I didn't go home for at least one year. Well, I missed them a lot, given the culture I grew up in. I'm very family-oriented. So I've been making my own forays back into the family, but they won't let me come home as who I am. I recently asked my parents—my father knows about me now—to meet me and Sonia on their way back from a trip overseas. I told them this is low risk, you don't have to come out to any of your friends. But they weren't able to arrange it. I was very disappointed. I said to my father, "Do you ever think you'll come to New York and meet me and Sonia?" and he said, "I don't know, I can't say." As if I shouldn't have feelings about it. My sister will say to me, "How are you going to come out to Krissy?" That's her child, my niece. She loves me and I love her. My sister says, "Well, I wonder what Krissy will do, I wonder if she will ultimately not want a relationship with you." She'll say things like that, and I'll start to cry. [After a long pause] Who are these people? Who do they think I am? They don't recognize the pain and the trauma that I go through trying to be connected to them.

[I asked Cheryl whether her problems with her family had anything specifically to do with Arab culture.]

Well, it's in part the culture. Something about honor, about honor and Arabs. I've shamed my family, and they won't forgive me for that. When I first came out to my mother, she learned that I was also involved with a lot of lesbian things here, that my name was going out on mailings, so she asked me to change my name. And I did. Now I use both names, Qamar [adopted name] and my family name; I hyphenate them. This is where I'm stuck. I haven't let go of my family name, and as I'm talking about it now, I think one of the reasons is that I don't want to lose them. So as superficial as it seems, or artificial as it seems, it's one way to stay connected.

[At the time we spoke, Cheryl told me she had no close Arab friends and no ties with the Arab community but that she was feeling more "Arab identified" than she had in many years.]

What facilitated the rebirth of my Arab identity was the women's movement and watching a lot of Jewish women come to grips with their [ethnic] identity and how it affected their womanhood. So it was through them that I began to look at my own culture and want to embrace it again.

Then with the Israeli bombing of Beirut in 1982, I had a resurgence of interest and desire to claim my ethnicity because I realized what was happening was so tragic and so frightening and that nowhere else in the world would we [the United States] stand by and let such a major world center [Beirut] be demolished like that. At that time, I was just getting involved in video, and I met a Palestinian film maker who became a terrific mentor for me in terms of video and in terms of Middle-East politics. It seemed that my worlds were coming together again, that I could be a feminist now and Arab and political.

So here I was, blending more of my worlds than I ever had before. It was a very exciting time and a very growthful time for me personally. But I got involved in [an Arab women's organization], and their brand of feminism was very different from my North American brand. They were talking much more about nationalism and only secondarily about working for women's rights. Feminism was almost a bad word for them. They didn't want to use it; they didn't want to alienate the rest of the Arab community. But I felt like I was being alienated. So given that being a feminist wasn't safe, I felt like I sure as hell wasn't going to come out as a lesbian here. So once again the potential that I thought was there, wasn't.

But it works the other way around, too. Being Arab marginalizes me in the lesbian community. Given that a sizeable number of lesbian feminists in this area are Jewish, they've done a lot to educate our lesbian community about Zionism and pro-Israeli politics. So when Israel bombed Beirut [in 1982], all of the stuff you saw in the general culture was happening in our culture as well. To criticize Israel was to be anti-Jewish, to be anti-Jewish was to be anti-feminist [because] to be anti any oppressed group is to be anti-feminist—even though the Israelis were the ones dropping the bombs.

But the lesbian community is very much like the Lebanese community I grew up in. It has all of the wonderfulness of knowing that there are people there who will support you and care about you and be invested in your interest, be invested in your development, want to share work, socializing, and so forth with you. That's been a tremendous source of comfort for me. But also like the Lebanese community, the lesbian community has all the pitfalls of being incestuous, where everybody knows everybody's business, all the gossip, but I'm used to that, it's not foreign to me. A lot of women have a hard time with it. To me *[laughing]*, it's just like home.

[So with which community, I asked Cheryl, does she now feel a stronger identi-fication?]
That's a tough one. In a way, my heart's with the lesbian community, but my soul's with the Arab community. Soul in the sense of "spirit." I think I have a very Arab spirit. I think the way I act, the way I move, whether it's my hands, or a certain flair, I'm Arab. And I like that about me, I like that my inner sense of self is very Arab-identified. But my heart's been too hurt by the Arab community, I've been too burned, so when I think of my heart belonging to the lesbian community, again that's where my sisters are, that's where my family is. I have really re-created family through my friends within the lesbian community. I think I've been more loved there and more ac-cepted there than I've ever been by my own family.

13

COLOR AND RELIGION

At recess, I couldn't take my eyes off Isabelle Essex, the only little girl I knew with feathery brown hair floating on her arms. I wished I could pat it.

My cousin Antoinette had reached puberty, and her older brother Mitch didn't like what he saw. "Ma," he growled, "get that stuff offa her legs!"

"You know, in some parts of the world, hairiness in women is considered sexy," the young doctor said, wanting to be kind.

Feminism has done one thing, if nothing else, for Arab American women. It has shown the absurdity of artificial standards of beauty that leave most women, Arab or not, dissatisfied with their bodies and that automatically exclude women on the wrong side of a color line—exclude them not just from the ranks of the lovely but from the company of real Americans. Arab Americans come in a range of colors. Some are nearly as dark as sub-Saharan Africans, a few are blond and blue-eyed, most—eyes brown, hair dark, skin tending to the olive—occupy that middle ground shared by other Mediterranean people. Dark pigmentation and, especially, dark body hair have traditionally been sources of shame to girls growing up in the United States. The desire to assimilate has foundered on this hard rock, this physical evidence of foreignness with all its irrational implications of moral inferiority.

In a short story by Joseph Geha, the female protagonist—a second-generation Lebanese American—sits in a laundromat, furtively eyeing a young man who has stirred her sexual imagination. She notes with approval that he is "the kind of American blond whose arms look hairless, smooth, almost shiny." A second glance reveals that "there isn't a sign of hair in the open vee of his shirt collar. Clean" (20). She, on the other hand, resembles her immigrant mother, "both of them dark-haired, hairy—every Saturday their upper lips tweezed identically red and sore" (22).

The connection between pigmentation and assimilation, and between assimilation and cleanliness, is clear in the recollections of Carol Haddad (founder of FAN), who remembers schoolmates asking if the thyme biscuit she brought for lunch was "bread with dirt on top." Even the "Arab warmth, food, music, and love," she found at home was not always enough to make her feel good about herself. "I found myself *wishing* that we blended into the dominant culture a little better," she says; "*wishing* that I had blond hair and lighter skin."

As she got older, Carol began bleaching her facial hair and the hair on her arms with a "burning solution of hydrogen peroxide and ammonia" that inevitably left a rash. But even a rash was more tolerable than being called "hairy ape" by her Catholic-school classmates (1984).

Catherine (the lesbian who bites her tongue on Arab issues) describes her family as very dark, except for herself and her father, a second-generation Scotsman. "The neighborhood kids," she says, "would call my mother the 'N' word." For Catherine and her siblings, the cultural message conveyed by the taunters took root. "Every one of us married somebody who was European, and many of them were blond. I don't think that was an accident. It was really clear to us that to be white was better. I don't think we ever questioned it."

Still, that preference for marrying light seems to have coexisted with a contradictory attraction to people in whom her family could see themselves. Self-love was never totally quenched. According to Catherine, every time her mother would say, "Oh, look at that handsome man," he was inevitably dark, with brown eyes, and curly black hair, a man quite unlike her blond husband. As for the men on her mother's side, "they would marry these blond women," says Catherine, "but then they would say how the women in our own family were all much more beautiful." In a final ironic twist, the blond wives have all labored to achieve "the elegant look" of their Arab sisters-in-law. "I don't know if they're competing or they just want to fit in," says Catherine, "but they all buy clothes and do their hair and wear a kind of jewelry [as if] they're trying to emulate the [Arab] culture."

In Catherine's childhood neighborhood, it was understood that Americans were not only white but Protestant. More problems! "All the Catholic children really stood out," she remembers, "because we had to go to catechism and confession and so we had to walk down the street from our house to the church at certain times during the week." Along the way, other children called them names, and it was hard until Catherine and her siblings got a little older, banded together for self defense, and learned how to make their tormentors leave them alone.

Religious bigotry is an old story in this country. Jews, Mennonites, and others have painful reason to know this is so. As do Muslims, the country's least understood and most feared religious community today. Since at least the Crusades, Islam has been held in low repute in the West, caricatured both by scholars and by purveyors of popular culture. In recent decades, TV pictures of Muslim crowds overseas, their faces distorted with rage, chanting anti-American slogans or jeering blindfolded American captives have given the public a nearly indelible image of Muslims as a hostile and savage people. The bombing of the World Trade Center in New York, evidently by Muslims, has only added fuel to the fire and prompted calls for restricting immigration from Muslim countries.

Nearly lost in the hysteria is the fact that Muslims—Arabs in particular—have been immigrating to this country for many decades without posing any threat to the United States; their children, grandchildren, and sometimes great-grandchildren are fellow Americans. Today, Muslims in the United States number approximately three million, including people with roots in dozens of countries around the world (most Muslims are not Arab) as well as "indigenous Muslims," the term used for African American converts and their children. If current trends continue, it is predicted that within a generation, more Americans will follow Islam than any other religion except Christianity.[1]

Among the *Syrians* who immigrated to North America at the turn of the century, Muslims were few and Muslim women even fewer. Fear of coming to a land of unbelievers often checked men's impulse to voyage and, prior to World War I, effectively prevented the effort by all but a handful of wives and daughters. With few women of their faith on the scene, some Muslim immigrants found brides among Christian Arabs or among native-born Americans of European stock. With each subsequent generation, this trend accelerated. At first, it was only men who married out; later, women followed suit, defying the Koranic injunction against taking non-Muslim husbands. Intermarriage tended to weaken attachment to Islam and observance of its teachings, as did the fact that in the early days the Islamic community as a whole was small, had few spiritual leaders or institutions to sustain it, and was hard up against the dictate of the day to "Americanize." These circumstances, in turn, made it easier to marry outside the faith.

Even the arrival of a new wave of Muslim men in the decades immediately after World War II did not do much to reinvigorate American Islam. As students or professionals, often from privileged backgrounds, they tended to be secular and nationalistic in their outlook rather than pious. This may be one reason—dearth of Muslim females is clearly another—why over two-thirds are believed to have married outside their religious community, and most commonly outside their ethnic community, as well.

Only in recent decades has a new religious spirit emerged, sparked first by new, more "purist" Muslim students from overseas and then by a dramatic increase of Muslim immigrants from around the world, many of whom consider a conservative brand of Islam central to their identity. Their large numbers, the neighborhoods they have formed, the mosques and schools they have established, and their refusal to be intimidated by mainstream American culture, all tend to reinforce bonding to their faith and may make it less likely that their children will so easily slip from its moorings.

Although there is little evidence that the newcomers have brought back within the fold the descendants of earlier immigrants, there is much to suggest that they have influenced policies and practices within the mosques whose establishment preceded their arrival.

In looking at these mosques and their members, newcomers have often been shocked at their deviation from traditional Islamic teaching. These deviations were the result of a decades-long process of adapting Islam to an American environment. In fact, sometimes the very impulse to build a mosque was a response to persistent queries from American-born children who wanted to know why they alone, among their friends, didn't have a "church" to go to. In that case, the mosque was a step toward acculturation, the American thing to do.

Once established, American mosques inevitably borrowed heavily from American churches, using them as models of what a house of worship should be and what services it should provide. Soon the mosque became the scene of weddings and funerals, of cake sales and dinners. Sunday Schools were established and the habit of community prayer on Sunday took hold (drawing more participants than the traditional but inconvenient Friday prayers). In the last two decades, revivalists from abroad have moved to root out those innovations that seem to them egregiously out of keeping with their faith and to restore the mosque as a place devoted exclusively to prayer, preaching, and Koranic exegesis. Thus, in some places, Friday prayers have been invested with new life, beer is no longer sold at mosque picnics, and teenage dances on mosque premises have been eliminated, as have political meetings and rallies. Where the conservatives hold sway, raffles and other forms of gambling have been banned as have bank loans and mortgages (since they are seen as inconsistent with the Koranic teaching against usury). Sometimes, too, as in a major Detroit mosque, the reformers have ousted American-born imams, replacing them with religious leaders from overseas whose views coincide with their own.[2]

Such reforms have not taken root universally. But where they have, the result has been conflict with those earlier immigrants and their families who built the mosques in the first place and the alienation of second-, third-, and fourth-generation Muslims in America, especially girls and women. From the first, Muslim women were instrumental in building American mosques and thus keeping alive their religion in this country. They cooked dinners, held bazaars, taught Sunday School, and helped administer the affairs of the mosques. To the reformers, the prominent role played by women in mosque affairs was inappropriate and unacceptable. Historians Yvonne Haddad and Adair Lummis report that in one mosque where women had been elected to the governing board, the results were invalidated and a new policy put in place, excluding women from eligibility (130).

The way Muslim women dress in America has also been a bone of contention. Traditionally, Muslim women have been enjoined to dress modestly, which according to conservative interpretation means covering everything but face and hands. (The veil was seldom worn by Arab immigrants, even in the land of their birth.) But according to Haddad and Lummis, "Few if any of the Muslims born in the United States dress in this fashion" except perhaps in the prayer room of a mosque. Haddad and Lummis quote one woman who sums it up this way:

How women dress outside of the mosque is their own private business. I don't want to go to college with my head covered, and wearing a short skirt does not make me a bad Muslim. I am a Muslim and I am proud to say it, but I want to say it in ways other than dressing in obnoxious clothing. . . . I want to look normal. (132, 133)

Recent immigrants, especially older women from rural areas, are more likely to conform to traditional dress and (men and women alike) to deplore the miniskirts, shorts, and bathing suits sometimes donned by younger, American-born Muslims. Such disapproval can carry weight. Women inclined to resist strictures on their dress (and to challenge other conservative dictates) may jeopardize their reputation and therefore, if they are single, their prospects of finding a mate. As sociologist Sharon Abu-Laban says, "The threat of unmarriageability is a potent form of social control over [Muslim] young women" ("Family and Religion" 29).

On the other hand, those women who do dress more traditionally may also encounter problems, especially in the work place. In 1996, for instance, the Council on American Islamic Relations (CAIR) reported several instances of discrimination against such women. Examples include a woman in Virginia, another in Connecticut, and a third in Texas who were dismissed from their jobs because they refused to remove their head coverings. In each case, after protests spearheaded by CAIR, the women were rehired. (In fact, the Virginia employer—a national hotel chain—issued an apology, compensated the women for wages lost, and also paid her attorney's fees.) In a more bizarre case, a woman in Colorado was denied access to a courtroom because of her *hijab*.

Much research still needs to be done on Muslim Americans. But it seems clear that many in the third and fourth generations are, for all intents and purposes, lost to the community, largely because of intermarriage in their family past; they may remember that one or more ancestor was Muslim, but they do not feel any personal connection with Islam. Others do feel that connection but tend to restrict their religious practices (primarily prayer and fasting) to the home, often ignore other injunctions (such as the prohibition against eating pork or consuming alcohol), attend mosque services only on special occasions, and commonly marry outside the community. Still others—where numbers encourage it—make the mosque and its community a more central part of their existence and pay greater heed to bringing their daily lives into conformity with Koranic teachings. But even they do not usually share the unwavering loyalty to tradition characteristic of some recent immigrants. Those born in the United States whose parents and sometimes grandparents or even great-grandparents were also born here may be Muslim and proud of it, but there is no mistaking the fact that they are also children of a nondenominational American culture.

KHADIJA

"When you dress sexy, you feel sexy, and you go out and anything can happen to you. But when you're all covered up, . . . you're so pure and protected in your mind."

Khadija (a pseudonym), former flower child, single mother, divorcée twice over, is the first to admit that she is not representative of her generation of Arab American Muslims. But as the granddaughter of early Lebanese immigrants, she started life typically enough, caught up in the rush to assimilate and knowing next to nothing about her religion.

TAKE ONE

I grew up in this town where everyone was Catholic, that's all I saw. So I wanted to go to church on Sunday, and, of course, I wanted to be a nun! My mother said, "We don't have nuns in our religion." "Well, what's our religion?" It was an invisible culture, an invisible religion. I'd come downstairs in a miniskirt and my mother would say, "You can't wear that skirt." "Why not?" "Because you're a Muslim." I said, "What does that mean? What is a Muslim?" All I knew from my parents was that we didn't eat pork, we weren't allowed to drink, and we didn't believe that Jesus was God. It wasn't until our mosque was built in 1964 that our parents started to learn about their religion and to really value what it was that they had themselves.

So the big value that was passed on to us was assimilation. We were going to go to college, we were going to be as good as everybody. Better! But in junior high school I noticed I had the plague. It was like everybody at the party was with somebody, but me. I had lots of girlfriends, but I couldn't get a date to save my life. I guess it's part of being an Arab American, I'm dark complected. But I don't really know, I never figured it out, I spent so many nights crying. Every weekend. In high school I tried out for cheerleader. Hundreds of girls tried out, and there were only two positions available on the squad, but they picked me. And I still couldn't get a date!

Anyway, I was heavily into assimilation. By the time I was fifteen, I knew everything I needed to know. I knew what to wear, how to walk, what to sing. The American way, that was it! And then I was gone. I went to college, I tried to get away. In fact, my goal was to marry a man who had a turned up nose and blue eyes. If I saw anybody who looked like me, I would run the other way.

After I graduated from college, I got married to a blond guy from Salt Lake City, Utah. He was thirty-two and had been in the Peace Corps for two years. He was supposed to be getting a Ph.D. in international education, but he never finished his dissertation. Then he was going to be a photographer, then he was going to be a filmmaker, then he was a song writer. He was the one who started me writing music.

We [had] a band, we traveled all over, we went to Europe and the South Pacific. At first, I thought his way of life was so adventurous and so exciting. But it wasn't like that. We'd go to Samoa—he had a friend there that he knew from the Peace Corps—and we'd end up sleeping in that friend's house, on that friend's floor, for a month. I wasn't used to living like that. We were married about three and a half years, but I couldn't live with this man who didn't like to work. My father pegged him when we got married. He said, "Jack, I like you, but you're a bum." So anyway that was that. He brought me back to New York, and we got divorced.

In New York, I began pursuing this dream. I was a talented song writer and singer, and I got a publishing contract with Paul Simon. One day I was playing guitar in this night club, and the next day I was sitting on the couch with Paul Simon, drinking champagne, and he's telling me, "Welcome to the family."

Then, when I was thirty, I had an identity crisis. I had done everything I wanted to do, and then *lhamdilla* [praise God] I came up with the question, "Now what do I do? Now what am I? Who am I?" There I was. I had a religious experience. I hadn't thought about God for fifteen years. But I felt so unhappy, so unsatisfied, and I ended up asking God to help me.

[Within a year Khadija had left New York, gone home, and started taking courses at a conservatory of music. Soon she met her second husband, another blond.]

We got married, and immediately I got pregnant. Suddenly I became the most responsible human being that ever walked. I started to look at this man I was married to and at our fundamental differences, which were huge! Just gaping! We had got together because we liked music, and the sex was really good. But other than that, there was nothing. Well, anyway, he's a wonderful person. And *lhamdilla*, we've had a great divorce. But he didn't believe in God, and I wanted to bring my child up as a Muslim, so we had big, big differences.

[After her divorce and the birth of her son, Khadija started working at a mosque, taking courses in Middle East history, and finally enrolling in a master's program in Islam and Christian/Muslim relations. Then, in 1988, Khadija had her moment in the limelight. Her picture was splashed on the pages of newspapers across the country.]

One day I was sitting here on my prayer rug, asking God to help me find a way that I could help the people in Palestine. [After that] a woman I knew called me up and said, "Do you want to be a delegate to the National Democratic Convention?" It was exciting. I could not say no. Then when we got our marching orders and I found out what we were doing there, I realized it was the answer to my prayer.

Our goal was to have the issue of Palestinian statehood and self-determination debated in a public forum. As soon as we got there, we were handed surveys. What we were doing there was finding out from among the delegates—there were over 4,000—who would be in favor of Palestinian statehood. There was nothing to it. Everybody was so friendly, and they loved to talk politics. Night and day! They couldn't get enough of it. And I was right in there. Everybody interviewed me, everybody. When I got up to talk to my state delegation, they brought in the cameras. I spoke about the situation in Palestine and how we can help, how we can change things, and stop all the killing. They had me on the noonday news, channel 4!

[Why all this attention? Because Khadija was the only delegate at the convention wearing a hijab *(a head scarf concealing the hair).]*

When I started working in the mosque, the imam said, "You really have to cover your head if you want to come into this mosque and work." So I started covering when I went into the mosque and then when I left I took it off. After a while, I started to feel kind of schizophrenic. And I felt like I was losing something when I would take it off. It took me a couple of years, but I finally decided I would try wearing it all the time and see what kind of reaction I would get. I got a wonderful, wonderful reaction. At the grocery story, the book store, wherever I went. People were very polite, they'd give me their seat on the train. Maybe they thought I was from another country.

But my mother had a fit. My brothers and sister had a fit. My mother said, "Take that rag off your head, you'll never find a husband." *[Laughing]* She's right!

*[In her Muslim garb—*hijab, *longish skirt, long or three-quarter length sleeves— Khadija feels herself a different person from the cheerleader who used to cavort in a skimpy skirt on the field.]*

How you dress makes a big difference. You can't deny it. When you dress sexy, you feel sexy, and you go out and anything can happen to you. But when you're all covered up, you go out there, you're so pure and protected in your mind. If you're in the grocery store with your kid and he has a tantrum, you don't lose your patience, 'cause everyone's looking at you. You're identifiable, you're an ambassador.

Yes, I am marginalized to a certain extent. But I'm secretary of the board of trustees at my son's very expensive private school, I'm at the Democratic convention, I'm in the middle of everything. But it's like swimming upstream.

Also, as a result of my wearing this head cover and being perceived as different, my son understands that he is different in certain ways. He feels he has a kind of special identity. I've taught him to be a little educator and to understand that people know nothing about our religion and that it's our job to inform them. That we have such a wonderful thing that we want to share it with everybody.

We were just down [by the ocean] riding along and looking at the sunset, and I said to him, "This is the exact time that we're supposed to pray, when the sun is going down and there's just a little bit of pink light left in the sky." He turned to me and said, "I'm glad I'm a Muslim." This is the beauty of our religion; it teaches you to appreciate God in that beautiful sunset.

TAKE TWO

[Three years later, Khadija and I had a follow-up interview. She seemed, if anything, more sure of her faith but also more subdued. The conversation turned first to feminism and then back to the hijab.]

In the 1960s I took off my bra. I said, "I'm going to do this if it's the last thing I do" because I thought it meant I would be liberated. I didn't liberate anything but my bra and my boyfriend. It was an illusion.

Like when they tell you to go ahead and sleep with whoever you want to. That was my generation. You shake hands with a guy and *[laughing]* you just go off in the next room. That was the norm for my peers, as it is now. You grow up, you figure out what's wrong with that. The *haram* [sin] in Islam is what you do to hurt yourself or anybody else. Think of all the things that can happen to you when you have sex outside of marriage. You can get pregnant, you can get AIDS, you can have to have an abortion, you can have an unwanted child. Your feelings can get hurt much worse if you slept with someone rather than if you just talked to him. They didn't tell us any of that. They just told us, "Do it, it's okay, you're liberated."

The one constant in every culture is that women are treated badly. This country is no exception. You might say that women here do not defer to men, but then look at the relationships between men and women here. They're killing each other. The more I realized what the reality was in this society about the place of women, the treatment of women, the exploitation of women, the more I became aware that no, I wasn't liberated, I wasn't emancipated, I wasn't being treated right.

[It was religion that helped Khadija arrive at this realization.]
The more in touch with reality I became through the teachings of Islam, the more of a feminist I became, meaning that yes I wanted to be free, free from all these lies they're telling me, free from cultural influences that tyrannize young people. I wanted to be emancipated from having to wear my skirts up to here or heels this high or being a slave to fashion, or showing fat legs when I have no business showing them. All this silly stuff.

[The change in Khadija's thinking has meant some sacrifice.]
It's a very lonely life, a life of abstinence. I don't date. The problem with the whole dating system in this country is that it's pretty much a foregone conclusion that you will have sex. I prefer to go over to my sister's house and meet a guy there, and we can get to know each other. Maybe we're in the next room privately, but we have people around us. So we know what we're heading toward is marriage, not just towards "I'm going to try you out like a television set."

The more I don't do the things that are forbidden, the closer I feel to God. So that's the way I live my life. And being modest.

[But for Khadija, being modest no longer entails wearing the hijab *on a regular basis. The garment, she finds, is a mixed blessing.]*
I always felt comfortable mixing with men and women when I was covered. It's really liberating, people treat you like a human being, you are protected. That's what the *hijab* is, it's a protection. But as soon as I have taken my head cover off, I'm very uncomfortable with mixed couples. You walk into a room, and women grab their husbands. Not that I'm a raving beauty, and not all women are so insecure, but some of them really are. And you're a target for gossip if you're standing in a corner with someone, getting carried away in a conversation, enjoying yourself too much. All that is what the head cover protects you from.

But what I didn't like was the idea that once you put it on, you can't take it off. If you're inconsistent, people don't trust you, they think you're insincere. For six years I wore it, and then one day I decided to take it off, and it was like everyone was traumatized. Except my mother. She was happy. No one in my family is comfortable with my *hijab*. If my brothers or my sister are sitting around with a glass of wine, they don't want me coming around with my *hijab* on.

So I still haven't made up my mind to go with the *hijab* all the time, the way I once used to, or to go without it all the time.[3]

[Khadija understands, she says, that some people are made uncomfortable by the hijab. *She thinks it may be because they don't want to be reminded of God. But what has most surprised her is the reaction of Muslim men.]*
I met this guy in New York, I went to New York purposely to meet him.

He was from New Mexico, he was Muslim looking for a wife. I wore my *hijab*. He took one look at me, and he said, "Why are you trying to be something you're not?" I knew that he didn't understand anything about me, and this was not going to work well at all.

And how many American women do you think I've met married to Muslim men, your basic American girl married to this great guy from Jordan or Algeria, this fabulous guy. Where did you meet him? "Oh, at the Top of the Hub." "Oh, at this bar or that bar." I wouldn't be caught dead in any of these places, but these guys are meeting these girls and *marrying* them! And living happily ever after, I might add.

So I am so discouraged. I am so envious of these American girls with their Muslim husbands, and I'm still roaming around, not married. I was sincerely thinking I was going to get a good Muslim husband with my head cover. But the message the men were getting is "This woman is a fanatic about religion, and I'm not good enough for her." They were threatened by it, these Muslim men were threatened by it. Like I was passing judgment on them. So I tried it with a head cover, and I tried it without a head cover, like my mother wanted me to. But having a mate for life, I believe this is from God. You're going to get one or it's going to pass you by, whether you're wearing a head scarf or not.

But if I have learned anything from wearing the head cover it is that it makes you think for yourself, something women aren't really accustomed to doing in this culture. Islam is a helpful guide. But you have to be willing to make sacrifices. I don't know how many people are willing or able to do that. Submission to God or to man? Luckily, if God opens your heart, He makes the choice for you.

Members of the Syrian Ladies' Aid Society of Boston prepare to march in the city's Armistice Day parade in 1925. Hannah is in the front row, second from the right.

Stitchers, some of them *Syrian*, work for a dollar a day at a garment factory in Spring Valley, Illinois, in the 1920s. One floor lady—first on the right, standing—is also *Syrian*. Photo (negative number 86–12831) courtesy the Naff Arab American Collection, Archives Center, NMAH, Smithsonian Institution.

Children of *Syrian* immigrants in Spring Valley, Illinois, dressed in their best 1920s flapper outfits. Photo (negative number 89–11909) courtesy the Naff Arab American Collection, Archives Center, NMAH, Smithsonian Institution.

After church, a Palestinian mother and grandmother teach a little girl how to make *tabouleh*, a traditional parsley and bulgur salad. While an older sister watches, the grandfather stands ready to help. Photo © Millard Berry/Photography;

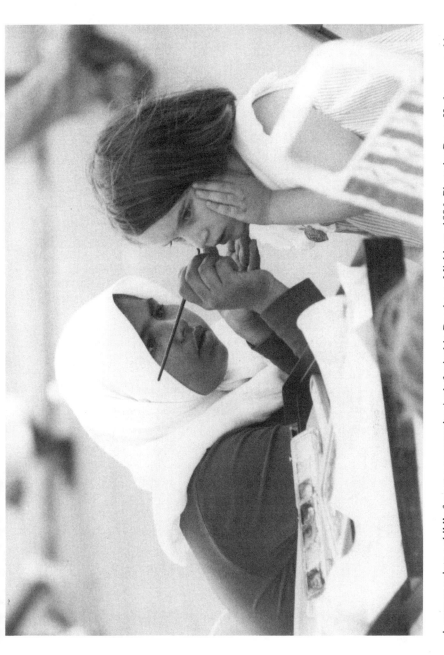

A woman paints a child's face at a community Arab festival in Dearborn, Michigan, 1996. Photo by Bruce Harkness; used by permission of Bruce Harkness.

Women gather in Washington, D.C., to protest Israel's 1996 shelling of a UN camp in Qana, Lebanon, in which over 100 Lebanese refugees were killed. Photo by Haajar Mitchell; used by permission of Haajar Mitchell; provided courtesy of ACCESS, Dearborn, Michigan.

A Palestinian woman in Dearborn, Michigan, watched by a little girl, studies in an English class at ACCESS. Photo by Jessica Greene; provided courtesy of *Detroit Free Press*.

Arab American children race across a street near their elementary school in Dearborn, Michigan. Photo by Jessica Greene; provided courtesy of *Detroit Free Press*.

A young Arab American woman, carrying the flag of Lebanon, marches in a Memorial Day parade in Dearborn, Michigan. On the banner is a logo that combines the American and Lebanese flags, with an olive branch between them. Photo by Bruce Harkness; used by permission of Bruce Harkness.

PART III

The Second Wave, 1945 to the Present

Since World War II, Arab immigration to the United States has included women from all parts of the Arab world, especially Lebanon, Jordan (including Palestine), Egypt, Iraq, and Syria. To devote a separate chapter to each national group made little sense since differences between women usually have more to do with class, education, and family than with country of origin.

Therefore, Chapter 14 selects one group—Palestinian women—for detailed attention both because Palestinians constitute one of the largest groups of second-wave Arab immigrants and because the situation of Palestinian women in the United States represents in clearest and most acute form the conflicts faced by many Arab women. What's more, given their numbers and their preoccupation with the political situation back home, Palestinian women have been among the best organized and most activist of Arab women in this country.

Chapter 15 brings together the voices of women from various Arab countries.

14

PALESTINIANS

These days it is easy to forget that to nineteenth-century Americans, *Palestine* meant not bullets and stones and bulldozed houses, but prophets of old and the promise of salvation. To speak of Palestine was to conjure up place names round and full in the mouth—Bethlehem and Nazareth, Gethsemane and Golgoth; it was to remember the Sea of Galilee where Jesus called Peter and James to be fishers of men, fields where he cured the lame and gave sight to the blind, pathways perfumed by the tread of his sandals.

It is no surprise, then, that the earliest Palestinian traders crossing to America were so well received since they brought with them olive wood crosses, rosaries, and other mementoes of the Holy Land. In fact, news of their success at the Centennial Exhibition (1876) in Philadelphia was probably one factor first prompting Arabs to seek wealth in America.

But once the movement westward started in earnest, it included just a tiny percentage of Palestinians. Only as the struggle between Arabs and Jews for control of Palestine neared a climax, did the statistics begin to change. In the decade before World War II, Palestinian Arabs, increasingly alarmed at the influx of European Zionists systematically squeezing them out of land and jobs, launched protests, riots, and, in 1936, a six-month national strike. That year, for the first time, Palestinians entering the United States out-numbered *Syrians*.

Since World War II, the Palestinian exodus to the United States has often been propelled—directly or indirectly—by the conflict between Arabs and Jews, primarily the 1948 war, which created hundreds of thousands of Palestinian refugees, and the 1967 war, which left over a million, Palestinians living in a depressed economy under Israeli military occupation. The revamping of American immigration law has also been crucial. In 1965, with liberalized policies in place, Palestinian traffic to the United States began a steady and often precipitous climb. Today, of the over 100,000 Palestinians in this country, the vast majority belong to families who were not here thirty years ago.[1]

In significant ways, these new immigrants differ from most of their predecessors, both those who came in the decades before the mid-twentieth century and those who came shortly thereafter. At first, the few Palestinians entering the United States were much like their Lebanese and Syrian counterparts: usually Christian, predominantly male (until after World War I), and likelier than most to take up peddling or shopkeeping.

In the twenty years following World War II, there arrived a new breed of Palestinians, generally better off, better educated, and already half "Westernized." Some were refugees, many were families continuing a chain migration, and many others were students (usually male). More than half, it would appear, were Muslim.

From the beginning, these newcomers had an easier time of it than had their predecessors. For the many with family connections in the United States, it was no great feat to find jobs or establish small businesses. For those who came to study, professional opportunities were waiting when they graduated. In fact, whatever their original intentions, educated Palestinian men (like their Egyptian, Syrian, and Iraqi cohorts) frequently decided to settle in this country, and, in large numbers, took American wives.

The United States was welcoming—or at least not hostile—in other terms as well. Although American public policy and popular sentiment were decidedly sympathetic to Israel, anti-Arab feeling in this country was not so virulent as it would later become; the stereotype of the Palestinian terrorist was yet to be born. For their part, Palestinians had a bitter enough quarrel with the United States (among the first nations to recognize Israel), but it had not yet festered into a blood feud.

Nor did difference in religion necessarily dictate alienation from other Americans, least of all among Arab intellectuals for whom nationalistic revival, not Islamic, was the passion of the day. Thus, through the mid-1960s, Muslim Palestinians in the United States seemed to be setting foot on the path followed by Christians and leading toward acculturation. But, as one scholar writes, "The period of semi-adaption did not have a long life; it became collectively unpopular again after 1967" (Cainkar 109).

The 1967 war embittered Palestinians—in fact, all Arab Americans, both Muslim and Christian. American glee at the defeat of Arab armies was a slap in the face; evidently, it was time to take a step back, to recognize one's enemy. Such feelings were soon reinforced by a new wave of immigrants, many of them fleeing the rigors of occupation. The thousands of Palestinians entering the United States since 1967—most of them Muslim—represent many walks of life and a range of political, religious, and social attitudes. But as a group they may be said to have fanned the flames of anger and made alienation politically respectable. Generally conservative in their understanding of religion and ethics, most newcomers are shocked by the immorality they perceive to be the hallmark of American culture. As a community in exile, which is how many think of themselves, they speak longingly of the day of return to a liberated Palestine. Meanwhile, most are determined to protect themselves and their children from the deadly blandishments of American society.

To Palestinians, 1948 is the year of the "Catastrophe," when Israel was declared a state, open warfare broke out between Arabs and Jews, and thousands of Palestinians lost their homes and their homeland. These events are central to the identity of every Palestinian in much the way that the Holocaust dictates Jews' sense of themselves and their history in the twentieth century.

For anyone whose defining moment is brutal, it can be difficult to feel other than a victim. The sense of impotence implied by that term grows not just out of the failure to avert past tragedy, but—as with Palestinians—out of an inability to shape the present, to persuade people of the legitimacy of one's cause, or to wring from them, at the least, an acknowledgment of one's pain.

Under such discouraging circumstances, many Palestinians (and other Arabs) in the United States have nevertheless persevered, learning to work and wait. Others, especially in the days before large-scale Arab American organizations rallied the community, have yielded to a sense of futility, in some cases going so far as to conceal their Palestinian identity from their own children, not because they feared their children but because they wanted to protect them.[2] To resort to such devices, as a few people did, was humiliating. To pay taxes to the American government (Israel's patron), as almost everyone did, was to feel like a collaborator against one's own people. In either case, it was an "unmanning" experience. Thus one man's comment that until he lived as a Palestinian Arab in the United States, he never truly understood his wife's complaints about living as a woman in a man's world.

For Palestinian women, political and gender-based frustrations have often gotten stirred into the same pot, simmering into a bitter brew that sometimes braces to action and sometimes simply demoralizes. Emily Shihadeh has known both reactions.

EMILY

"What do you want them to throw? Felafel?"

Emily Shihadeh, a native of Jerusalem, is a professional storyteller who makes humor out of trauma. In 1948, when she was seven, her family (Quaker Palestinians) fled the fighting in Jerusalem, resettling a few miles away in her

*father's hometown of Ramallah (now under Israeli occupation). Ten years later,
she married and came to the United States. I first interviewed her in 1989,
when she was doing a comic routine on the* intifada *(popular uprising against
Israeli occupation), which had started a year earlier. Emily began by recalling
her childhood home.*

TAKE 1

It took my father two, three years to build our house. You know, building
a house in Palestine is not an easy matter. You have to go to the quarry and
get big boulders. As a child, I remember seeing the men sitting and chiseling
away at that stone over and over and over again until they flattened it. Then
there's a big, big celebration when you put up the roof because to Palestinians a house means family, it means security, it means the man has provided.

We stayed in Jerusalem until about 1947, 1948, when there was the fighting between the Arabs and the Jews. I remember being afraid and hiding in
cellars and hearing the bombs and hearing ambulances and hearing sirens
and watching them dig out bodies—arms and legs—especially when a hotel
behind our house blew up.

*[Emily's family escaped north to her father's people in Ramallah. While Emily
attended a Friends school there, her father, a physician, worked for UNWRA, the
United Nations agency charged with caring for refugees.]*
My father went around villages and refugee camps, and once in a while I
would go with him. So I saw those kids that grew up to be PLO, grew up
to do, quote unquote, terrorist activities. I saw them in those camps. It was
very difficult conditions, living ten, twelve [people] to a tent. And hardly any
food. UNWRA tried and were kind, but it wasn't enough, of course.

So the loss of Palestine became very clear to me early on, the people
talking about the loss of their homes and lands. You'd see the lights [across
the Israeli border], and my mother would say, "This is . . . was Palestine."
You felt like you were bludgeoned, someone has taken what's yours. That
feeling was with me all during childhood and growing up.

*[At fifteen, Emily was sent to Beirut College for Women in Lebanon, but after
two years she dropped out to marry. Her husband, a friend of the family, had
become a refugee to the United States in 1948. Now a decade later he returned,
looking for a bride.]*
It [the courtship] was very quick, forty days, like Jesus in the desert. It
wasn't quite arranged, I had a say in it. And I said "yes," I guess. I was young
and bored with school and wanting to fall in love. He was kind to me, and
gentle, and it seemed like adventure. We went to Damascus for our hon-
eymoon, and then he left for America. Two months later, I [followed] all by

myself. In New York the porter carried my suitcases, and when he finished, he held out his hand. So I shook it and said, "Thank you very much." I thought he was welcoming me to America.

[Before their marriage, Emily's husband had earned a bachelor's degree in busi-ness and opened a grocery store in San Francisco.]
I started working in the store with him. And started having babies. And all this time, Emily *[referring to herself in the third person]* had never emerged yet. Emily was playing this role of wife and playing this role of mother and was restless and searching and wondering.

So in 1970 [at age thirty] I went back to school. The first semester, I was scared to death. Then it was fine, and I went slowly, two courses at a time, and got my degree. And found out that I have a brain, that I could do well. But I felt total guilt all the time. [I kept thinking] "I shouldn't be in school, I should be at home, I'm not a good enough mother, I'm not a good enough wife." I think definitely there was a big connection with what happened to Palestine. I felt the inadequacy, I almost became like Palestine. Palestine lost, I lost. I am no good, I am guilty, I am bad.

So I've been involved with my own personal story for so long, four at-tempts at divorce [before making it final], doing therapy, starting to like and respect myself. Then slowly I became more aware of the humor that I had. I remember on campus once, there was a flyer. It said, "If you like to make people laugh, if you have a big nose, call me." So I called him, and he was a comedy coach. I worked with him on a routine about my marriage. Then one day he called me up. His friend was starting a comedy club. He said, "Do you want to perform?" So with a lot of trepidation and fear, I said, "Yes, I'll do it."

It was fun. I was getting laughs, and I love laughs. But then one day I decided to stop that routine because my husband, he and I are on good terms, and I don't want him hurt. So I went back to the comedy coach, and I worked on another routine that was more political. It was on the Middle East.

[In the routine] I say things like "Some say that throwing stones on the West Bank and Gaza is violent. What do you want them to throw, felafel? What do you want, a potluck or an uprising?" Things like that. Or "Did you hear that Palestinians have been hospitalized for schizophrenia? They keep saying 'I see my house, I don't see my house.'" There's one line that I love. Progressive Jewish people like it, too. It says, "I was speaking on the Middle East and a Jewish American man asked me to recognize Israel. I said, '*I* recognize Israel. *Here's* my house, *there's* my land.'" So it's done with humor. I don't want to hurt people's feelings—Jewish people or Arab people.

So what used to make me cry and cry, now is making other people laugh and making me laugh. It's almost cathartic. It's like I'm able to speak some of my frustrations. As if my arms were tied behind my back and now they're loose. I can express myself about the pain of what's happening back home. I say, "Did you hear about the Arab man who robbed a bank? He slipped the teller a note that said give me all your cash, I have a stone in my pocket." Those stones *[thrown by young protestors]* are so important to me. Seeing those kids with the stones, it's almost liberating, it's like we're not any more cockroaches as the Israelis have called us, we are human beings. We're saying, "We're here, we're alive, we're human."

I've done some speaking also, here and there. Again, I got good reaction from people. I speak about my own experience, my own feelings. I talk about the unfairness of the way Israel was created. I speak about the devastation that happened to Palestinians. I speak about my own pain growing up, and my pain in this country about the way Palestinians are depicted—the calling us terrorists and ugly Arabs. Then I speak about the work I've done getting to know my quote-unquote enemy, learning about the Holocaust, learning about Jewish culture, joining with people in the Jewish community, letting them know who I am. I've talked at Yom Kippur, I've talked at the seder, I've talked at temples, I've talked to a group of sixteen-year-old Jewish kids. I gather my stuff from my house, the embroidery and the olive-tree wood and the mother-of-pearl and the pictures. I take them and I speak and I try to give a positive image of the Palestinian to combat all these horrible images.

Because I cannot stand oppression. I have myself oppressed others. I've oppressed my children, I've oppressed my husband, I've oppressed my sisters when we were younger. So I know what it is to be the oppressor and the oppressed, and I feel sorry for both. I understand both.

I don't know which is worse; I can't really say because when I oppressed, I didn't know how else to be. I was frustrated and angry. And that's how I took it out. Jewish people [act] out of their own desperation, out of their Holocaust, out of their wanting a homeland. I understand why. But I also understand that that's not the way you do it. You don't take other people's homes and lands. People have done that way for as far as we can remember, right? Colonization. But I want, for once, for us to stand up and say that is wrong. Let's find another way.

The humor allows me to say these things. They go down a little easier. Because I don't want to tell [Israelis or Jews] they're bad people. They are doing wrong things, are doing hurting things. But Shamir *[then prime minister]* lost his family in the Holocaust. How else is he going to think? He helped build Israel in terrorist activities. He's going to be the way he is. He's closed-minded, he's worried about his people, he wants to survive, he's miserable, how else is he going to act? There's no other way.

For the Palestinians, I don't look at big solutions because they're not here yet. I look at little victories, and I think they build up one on top of the other. It happens when people communicate with one another, when an Israeli and I talk, and when he says to me, "Ah, the wonderful, wonderful day of the War of Liberation," and I'm telling him, "That day was a miserable day in my life." And he hears me.

TAKE 2

[When we spoke again, in 1995, Emily was happy with the direction her career had taken, specifically her new one-woman show "Grapes and Figs: A Palestinian Woman's Story." Based on her own history, the performance is a deft blend of humor and pathos that showcases Emily's considerable gifts as a storyteller.]

I am following my bliss, my dear, I'm doing what I love to do. I'm doing "Grapes and Figs." I did it in the Zionist Theater in the center of Tel Aviv and in front of my old high school friends in Jerusalem. I'm working on a new performance called "Me and the Jews." And I'm speaking in peace conferences.

Actually, I tell you, when this [the latest peace process] started, I went into mourning because it was like they forgot what happened in Palestine, like they canceled all the refugees, all the Palestinian homes lived in by Israelis, the Palestinian land tilled by strangers. I always ask for acknowledgment by the Israelis of what happened to Palestine, just saying, "We were in desperation and we didn't see you in our way, we just stepped all over you, forgive us." That kind of thing. That's what's lacking, and what will create the healing and a real way of making peace.

[In one sense, Emily was lucky. Her childhood displacement, however painful and emotionally disruptive, did not land her in a refugee camp or move her many miles from home. It was a different matter for Ihsan, about five years older than Emily, and, like her, a native of Jerusalem.]

IHSAN

"There'd be a whole bunch of women busy talking something interesting, frying something delicious."

Ihsan (a pseudonym) comes from a relatively privileged Muslim family, one in which her grandfather, a Koranic scholar, made sure that not just his sons but his daughters, too, received a good education. Her father, in fact, studied in England, where he met his wife. Together they came back to Jerusalem to take their place as part of a lively extended family. But the idyll of connectedness that Ihsan remembers from her earliest years in Palestine would be shattered by the 1948 War. Soon, faraway people and places would change her, complicating her connection to the past. But even before 1948, when she was still a little girl not old enough to understand colonialism and its legacy, Ihsan was already commuting between two worlds.

We lived on the western edge of Jerusalem, on a dirt road [where] the fruits and vegetables came on donkeyback in from the village. When I was a bit older, I used to walk to the asphalt road and catch a chocolate-colored school bus and go into the old city to a convent school, where I was reprimanded if I was caught talking Arabic. It was run by a French order, which had an orphanage for Armenian children who were dressed in a different uniform from us and who used to peel the vegetables for our lunches. Middle-class families [both Christian and Muslim] would send their children to a good school like that to get a French education, and I think it probably started right there, this not knowing who you are.

The [school] bus would stop outside St. Stephen' Gate because it couldn't go into the old city. So we'd have a crocodile of navy blue girls, two by two, walking through the Muslim quarter, and little Arab boys would come and spit at us because we were "Christians." Once at the school, it was up two steep steps, and a big door would sort of clang shut, and it would be so still. You had to bow your head when the nuns passed, and curtsy when Mother Superior passed, and you couldn't do this and you couldn't do that.

And oh, you got praised for giving up things. There was something called *sacrifice*. So instead of eating your snack, you gave it up just for the good of your soul. Except that we started getting two snacks, one for *sacrifice* and one to eat ourselves. You'd get special appreciation if, for example, you chose not to play in break time; if you were able for a week not to speak on the bus home, that was extra good.

There was a lot of humiliation. Somebody who did homework badly would have the notebook open at the page with the zero on it, pinned to her back. All day long she'd walk with that book on her back. I hated the school, I hated it.

[School might have been grim, but summer vacations were happy times, peopled with extended family, including six sets of aunts and uncles and dozens of cousins.]

What I remember [most] of my life in Palestine is all the holidays, the long months we spent [in the country] where there were several households of the family, that wealth of people—old, young, married, unmarried, good, bad, funny, fierce. My memory is just feasts and laughter and lots of people in and out, and the uncle who was a schoolmaster, in charge of beating the boys if they were caught smoking, so you kept out of his way.

Then on the coast, one of my uncles had an orange grove, and that was also fun to go [to]. There was this big, sort of rambling house and a dormitory for the kids, and there were all sorts of things to mess around with outside, mud to play with when they were watering, and you could climb the orange trees. If you felt hungry, you'd go into the kitchen and there'd be a whole bunch of women busy talking something interesting, frying something delicious. And then all the appendages—young maid servants, people like that. So it was a whole city, it was boiling.

[Then came 1948. Ihsan's first intimation of danger came on an otherwise happy day.]

My father was a teacher, and [Palestinian] people appreciated education, so presents of melons and stuff would often come to the house from students whose parents were in the country. I remember once we were invited to a feast at the house of one of his students in a little village outside Jerusalem. His father wanted to kill a sheep for us, so off we went. I remember we played and played and played. Then there was an enormous muffled sound, and we looked toward Jerusalem. We saw a big, black cloud; that was the King David Hotel being blown up [by Jewish terrorists]. [Later] at home, I remember we actually had bullets going through the house. I remember having to crawl on hands and knees—I think we went into the stairwell—because it got rough around where our house was. Then we moved to my uncle's house in Nablus.

All of my family who were on the coast also came inland. Actually, for me that was a very happy time while we were refugees at my uncle's house because there were a lot of us all cooped up together and then always more people coming. In every corner, there'd be one of the old ladies reading her Koran or making coffee on one of the portable charcoal braziers and praying. I was aware about the air raids coming in over the town, usually on moonlit nights, but I don't think I understood what it was really.

[That huge family campout could not go on indefinitely. Within a year, Ihsan's father had found a job in England.]

Everything was different in England. I would wake up at night very upset and crying from a dream of the Middle East. I really pined for it. It was just the quantity of people to whom I belonged that I missed. But, of course, the school in England was much better than schools I'd ever gone to. Everybody was very kind, everybody was wonderful, I never felt discriminated against at all. So I can't say there was anything [to complain of], except that I didn't have all the cousins around. And it wasn't home. You're treated very nicely, but you still know you're different.

[Ihsan continued her schooling in England, visiting home once after graduating from secondary school and then, after college, moving back to take up residence in Jordan, where her father had found a new job. For Ihsan, it was not an easy transition.]

There was no freedom of movement. Because I was a girl, I couldn't just get on a bus and go somewhere; somebody had to go with me. I got rather annoyed because it's got to do with the "what will people say" factor as much as with religion. I once accepted a lift to the riding club, and the mother of the [young man] who gave me the lift assumed that this was an engagement already.

[And always there was the question of Ihsan's future.]
On the one hand, it seemed a good idea to be independent. On the other hand, there were neither career opportunities nor could I go do what my cousins who hadn't moved all the way to England do, [which] is just marry one of the suitors or enter into one of the arranged marriages. My aunts were charming. They'd say, "There's this engineer, he's visiting, he's got an excellent job in Kuwait, he earns this much. I know you're modern, we'll do it the modern way. We'll be having supper, you'll [happen to] be there." Very, very nice, but again I had different ideas about my life.

By 1967, I was working. It was fun to work, fun to have a job. By the way, all my aunts would say, "Praise be to God, your father can afford to keep you at home. Why are you taking a job? It's not done." And I had come back to Jordan thinking, innocently, that I would have my own apartment! It was very difficult—after college and summers spent traveling in Europe—to go back and live in your father's house under those conditions.

That is the saddest thing about being a displaced person. Eventually one feels out of place in the land of one's birth, the very place one has so longed for from afar. It warped my whole life—I think you would hear that from everybody who's been displaced, not just from this particular place. It took a long time, it took until very recently before I sort of got a sense of who I am, and coming to America was very good for me, I think.

At first, the thought of coming to the U.S. seemed bleak and daunting. Such a long way away. So much further than Europe. How long would it take to adjust? It does take a long time, and it is difficult. But for all that, one is never a misfit. How liberating it is to know that almost everyone here has lived through some kind of dislocation or carries a memory of a distant home in some other place.

Since I came in 1967, more and more Arabs have been coming as a result of wars in Lebanon, Yemen, Iraq. So in New York now I speak Arabic daily. The [immigrant] news vendor will remember to wish me a happy new year on the first day of Ramadan. He speaks Arabic, yet he wears a baseball cap at a jaunty angle.

For Ihsan, the tension between cultures came to a head in the Middle East. For most immigrant families, it is acted out in the West and is based less on pragmatism than on passionate conviction.

Though de Crevecoeur held that in America the immigrant is gladly born again, the fact is that people do not easily relinquish the customs and convictions that have long defined them and in which they find their dignity. Nor do they easily give up hope of passing their values on to their children. All the while, of course, American culture attempts to claim those children as its own. Sometimes immigrant and mainstream American values converge or else differ in relatively unthreatening ways. But when standards of female behavior are at issue, Arabs have usually dug in their heels, mindful that a sexual misstep by a daughter, whether actual or merely suspected, could mortally wound their standing in the community.

In the 1930s, questions about what a girl could do and still be a "good" girl were thrashed out in the pages of the *Syrian World* magazine; editorials and letters to the editor traded shots over the lingering institution of the arranged marriage (meant to protect both the girl and her family) and whether daughters should be allowed to date. By the 1950s, and 1960s, the debate was largely over; acculturation had won the day. To later immigrants from the Arab world, this outcome was an example and a warning. In the mid-1980s, a study of Palestinians in Florida found community elders worrying that "soon our children will be 100% American, just like the *Surieen*" (Kazaleh 124).

The lesson here may be that history repeats itself and that, in a generation or two, most Palestinians will be as Americanized as the descendants of early *Syrian* immigrants. But in the meantime, Palestinians contend with obstacles of a different order than those faced by *Syrians*. In the first place, many are Muslims of a conservative stripe; religion alone, then, makes them suspicious of Americans, and Americans suspicious of them. At the same time, the ominous impression of Palestinians, held by most Americans, does not invite mutual trust, nor does Palestinian anger at American support of Israel. Furthermore, for those Palestinians who consider themselves a community in exile and who think about returning some day to an independent homeland, wholesale adaption to American culture makes little sense. It is true that many early *Syrians* also thought of their stay here as temporary. But there is a difference, and it lies in the Palestinians' sense of themselves as a people and a culture under siege, threatened by an enemy that has sometimes denied their very existence. They remember well Golda Meir's pronouncement that there is no such person as a Palestinian.

Thus, the compulsion to hold fast to markers of Palestinian identity— language and religion, food and folk arts, etiquette and poetry. (Thus, too, the value placed on education, which—unlike land—cannot be confiscated.) The injunction to honor heritage places a particular burden on Palestinian women since, as homemakers and mothers, they are the traditional conveyors of culture from one generation to the next. Should they break old taboos, rehearse new roles, or become more permissive parents, they may be accused of contributing to the erosion of Palestinian culture and thus, at an extreme, committing an act of political betrayal.[3]

Women residing in Palestine are subject to the same pressures, but for immigrants, living cheek and jowl with foreigners, the threat of cultural contamination may seem especially real and the need to resist it more urgent. This is why communities in the diaspora are sometimes seen as breeding grounds for conservativism.[4]

When Maha (a pseudonym), a native of Ramallah (on the West Bank) came to the United States in 1974, she found "something strange": people here *from* Ramallah, she says, were much more conservative than people *in* Ramallah. "And I think we'll end up the same way," she muses, "not really moving [changing], because we want so hard to keep our roots."

In fact, Maha has not been one to cling compulsively to tradition. At first, she was determined not to become Americanized since she had emigrated (with parents and sister) unwillingly.

I felt we shouldn't leave, but I wasn't independent enough to stay by myself. I still remember the day we left *[she begins to weep]*. That was the hardest day of my life. But little by little, even though I thought I'm going to resist and I'll stay Palestinian, little by little you start to adjust to this country.

But, as Maha explains, the adjustment is never final. One is forever weighing and comparing, seeing the up side and the down. "In Palestine," she says, "you never feel alone, but at the same time, the neighbors find out every small thing in your life. Here, you're more free." When she's well and healthy, Maha enjoys her newfound privacy. But when she's ill or in need, she misses the caring, if snoopy, ways of home. Democracy, too, is a boon. "Here we have freedom of speech," Maha says. "We talk, we go on demonstrations, we really do so many things that we're scared to do there [under occupation] because we might get killed." Freedom is nice, she concludes, "but even freedom should have some limits." She is thinking of her children and worrying about young people's ready access to drugs.

When Maha thinks about events back home, a different kind of ambivalence sets in. On the one hand, she writes passionate poems about Palestine, does intricate drawings depicting the Palestinian struggle, and proudly wears, around her neck, an amulet given her by a Palestinian "martyr." On the other hand, she is almost glad that her young son cannot share her political passions.

I don't want him to go to school and get in trouble, I want him to make a difference [distinction] between Zionism and Judaism. If he has Jewish friends, I don't want him to build barriers. I'm open minded, I want him to be open minded, too.

Maha points to the example set by her parents. Though Muslim, they sent her to a Catholic school in Jerusalem (where her best friend was a Christian girl), and later let her leave home to study in Beirut. "All my father told me was 'I trust you,' and that was enough for me to set my own limits."

Maha was fortunate in her parents. They made it easier for her as she was growing up, not harder. Najeebi, who also emigrated in 1974, has a different tale to tell.

NAJEEBI

"I wanted to get the hell out of there. I didn't want to stay in my parents' house, not one minute."

Najeebi (a pseudonym) was born in 1948, the year in which the state of Israel was established. Her family were among those Palestinians who fled the fighting between Arabs and Jews, leaving their homes and businesses behind. Like many others, they relocated in Lebanon, where Najeebi grew up in a refugee camp on the outskirts of Beirut. Born in wartime, Najeebi speaks of her life in terms of battles waged and often lost. In her earliest combat, a kind of guerilla warfare, her parents were her adversaries.

My father and mother were very religious, both of them, religious to the extreme. [They believed] Muslim women should be wearing long dresses to the ankles and to the wrist. The hair should be covered. Only you could show your mouth, your cheek, your eyes. [They believed] God want us to do this way, our prophet Muhammad—peace be upon him—want us to do this way, the Koran say we have to do it this way, so we have to follow. Blindly, blindly, no question about it.

So when I was eleven, twelve years old, my father wanted me to wear a scarf to cover my hair. I was embarrassed because most girls, they start later, at thirteen, at fourteen, at fifteen. So what I did, I wore it when I left the house because my father, he'd be waiting outside to see. When I walk about a quarter of a mile from the house, he won't see me any more. So *[laughing]* I start to pull it on one side until it's all down and take it and put in my bag.

We used to wear uniform for school, one color, one design. My father wanted me to wear it very long, cover my ankles. Other girls, they wear it up to here *[indicating her knees]*. So I used to roll it underneath the belt when I *[was]* a little bit far from the house and he doesn't see me any more. I used to roll it and roll it until it gets short to the knee.

And I always wore a sweater, even in the hottest days, so when I roll up my uniform, it doesn't show. All the girls, they said, "It's so hot. How come you are wearing a sweater?" I said, "It's Okay, I'm cold, I'm cold."

Anyway, it was the most tough time in my life. When you are ten, eleven years old, you want to play, you want to be free, you don't want to worry your scarf fell or your knees shows or your legs.

[With the injunction to cover up, came other restrictions as well.]
Like not to talk to boys in the school. If you need a question about home-work, you can't even go and ask a boy because it's a no-no to talk to boys. It's shameful. If people will see, it will be a lot of gossip in the town, and

you'll be humiliated. And if the girl has bad reputation, sometimes her family got stuck with her the rest of the life. Nobody will ever come and ask her to marry him.

It's not like here in the United States. Here the girls, they experience sex before fifteen, before sixteen. Over there, people get married and they don't even know what sex is. My husband, he didn't know how to marry me because he was virgin himself. I was virgin myself. And both of us [laughing], we didn't even know how to think about it. It took him two days to know how.

[In 1974, after eight years of marriage and three children, Najeebi and her husband came to the United States, hoping to improve their financial situation and to finally have a home of their own. Three years later, Najeebi decided to train as a hair dresser.]

My husband was overseas—he had a job [in a Gulf state] for about four years, and I was here with the children. Then somehow I felt lonely. The children are in the school, I'm home by myself in the daytime, and I felt bored, useless. I felt like cooking and cleaning is not enough for me, I wanted to do more. So I went to school for hair design.

I told the kids, "If your father ever call, don't you ever mention that I go to school" because I know he's not going to like the idea. So one time he called in the afternoon, and my daughter happened to be home. He said, "Where is your mother?" She said, "She went shopping." So he called back after one hour, and she told him, "She took the car to the garage, something wrong with it." He said, "Okay." [A third] time he called. Then [laughing] he got suspicious. He said, "Where is she now?" So she said, "Well, dad, she's in school."

All of a sudden the phone rang in the office in the school. The principal came to the class, and he said, "You have a long distance phone call." I was scared to death. I said, "What I'm going to tell him now?" I had only two, three months to graduate and I was putting more time than I should so I will graduate earlier so he doesn't find out. I was putting a lot of pressure on me, taking care of four children and going to school double time until nine in the evening. It wasn't easy. And [I was] worried all the time, honest to God. Always I'm in the class listening to the teacher and studying and my mind somewhere else.

But anyway I went to the office and I got the phone and he said, "Where are you?" I said, "In the school." I couldn't lie, I was on the spot. He said, "What school?" I said, "School for hair design." He said, "How long you've been going there?" I said, "Recently, I started recently." I didn't say exactly when. He said, "And you're leaving the children by themselves at home?" I said, "They are old enough. You know, fifteen and sixteen, they are not really babies. They don't need me, and they are well behaved and they know what to do. And soon I'll be home." He got mad and he started saying things that I don't like.

But with everything that went against me I finished school two months early, with high honor. Not even one step [was] easy for me. But I used to jump over everything and just go. Then, when I graduated, the same night I had [a job] interview, the same night! And the lady said, "Can you start tomorrow?" I said, "Sure."

When I start working, I told my husband. Yeah, he had to know. I explained to him I'm working just the hours when the children are in the school. Just something to make life a little bit more exciting, something to look forward to in the morning when I wake up. So he accepted a little bit.

I work five full years. I enjoyed every second of it. Then one year or two year after he came back, I stop because every day I'd be ready to leave to go to work, [and he would say], "Do you have to go to work really? Do you have to?" I got sick and tired of [his nagging]. I gave up my job. There is certain time of your life you could fight, but there is also time that you feel like you don't want to fight any more.

[Meanwhile, Najeebi's daughter was also having a hard time with her father.]
Very difficult. Very difficult. She can't take it. She came here [when she was] five years old. It's not like the way I grew up. I don't tell her every day to put a scarf over her hair when she goes to school, I don't tell her to wear long dresses, I don't tell her to go to mosque and pray every day. I know I should, but I don't. So she has very difficult time with her father, too. I seem to be little bit more loose than him, and I accept, [a] little bit, teenager problems here. Because to think about it, you can't just put something over boys' and girls' eyes and have them sit in the corner and protect them from seeing anything or hearing anything.

But he doesn't accept. He keeps saying, "Oh, I wish we never came to this country, I wish we never. . . . It's too much freedom here. . . . ['] *[his voice modulates into hers]*, too much liberation here, especially for women. That's no good, you know. I came here old—I was twenty-five years old— and I could never forget the background. Always in my ears, always my father's voice and my mother's voice. But when you raise up your kids here in this country, it's different. They are not going to look at things the way we look. And he doesn't understand.

And me, myself, I would say I wish I never came here. Even though I wanted to come here so bad because everything [there] so difficult to deal with. The war, the money problems, the family pressure, the gossip. No privacy, none whatsoever.

But when it comes to raise children, over there is easier. If I tell my daughter to wear longer dress, everybody in the neighborhood is wearing it, she's not going to feel embarrassed or humiliated. If I tell her you have to pray, everybody pray in the neighborhood. So anything I tell her to do it, everybody is doing it. Even though less [strictly] maybe, but they still doing it. And [the children] accept it.

But here you tell them something and they go to school, they go meet their friends outside, [they hear] something different. So it's like a war between the parents and the children, and especially the mother. I can't make my kids understand my point.

Let's say my [oldest] son. He's not baby, he's twenty-four years old now, and he could do whatever he wants to do. He dates; he dates even when he was sixteen, seventeen. It kills me. I can't accept it, I can't accept it. Every night he goes out, it feels like knife into my heart. Sometimes I fight with him, and I tell him, "This is against the religion, this is sin. You are doing something wrong, and I'm letting you do it. I should teach you that this is wrong, and you shouldn't do it." But I can't stop him. It's like a war, it's a fight every day.

My [middle] son got married to an Italian girl, too. For long time, we didn't talk to him. Now when he's going to have kids of his own, how we going to know that his wife is going to keep up our tradition? Am I going to be able to go every day to teach her how to do, to teach her boy or girl about our religion? I'm sure my son is not going to do it either. Because he came here [when] he was six years old, what does he know? You see?

[At this point, reaching toward summation, I asked Najeebi what she likes best about the United States.]
The best is the business. This is the most important thing, I guess. And the peace here. You don't have to worry about bombing and planes and war. You sleep at night, you know nothing is going to happen to scare you. Over there we always worried—maybe we'll wake up in the morning, maybe we'll not.

[And what, I asked, is worst about the United States?]
[Laughing response] Raising up teenagers. And *[more soberly]* also being far from your family is very lonely. Sometimes you get sick or you feel like you need your sister around you or your brother around you or your mother. Sometimes I be cleaning the house and I be sitting down looking at it, and I say, "Oh, I wish my mother could come over for a cup of coffee," or "I wish my sister could come and we go shopping." It hurts so much inside, you have no idea. In the summertime, I went to the beach every day. I said, "I wish my mother is here. I could bring her to the beach with me, she'll have fun, she'll have ice cream."

[At this point, we shut off the tape recorder, had coffee, and chatted. Najeebi began telling me a story about a girl she knew back in Lebanon. I turned the recorder back on and asked her to go on with the story.]
She was about fifteen at that time, and I was about fourteen. And she was

pregnant. Her mother found out because the girl, she didn't get her period. Usually the mothers over there, they observe the periods for their daughters very carefully because on her wedding night, they'll be humiliated if their daughter is not virgin.

So her mother, she asked the girl once, twice, about her period. The girl, she was scared to death. She kept saying, "It's not the right time yet for it." But after few days, she couldn't hide [her condition] any more because her sickness in the morning, it showed. Then the mother's duty and responsibility is to tell the brother.

So the poor girl was trying to cook something, she was trying to build the fire on the grille, she was kneeling on the floor in front of it. All of a sudden, she lie down on her back, and she was bleeding. Her brother in just two minutes [snaps her fingers] took her life. He shot her.

If they ever let the girl get away with it and don't kill her, everybody's going to gossip about the family and they don't respect them, and they don't go to visit them any more. So they will be isolated in their own neighborhood. So this way [by killing the girl], the family think they regain their honor back and their respect back from people because they show they won't allow something like that to happen in their house.

[*Still, it must have been hard on the mother, I said, meaning her daughter's murder. Najeebi misunderstood me.*]
Oh, yes, definitely, definitely. No mother will accept her daughter act like that.

[*And would Najeebi feel about it as the girl's family did?*]
In general, yes. Because I live in the same camp with the same type of people, and it is in my blood. So I will take it as tough as they did.

[*And if it were her own daughter, killed by her own son?*]
Oh, I can't handle it! God forbid! It will be very tough situation. I'll be worried about my son. Here in this country it's different, they don't understand these things. I mean, if the girl got pregnant, they say, "What's the big deal?" If the brother will come and shoot her, they'll take him, put him in jail maybe thirty, forty years. They don't respect the tradition and the religion over here as much as we do over there. Because in our Koran if the woman commits sin, she has to be stoned to death.[5] Even the man, both of them. And the courts and the laws, they go by the Koran.

[*I wanted to be sure I understood. "You would understand," I said, "if your son did as that brother did?"*]
Yeah. Oh, yeah, definitely. I won't blame him, no. It's a very strict religion, our religion.

[But in the next breath, Najeebi seemed to distance herself from those who would condone the brother's act.]

People over there, they are not exposed to the outside world. And 99 percent and a half of these mothers, they are not educated. They don't know how to read or write. They know few rules and regulations from the Koran because they hear it in the mosque every Friday. That's all. They don't read books, they don't know about psychology, they don't know about freedom, they don't know about education, they don't compromise as far as [how] their girls and boys grow up, how they change when they go to school, how their knowledge is going to get bigger and expose [them] to other things in life. They don't understand these things. They are very limited. They know very little from the Koran and they go by it and that's it.

[After that analysis, Najeebi shifted ground again, positioning herself a step closer to the uneducated women back home.]

That's why we are facing a lot of problems here. If I put on the television, I be scared, I be offended, very much so. Now sometimes my youngest son goes upstairs, and I follow him to see what he's watching. I pretend like I'm doing something in the room, and my eyes on the TV. I always worry. Maybe he will see people [with] no clothes on or people in bed together. If he finds it this easy on TV and if they could do it in front of the camera, next year "Why can't I do it?" he'll say. To expose twelve year old, eleven year old, to something like that . . . it scares me. Let me tell you this story.

[Like the story of her childhood trials, what follows is a typical Najeebi tale, serious in intent but spiced with laughter.]

Last year, at Halloween, they had a dance in my son's school. All students were invited. He was only twelve and a half at that time. He came home, and he said, "Ma, I'm gonna have to go the school dance tonight." I said, "Whose idea was it?" He said, "I don't know." I said, "Okay, I'm going tonight to the school and see whose idea was it." He said, "No way, you are not going with me to school." I said, "Of course, I'm going."

I went with him in the evening. We were living only one block away from the school so it took me five minutes walk, that's it. *[Laughing]* he was pushing me back, and I was pushing forward. But anyway we got to the school, and I saw the principal outside, and I said, "What is this school dance tonight? What is it about?" He said, "Well, the kids want it." I said, "And you do whatever the kids want? You think it's right?" He said, "Yeah, let them have fun." I said, "Okay, I'm going inside to see what the fun [is]." I went inside and I saw the girls, twelve year old, eleven year old, ten year old, wearing fancy dresses, sexy dresses even, putting their hair up in the air, spray their hair red and blue and yellow, wearing all kind of make-up. It's unbelievable. They looked like prostitutes.

Every three, four girls, they grab one boy to the dance. And they dance just like twenty, twenty-five years old. The minute I saw that, I got very, very scared, and I said, "My God, I'm not going to allow him to do this." Let them go to hell the other kids, I can't be mother for all these kids here. I don't know how their parents allow them, but I'm not going to allow my son here. I mean what if a boy and a girl, they sneak to the bathroom or they sneak outside the school and do something, who could watch them? The teachers were drinking coffee and having doughnuts, and they could care less what's going on.

The girls they are so wild. The minute we walk into the room, they grab my son from my hand. One minute later, I couldn't even see him. I couldn't even see him from the lights, from the color of the girls' hair. They were wild, wild. I felt like I'm in a zoo. Honest to God! And I didn't believe that was any kind of civilization. So I grabbed my son, and I said, "We're going home right now." He said, "No, I'm not going home." He's so stubborn, he wanted to enjoy the dance. I said, "Okay, fifteen more minutes we stay, and we're leaving." So altogether I allow him maybe about half an hour and I took him home.

He was mad for a few days. He said, "I was the only one to leave early. The other boys and girls, they stayed until 11 o'clock. I looked like five years old." But I talked to him in my own way. I told him, "How many pregnant thirteen and fourteen year old there is in the school?" He said, "Plenty." I said, "Plenty, but the teachers and the principals are making it easy for them." He said, "You know something? You opened my eye, you got my attention to something that we never thought it's wrong."

But always whatever we do, we are against the reality here in this country. Whatever we do. Very small chance to win. They always win, the kids and the society here.

"Honor killings" of the sort Najeebi describes have never been common-place, even among rigidly moralistic families.[6] Traditionally, just the threat of such punishment or of social ostracism has been enough to keep most girls in line. And even for those who stray, strategies for concealment have been worked out, ranging from the traditional (hasty marriage of the guilty couple) to the technological (surgical repair of the hymen). Still, several middle-aged women I have spoken to—especially those from rural areas or refugee camps—know personally of an "honor killing." On rare occasions, such crimes may even occur among immigrants to the United States.

In 1989, a Palestinian father in St. Louis, aided by his wife, stabbed to death their sixteen-year-old daughter. Tina (short for Palestina), was apparently becoming too "Americanized"—playing high school soccer (against her father's wishes), attending her junior prom (until dragged away by her family), taking a job in a local fast-food restaurant (instead of working in the family store where she would be under her parents' surveillance and protection), and spending time with a boyfriend. In short, Tina seemed headed down a path that would inevitably lead to dishonor or, rather, in her parents' eyes, that already had. Tina's father was tried and convicted of first degree murder. When a judge imposed the death penalty, an older daughter cried out, "If my father is sent to death because he is a Muslim, then he is proud of himself to die that way!"

But in equating "honor killing" with Muslim piety, the sister—like Najeebi—was mistaken. According to Jeanette Wakin, professor of Islamic Studies at Columbia University, " 'Honor killing' is not Islamic at all, there is nothing in the religion that sanctions it. And I have never heard of any Islamic scholar saying it is permitted"[7] (interview).

Palestinians are, of course, most conscious of (and troubled by) "honor killings" when they occur in their own community. In such cases, they may feel called upon either to defend the practice, as does Najeebi (though her ambivalence is evident) or, more likely, to condemn it, as does Amal Amireh, a Muslim Palestinian pursuing graduate studies at Boston University. "There's nothing honorable about a man killing his sister because she's pregnant," says Amal. "That's murder. And it's a tragedy because the woman is dead, and the brother (or father) is in jail. No shred of honor here." But, she adds, to condemn only the individual perpetrator misses half the point. "We [society] told him it's an honorable crime so we bear the responsibility."[8]

Amal's abhorrence of "honor killings" is shared by Karima (a pseudonym) who, like Najeebi, grew up in the socially conservative atmosphere of a refugee camp. 'I don't understand it," she says, clearly appalled at her own tale of a father who slit his daughter's throat. Her only explanation is that the father was not "fully up here," not mentally balanced.

For her own part, Karima does not believe that premarital sex is morally criminal. "But you have to be mature enough," she says. "I think the age of eighteen is old enough for my daughter to decide for herself." Asked about the fetish of virginity, she replies, "I don't care about that. But if my family know I talk like this, they would despise me."

Between the extremes represented by Najeebi and Karima lies a vast middle ground of compromise like that worked out between Alia and her parents. When I spoke to her a few years ago, she told me they wanted her to finish college before thinking of marriage, no rushing to move her out of harm's way by marrying her off. On the other hand, Alia and her parents agreed that American-style dating was out of the question.

Seeing eye-to-eye with parents is one thing. Finding acceptance outside the home is another. When Alia first came to this country, her new classmates teased her about being Palestinian. "What do you have in your bag," they would ask, "a bomb?" Her unstylish manner of dressing and doing her hair also set her apart. As time went by, she updated her wardrobe, learned to shave her legs, began using hair spray, and even a little make-up. "So they won't think I'm an alien," she explained. As a result, Alia commanded new respect. "They used to call me Miss Serious, now it's Miss Fashionable; they even ask me to do their hair." Still, it was hard to make best friends. "They always want me to go places I can't go, like discos and out dancing and drinking." It was hard also to be open and frank. If a boy asked her out, she told him that she was seeing someone else. "I can't tell American people I'm not allowed to have a boyfriend. They'll think we're crazy."

By the same token, it took a bit of subterfuge to avoid alienating other Palestinians, who—like Alia's schoolmates—judged her by the clothes she wore.

When we go to Florida on our vacation, we wear bathing suits, my mom and me. My dad lets us. "You deserve to have fun," [he says]. But when we come back here, I can't even wear a mini-skirt. And I don't wear shorts in front of guys in the community. They might get the wrong idea.

So Alia has learned to maneuver on two fronts, skillfully, cheerfully, and with the tacit approval of her parents. They are "cool," she said; "they understand."

SUHAIR, SOUAD, NUHA, AND NAWAL

"It's respecting [your parents], respecting their ideas."

"Okay, respecting their ideas, but it shouldn't stifle you."

Nuha and Nawal, like Souad and Suhair (all pseudonyms), are sisters whose parents immigrated from Palestine to the United States in the 1970s. At the time we spoke, the young women—then ranging in age from seventeen to twenty-three—were attending school and also holding down part-time jobs. One was married.

As the girls (who knew each other well) talked, they struggled openly with issues common to their generation of Arab girls, while, at the same time, discovering (or rediscovering) important differences in their parents and in their relations with their parents. I began the conversation by asking how strict Palestinian parents are with their daughters. (I appear in the conversation as "Evelyn.")

Souad: It depends on the background of the family. For example, my family comes from a village, while I have a Palestinian friend, her family comes from a city, and they have two totally different perspectives. My parents are harder, they're stricter. Her parents, when I tell them how my parents are, they're shocked. If I can give you an example: about two weeks ago I was going to go to a nightclub downtown with some friends. And I was planning to stay until midnight. When I got there, I'm like, "I didn't tell my parents where I'm going, and if I tell them, I don't want to lie." So I stayed there for one hour, and the whole hour I was feeling so guilty. So I just picked all my stuff up and I left.*

Nuha: Lately I've been rebelling against my parents.

Nawal: You have not! You got engaged. She got engaged to this dufis.

Nuha: Well, that's what my parents wanted. He was a friend of the family, he comes from the same village they do. And I was like, "Well, I should please them." At that point, my life revolved around my parents.

Nawal: No, her idea was it's an easy way to get out of the house.

Suhair: A lot of Arab girls do that.

Nawal: You shouldn't do it that way. You have your education.

Nuha: My sister, Nawal, she pointed out the light to me. I broke up with him.

Nawal: *[Turning to Suhair]* I have to ask you this. Why . . . ? Why did you get married? I mean, Radwan *[Suhair's husband]* is a great guy. But you had so much going for yourself!

Nuha: Hey, just because she got married doesn't mean her life's over. She's supporting herself through school, she has a job. Radwan's not putting a halt to her life.

Nawal: No, no. But *[turning again to Suhair]* I know that you went through a lot when you married, just to go back into school.

Suhair: I know, I know. The thing is it's not him that is the problem. He actually gets mad at me sometimes if I get a C in a class. The problem, it's with his family. My father-in-law—he's my uncle—he doesn't believe in girls going to school. His first daughter, his eldest, he forced her out of school into marriage. But her husband was encouraging enough to let her go back so that she was able to finish school. When she had her kids, her mother-in-law took care of them. With me, my husband was encouraging too, but his family was very discouraging, and they lived with us at the beginning. They did everything they could to make it hard for me. Now my father's telling my sisters, "None of you can even think about marriage before you finish school."

Evelyn: How did you happen to marry your husband, in the first place?

Suhair: Well, he's my cousin.

Evelyn: Is that still considered the best thing to do? To marry your cousin?

Suhair: Yeah. With most girls I know of, the families would prefer you to marry a cousin or someone from the village before you marry outside.

Nuha: If you marry outside the village, you're talked about.

Suhair: They think there has to be a reason why you went outside. *[Other voices agree.]*

Nawal: Yeah, they're like, "I wonder what happened to her." Or, "She must have been not a virgin." Or "Nobody else wanted to marry her."

---

*At this point, Souad was called out of the room for a while, which accounts for her extended silence.

Suhair: They're like, "That's why they found her a husband from outside."

Nawal: Have you noticed she says, "*they* found." Not "*she* found." I could never do that, I could never have my parents select my husband. If my parents said, "This guy is perfect for you," and I was actually in love with him, I would not do it because they chose him. It's because I want to make a stand. I want to tell my parents, "Listen, you can't rule my life."

My oldest sister, she's married; she gave up at fourteen or fifteen; she had nobody. She didn't have what we have here today. She didn't have Arab friends who can help her through—people of the same origin, who can understand your problems.

[Voices in general agreement]

Suhair: That is very important. Some of my best friends happen to be three Americans. But sometimes I can talk to them about everything that's going on and they still will *not* understand because they're not Arabs.

Nuha: I have friends at work, they're all American. I tell them what's going on, how it is. And they're like, "Why don't you just leave?" Or [they say], "If I grew up like that or I were ever born in your religion, I would never survive." I'm like, "Well if you've grown up in a different environment, you wouldn't have the same attitude that you have now."

Suhair: Exactly.

Nawal: Okay, our parents lived in Jerusalem in the 1970s. And my dad, he's trying to fit it into the 1990s. "Dad, I'm sorry, that does not work now." I mean even in Jerusalem right now, the kids are different. When I went there, I was shocked. I'm like, "Wait a minute! Where's this that my father keeps on talking about? Where are the girls who are still at home?" "Dad, they're out there getting an education, there's no more forced marriages." Oh, my God, talk about a generation gap!

Suhair: There's only twenty years between my father and I, so we can sit there and talk.

Souad: When it comes to political issues, I mean we can sit there and we argue and discuss. I understand his point of view, and he understands my point of view.

Nawal: You guys are lucky. One time recently, I bring up a subject about politics to my dad. "Well, dad, this is what I believe." And he just looked at me like I was a total stranger in the house. "What do you know about politics?" "Dad, I know a little bit. I mean, give me some credit here."

Evelyn: But do your mothers encourage you?

Suhair: My mom knows a lot, she's always reading. We must have got our love of reading from my parents because my parents read and read and read, and they love books. Or magazines. Anything they can get their hands on, Arabic and English. But the thing is, they are still from the old country; we're from here.

Souad: Can I tell you what it is, really, really, really? They're afraid of what "the people are gonna say" and "the people are gonna do."

[General groan of agreement].

Suhair: Yeah, that's true. I went to a concert, and my father let me go, but he didn't want our relatives to know.

Nuha: One time me and a few other friends went to this little café by the university. Somehow someone saw us there and went back and contacted my mother. "I saw your daughter. . . ." And we were just having fun, laughing.

Suhair: But you were out; you see you're out of the house. The girl is actually out of the house! If it's a son, it's different. But a daughter! "You're letting your daughter go out?! Where people can look at her?! Where she can talk to people?!"

Souad: We just have to keep watching out, just in case we see anybody.

Suhair: People are looking over your shoulders all the time.

Souad: You know, right now, I'm always in meetings. My father knows where I am, and he still gets really ticked off. I'll even show him the agenda. He goes, "Lookit, I accept it, I know what you're doing, but now your relatives who live right down the block might see you come home late, and they're going to say, 'Oh, look, I wonder where she was, and I wonder what she was doing.' "

Suhair: It reflects a lot on the father. They [the relatives] blame him as it is for not marrying us off when we were thirteen years old.

Nuha: See, from what I heard, your father is starting to not give a damn about what people say.

Souad: Well, in a way, but in a way he still does.

Nuha: I can't say I love my parents because they were never there for me. They never understood what I went through.

Nawal: Who was always there for you?

Nuha: My sisters. My sisters were always there for me. Now I see Souad as my best friend. She always gives me good advice, that's why I love her so much.

[General laughter, gentle]

Not like my mom. I was afraid to ask her if I can even go to the movies tomorrow because I know it's going to go right back to my father.

Nawal: See *[addressing me]*, that's [Nuha's] fault. I stand up to them, and I just tell them, "Listen, I'm leaving." She can't do that.

Nuha: I want to go to a New Year's party tomorrow with my friend. She's like one of my best American friends, even though she hates the fact that I'm a coward.

Nawal: You *are* a coward.

Nuha: She's like, "Come, come [to the party]." And I'm like, "No, I'm not going to ask my mom 'cause I know she'll make me ask my dad, and I'll get my butt kicked."

Nawal: No, just tell her, "I'm going."

Nuha: You see, I admit I am a coward. Like today, coming here, I was so scared. My father, he goes to sleep at eight o'clock; right at eight o'clock he's in his bedroom. When he's ready to pray, he sleeps. He's praying, and I'm out the door coming here for *dabke* [dance] practice. He doesn't know.

Evelyn: Why would he object?

Suhair: Some people begin talking. They say you come here only for one thing, looking for a husband.

Nuha: That's my mother's concern. "Oh, they're going to start talking about you." I told my parents many times, "I don't care what the people say any more." Even though I really do care, but sometimes I'm like to the point where I don't.

Souad: I came here without telling my father. Now I know I'm going to go home, I'm going to feel guilty. But he knows I'm not doing anything wrong.

Nawal: So why should you feel guilty?

Suhair: Because my father's going through so much right now.

Nawal: You know what? Our parents are putting *us* through so much b.s.

Suhair: No.

Souad: No, it's not always so.

Nawal: [Your dad is] helping you, my dad is not helping me.

Suhair: See, that's why we feel guilty if we do something and it's going to hurt my parents. Because they try to do a lot for us.

Nawal: See, to be honest—you guys can argue this point with me—that's where I think you guys are wrong, still being scared of your parents.

Souad: It's respecting them, respecting their ideas. . . .

Nawal: Okay, respecting their ideas, but it shouldn't stifle you.

Souad: It's not stifling. It's not putting a major change to my life.

Nawal: In a sense, it *is* stifling you. If you want something, you should be out there getting it. Your parents should support you 100 percent. Like, I think the girl should date.

Souad: I'm not against it, I'm not against it.

Evelyn: Is it that your parents are afraid that if you date you'll lose your chastity?

Nawal: I have to say one thing: I lost my chastity a long time ago. But if you're going to have sex, use something.

Souad: Fine, I don't think there's anything wrong with having sex before marriage; I don't think there's anything wrong at all. But you have to be careful. A lot of girls just want to go out there and just indulge themselves, each time with a different guy.

Nawal: They're more self-centered. We're not self-centered. We all know that we're not self-centered. If we can think in a political atmosphere, if we know that we're practically living a political life here, especially with what's going on in Palestine, we're not self-centered at all. I mean most of the American girls, they sit there and they think, "I gotta go shopping, dude, I gotta go to the mall." We don't have that ideology. We don't think that way.

Souad: I don't know. I don't believe that if you want to go do anything, just go out there and do it even though it's against your parents' will. No.

Nawal: If my mom told me, "You cannot do this and you cannot wear this," and I believe it's perfectly fine to do it, I'll just go ahead. [I'll say], "Listen, mom, I think this is right, and I'm going to do this. You cannot stifle me."

Souad: Fine, but they still disagree, and it's hard to say. . . .

Nawal: If they disagree, but I think it's right, [I'll do it], and if I make a mistake, I learn from it. I don't think [pre-marital] pregnancy is right. I don't think it's proper for a girl to go out there and wear a miniskirt, I mean a real short, short miniskirt because guys are going to hit on her because of that reason. It's not because my mom says "This is wrong and it's against the religion." No, it's my own thinking. Do you understand what I'm saying?

Souad: But you know, it's hard to still go on and just do whatever I want to do. I mean, I'll do it. You guys know I still do things even though I know my parents disagree with it. But I feel really guilty.

Suhair: [In my family] we all have this guilt thing, maybe because we know what my father has struggled through.

Souad: You know, my father came from one of the poorest families in the village. His father was killed when my father was small. He had to get out of school, he had to go two miles, three miles, just to get a barrel of water. And my father, when he was in school, he was always at the top of his class.

Suhair: He's very, very smart, but he was not given the opportunities.

Souad: You know, I noticed there's a big difference between our two families. First of all, since we were younger, my father used to encourage us; like we used to sing and make up all these political songs about Palestine. . . .

Suhair: And he bought me a guitar when I was younger. . . .

Souad: And he used to teach us about Palestine, he always taught us history.

Nuha: [Our father] never taught us anything. He won't even help me in Arabic sometimes.

Evelyn: But you all speak Arabic, right? It sounds like you speak it well.

Suhair: I spent two years there in Palestine, with my grandmother.

Nawal: When I went to Palestine, I paid for it all by myself. When I said, "I'm leaving," my dad's like, "Why are you going? It's useless." I said, "Dad, I'm going to where you were born, this is my culture, my heritage." He says, "Why go back? You'll just get in trouble over there."

Souad: Can I say a problem that's going on right now for a lot of Arab Americans because of the crisis [the Gulf War] in the Middle East. For instance, we go to the university. We've had threatening letters to our student office—which is the General Union of Palestinian Students—threatening to rape Arab women, Palestinian women. So a lot of the guys are like, "Whenever you go walking around, you gotta be careful."

Suhair: And *[laughing]* they probably want to walk around with you, I bet.

Souad: Yeah. They do. It's all so tensed up right now in school. They had these T-shirts in the bookstore that said "One thousand miles to kill an Arab" with a camel and an Arab on top of the camel and a target, like shooting right at the Arab.

We wrote thousands of letters to the company that was making them, and about two weeks ago they had these T-shirts removed from all the shelves. When we told my father what we did, he was happy. He's supportive in a lot of things. It's just he's afraid . . . I don't know.

Suhair: How about the truth, Souad? How about the truth? How about we don't know who of our relatives will hurt one of us next because of what our sister Alia did, running away from home.

Souad: We've been getting [anonymous] threatening letters to the house.

Suhair: Right. My relatives, some think my father should have killed my sister when she left home. And to this day, they're against us.

Souad: They're like, "Your daughters are going to pay."

Suhair: And my father's always afraid for us.

Souad: Now, like right now I'll go home, he'll be up watching TV.

Suhair: He's *afraid*. I used to see him worried but never as much as he does now.

Souad: Now he's more cautious.

Suhair: A lot more cautious.

Souad: They hated my father for such a long time, and you know why? Because he believes in educating his daughters; he believes that his daughters are human and that they have their own minds and that we can sit and argue with my father. Many of the girls are married off at the age of thirteen and fourteen. The girls that we used to play around with are all married with five or six kids each. And my father is, "See, I don't want you to be like that. I want you to have a career, I want you to have a happy life, a home, and I want you to be very comfortable in the future. And I don't want you to depend on me."

Suhair: People have been against him from the beginning because of this. Now with my sister's leaving home, they blamed him even more. "We told you don't raise them in this country." A lot of times, the [Palestinian] men are here, while their wives and kids are over there, especially in our village. My husband's family, because my sister left, they don't think I'm good enough for them, I'm trash.

Nuha: [*Changing the subject*] You don't know how scared I am [of] my dad. He's really big, and he's got a big hand.

Suhair: I guess you're afraid of your father. We're never afraid of our father in any physical way.

Souad: He never hit us.

Suhair: As a matter of fact, if my mother ever lifted her hand to hit us, my father would yell at her. I mean if we're scared of my father, it's not that. It's just scared of making him feel bad.

Nawal: Let me tell you this story. My brother-in-law, he comes over. I wouldn't say hello to him, and I didn't make coffee for him. I was in an angry mood. You know, we're moody when we're kids. And then I kinda mumbled "asshole." I didn't know he was in back of me. He beat the shit out of me.

Suhair: God!

Nawal: My father walks up. "What did she say?" "She wouldn't make coffee and she swore at me." [My father says], *"Drubha!* [Hit her!]." My brother-in-law beats the shit out of me, breaks my bicycle—which was my freedom then.

Nuha: It was like your wings, to fly and go wherever you wanted to go.

Suhair: We have extremely different families.

Nawal: [Turning to me] If you sense this, it has nothing to do with being Palestinian, it's just having the different fathers.

Suhair: Exactly.

[It was time to end the interview.]

Nuha: [Turning to me] So did you get what you wanted [from the conversation]?

Nawal: I think it went around in a big circle.

Evelyn: No, we covered a lot, it was good.

Nuha: Did you get a Palestinian aspect or a family aspect? Or both?

Suhair: I think it is [both] in a way.

Evelyn: Yeah, I think they come together. I think the culture sets certain limits, and then the individuals operate within that. Some are right at the center and some are on the fringe.

Suhair: Exactly true.

Evelyn: Thanks everybody, so much.

Nawal: It's been a pleasure.*

When Nawal describes herself and her friends as leading political lives or sneers at the "mall" mentality of her American schoolmates, she voices a political consciousness that permeates the Palestinian community and sets many of its young people apart from other American teenagers. That consciousness is encouraged by family, by student organizations, and by institutions such as the Arab American Community Center, where I met with Nawal, her sister, and friends. Here maps of Palestine hang on the walls, as do Palestinian flags, testifying to the people's attachment to the land and

---

*For more current information about these four young women and their afterthoughts about this interview, see the Appendix.

defining the contours of the state they hope to achieve. Palestinian newspapers and political literature, scattered on tables in the main meeting room, deliver the same message.

In these surroundings, young people become politically literate, and at the same time, young women can find mentors among members of the Union of Palestinian Women's Associations (UPWA), which meets at the center. Like the Ladies' Aid of Boston, the UPWA was created in response to crisis back home—in the one case, disease and starvation brought on by the first World War; in the other, the occupation of the homeland and ills attendant on that occupation. A major difference lies in the degree of moral support provided by the host society—the United States. In 1917, the year the Ladies' Aid was founded, popular sympathy toward *Syrians* was encouraged by press reports on their plight and by a government-supported campaign to raise funds for their relief. In 1986, when the UPWA was established, hostility or, at best, indifference to the Palestinian cause was the rule.

Still, in comparison to the early *Syrians*—most of humble origin, many illiterate—Palestinian women have had advantages, most notably a cadre of well-educated, politically sophisticated leaders, able to forge alliances with political, religious, and feminist groups outside their own community. Palestinian women have also inherited, to their profit, a decades-long tradition of political activism.

As early as the 1920s, women in Palestine were participating in political attempts to limit Jewish immigration to Palestine and prevent a Zionist takeover of their land and their economy. After 1948, with Israel a *fait accompli*, women turned to immediate humanitarian needs, establishing orphanages, clinics, and first-aid stations for a flood of refugees who overnight had lost their homes and means of livelihood.

After the 1967 war, with all of the West Bank and Gaza Strip now under Israeli occupation, a new generation of women activists came of age, many of them reared in villages and refugee camps. Dismissive of charitable work per se, they took to political protest and, in a few cases, to guerilla operations. In larger numbers, they promoted literacy and health education among the poor, became active in student and trade unions, and started kindergartens and day care centers, as well as work rooms where women could learn skills and crafts, and cooperatives through which they could sell their goods. By the late 1980s, the women's committees, with their broad-based membership, were well poised to participate in the *intifada*.

Once it erupted, they cared for the wounded, set up alternative classrooms when schools were shut down by the military, spearheaded boycotts of Israeli goods, and cultivated victory gardens. Furthermore, in larger numbers than ever before and despite cultural inhibitions against doing so, women (many clad in traditional dress) took to the streets, helping to throw up barricades, supplying stone throwers with ammunition, and stepping forward to protect young people from arrest or beatings. During the day, women monitored

the closing of shops according to a schedule decreed by the leadership of
the uprising; after dark, they smuggled in food and fuel to villages under
punitive curfew. By the end of the first year of the *intifada*, some 100 Palestinian women had been killed, and many others had been arrested.

Rita (a pseudonym), now a graduate student in the United States, was one
of those women actively involved in the *intifada*, not in street demonstrations
or confrontations, but in behind-the-scenes stealth. Even as a child, Rita was
preparing for the role she would later play. Some of her earliest memories
are of visiting her uncle in an Israeli-run prison, where he was serving a
seven-year term for planning to sabotage an Israeli military installation (a
charge he denied). In her eyes, he was a romantic figure. "Everyone in the
family told us, 'Your uncle is a hero.' "

By the time her uncle was released from prison, Rita was in high school,
and every day after school was out, she and her brother would stop by to
see him, hungry for stories about his time in jail. When he spoke of women
prisoners who were "stronger than the men," Rita paid close attention.
Meanwhile, her parents, who had sung the uncle's praises when he was behind bars, now worried as they saw their teenage children falling under his
spell. Heroism was fine in theory, but its consequences could be unpleasant.

My father went to him and told him, "I don't want you to talk to my children, I
don't want your influence on them." And to us, my father said, "Your uncle is good,
I don't say that he's not. But do you want our house to be demolished by the Israelis?
Do you want me to lose my job?"

It was too late for such warnings; already Rita was taking part in student
demonstrations. On days commemorating the massacre of Palestinians, the
seizure of their land, or the burning of mosques, she joined in throwing
stones at Israeli soldiers, who responded with lobs of tear gas. When such
skirmishes became an everyday affair, the *intifada* had begun.

By then, Rita was attending college in Jordan and had joined a Marxist
Palestinian party at whose behest she undertook a series of risky missions.
Her usual assignment was to pick up instructions from Jordan-based leaders
of the *intifada* and carry them to activists inside the Occupied Territories.

As she tells it, these errands had all the trappings of a spy thriller, complete
with passwords, code names, and surreptitious meetings in crowded public
spaces. In preparation for her first mission, she watched a woman leader pen
messages on two sheets of exquisitely thin paper, then roll them tight and
slip each into a capsule about one-inch in length. After sheathing each capsule in plastic and sealing the plastic with her cigarette lighter, the woman—
to Rita's astonishment—instructed her to swallow them.

It was the only way—at the border, her clothes and baggage would be
searched and a metal detector run round her naked body. The next day, after

passing the capsules, Rita handed them over, unopened, to someone whose name she never learned.

In undertaking such missions, Rita felt she was following in the footsteps of her uncle, doing something serious and important. Certainly, it required strong nerves, not just the smuggling, but later, when she fell under suspicion, the standing up to interrogation by Jordanian authorities.

But it seems clear that Rita's political life was also both exhilarating and personally liberating. When party members called her "comrade," she was proud; it felt good to sip vodka while toasting the health of the comrades in Russia. Her brother's support made everything sweeter, too. He was the first to bring wine (forbidden by Islam) into the apartment they shared in Jordan, and far from guarding her virginity with a jealous eye, he encouraged her to find a boyfriend. She already had one.

In its combination of political commitment and social experimentation, the experience she describes in Jordan is reminiscent of nothing so much as the student subculture of the 1960s in the United States. The apartment she set up with her brother says it all. "The keys used to be with many people," she recalls, "and when we would go home, we didn't know who would be there. People used our apartment to come and drink and do whatever they wanted to do."

By the time Rita's political activities had made her unwelcome in Jordan, she had already made plans to attend graduate school in the United States. Now happily involved in her studies here, she has also found a set of politically committed friends with whom she feels at home. She is active, too, in campus politics, attending meetings, participating in student protests, handing out flyers. "This is very easy," she says with a laugh, "not like swallowing those capsules!"

When Fadwa (a pseudonym) came to study in the United States, she had a harder time finding kindred spirits. "Political debate," she says, "intellectual discourse—I missed it so much because I didn't feel it here on campus." She had been used to it at home, having grown up in the university town of Bir Zeit, where questions of culture and political ideology were intensely debated by students and by teachers drawn from Arab countries, Europe, and the United States. Another source of distress was Americans' ignorance about the Arab world and, in particular, Arab women. "Do you have a camel?" she was asked. "Does your father beat you?" It was like having someone in another country—someone familiar with the steady stream of news reports on battered women in the United States—ask a visiting American, "Do you have a restraining order out on your husband?" "Has he ever tried to kill you?" As if aberrant behavior defined the norm.

To Fadwa, the questions that came her way seemed not just offensive but ironic since personal observation had convinced her that women back in Bir Zeit were often more publicly engaged and more assertive than women in the United States. The query "Do you wear a veil?" (and all that it implies) seemed especially ludicrous. In Bir Zeit, she had worn shorts and tank tops, raced against boys in school tournaments, and even brought boys home. Her sisters did karate and played on a co-ed basketball team. Her girlfriends belonged to a co-ed dance troupe that toured Europe and the United States.

When the *intifada* took fire, Fadwa was already studying in the United States. But back in Bir Zeit, one sister was instrumental in setting up a home guard; another sister, just fifteen years old at the time, helped pile boulders and tires in the middle of a road and then, from behind that barricade, joined in the signature act of the *intifada*, throwing stones at Israeli soldiers. Fadwa was stunned by her sister's daring (observed on a visit home one summer) and by that of older women out on the streets, rocks in their laps, who directed street battle, telling young protesters what to do, when to run, and where to hide.

Still, according to Fadwa, the *intifada* was not so much about hurling stones as about building institutions through which people could claim control of their own lives, women could become more self-sufficient, and children could expand their intellectual and cultural horizons. Her sisters, for instance, helped start a summer camp where young people were taught to play sports and to stage plays, to paint, and to draw, as well as a town library for children whose schooling had been interrupted by the *intifada*. As Fadwa describes it, then, the uprising was a spark igniting enormous energy and imagination, especially in women.

For as long as it lasted, the *intifada* rallied the spirits of Palestinians, both at home and abroad. Day after day, TV pictures of stone-throwing youths confronting gun-shooting, club-wielding soldiers stirred admiration and pride. At the same time, shots of women talking down soldiers or protecting young men with their own bodies provided Palestinian women in the United States with new heroes and with graphic evidence that in the name of nationalism (if for no other reason) women could legitimately invade the male territory of the streets and take action in the public arena. If women in Palestine were exercising such options without any loss of honor, certainly women in the diaspora could do the same.

Activism can take many forms. Fadwa, for instance, helped organize a Palestinian Academic Freedom Network, which has shipped computer software and thousands of books a year to Palestinian universities, helped to hook them up on the Internet, and sent them delegations of graduate students to teach summer seminars in science and technology.

Amal Amireh provides further example of how Palestinian academics and intellectuals in this country have found ways—within the context of their own disciplines—to help their people. In 1989, Amal arrived in the United States to pursue a graduate degree in English literature. From the start, her professors at Boston University, whom she describes as "nice, well intentioned people," encouraged her in her studies. But although her arrival coincided more or less with the outbreak of the *intifada*, neither they nor her fellow students ever expressed any concern for what she might be suffering or any awareness that her friends and relatives were living in a war zone. "Not one member of my department asked me, 'How are you doing?' 'How's your family?' "

Yet, when "Tiananmen Square" happened, a panel was organized at B.U., Amal remembers, giving Chinese graduate students a forum to tell about political repression at home. "I was never given that opportunity," says Amal, "and so I felt really very lonely and invisible."

Her response was to begin writing newspaper and journal articles on Arabs and their literature. It is, she says, "an interventionist act."

In writing a book review about a Palestinian novel or in writing an essay about Arab women, I'm interrupting a certain way of thinking that's prevalent here, the way we are understood as Arab women or the way Arab culture is understood and written about. I am not defensive. I just try to make people see us [Arabs] as fellow human beings. It's a way to make it easier for them to ask me, "How's your family at home?"[9]

As the *intifida* heated up, the UPWA was also swinging into full gear, its members participating in demonstrations and rallies, sponsoring tours by women from the Occupied Territories, and finding common ground with progressive Jewish women and "women of color." At the same time, the UPWA was providing direct aid to women's projects in the Territories and instituting a family sponsorship program, with an office in Jerusalem, to provide food, clothing, shelter, and health care to families living under occupation.

As a matter of policy, the UPWA was committed to enlisting members of every age and class and of all political and religious views. (At UPWA conventions—the last held in 1993—women in jeans and T-shirts mingled amicably with women in head scarves and traditional floor-length dress.) But from the beginning, many UPWA leaders have been self-declared feminists, who watch with interest and concern the progress made by their sisters abroad.[10] Like feminists there, they are concerned that women have not achieved leadership positions in the Palestinian political hierarchy, and they are worried by the kind of antifeminist backlash that, a year or so into the *intifada*, pressured women in Gaza into donning the *hijab*.

Also troubling to many is the familiar argument (sometimes put forth even by members) that women should postpone their feminist agendas—narrowly defined—until national liberation is achieved. In the words of one woman, "How much time can we give to [working for] other rights when our sons are martyrs and our husbands are in prison?"[11]

Her impassioned statement was made at an annual convention of the UPWA, which has provided a forum for debating such issues, usually with the spirited participation of women from the Occupied Territories. (Indeed, the degree of identification between Palestinian women here and abroad is deep, and the commerce between them steady.) At any rate, it has been at such conferences, rather than in circles of third-generation Lebanese and Syrian American feminists, that one is likely to encounter a critique of the Arab woman's position within her own society.

A panel on feminism at the 1992 UPWA convention provides a case in point. On the one hand, panelists agreed that Western-style feminism was inadequate to the needs of Arab women and incompatible with certain of their cultural values and ideals. Many Arab women, for instance, disdain a creed that seems to them to endorse individual autonomy and self-expression (sexual and otherwise) as ultimate values to which other claims—of family, community, nation—and deeper sources of satisfaction must give way. Another point of agreement was the panel's indignation at American feminists who have been quick to lambaste Saudis and Kuwaitis for their treatment of women, but silent on Israeli brutality toward Palestinian women living under occupation.

But such complaints were old news. The most pointed message from the panel was the necessity to be self-critical: "We should be more vocal than NOW about Muslim fundamentalism and about Saudis and Kuwaitis and the way they treat women." Better to take such criticism into one's own hands than to leave it to unfriendly others.

Self-criticism has also meant questioning the UPWA's priorities. Is it primarily a women's organization or a Palestinian organization? Is its center of concern Palestine or the Palestinian community in the United States? Specifically, is it possible that the obsession with Palestine has diverted attention from serious social problems in the Palestinian American community?

That such questions have been raised in open meetings indicates the direction in which the UPWA and, in a sense, the community at large is evolving. Like other Palestinian American organizations, the UPWA began as a solidarity group. According to one leader, "The idea was how can we living in exile help our people living under occupation." Women, so the theory went, would be empowered simply by participating in that work. But over time, the UPWA has come to realize (as did the Ladies' Aid some seventy years earlier) that it must put more effort into addressing the needs of its local constituency, especially women and children. "Our community has always invested its resources over there [in the Middle East]," says one member. "We have to show them that they need to invest in the community here."[12]

Ultimately, investment must mean tackling the most sensitive problems in the community—too many girls still forced out of school and into early marriages; too many wives prevented from working outside the home or resuming their educations; too many women of any age unreasonably constricted in their dress and behavior; and finally, as is true throughout American society, too many women still victims of domestic violence (and too many children vulnerable to the dangers of drugs, gangs, and AIDS).[13]

As much as anything, what UPWA has tried to offer women in trouble is moral support from people within their own culture and hope for change. The message, says one leader, is "You can't do it alone, and I can't do it alone, but together we can have an impact on the community." With support from others, women and girls can begin to say, "I do want to go to school," or "I don't want to get married now."

Certainly, there are forces in the community working against change. Religious extremists, for instance, are quick to criticize women who take on activities outside the home (be it no more than selling tickets to club events or distributing fliers) and may preach that obedience, even to abusive husbands, is pleasing to God. Men and women committed to a particular religious or even political agenda may accuse the UPWA of encouraging women to leave their husbands, of encouraging girls to run away from home, or of simply surrendering to Western cultural values.

To avoid such charges, the UPWA relies on mediation and quiet intervention rather than on confrontation, sometimes enlisting the aid of sympathetic clergy, community leaders, or progressive men who have influence with a particular family or clan. When such efforts fail, the UPWA may refer women to programs or shelters for battered women. But a woman who takes the ultimate step of divorce knows that she runs the risk of having her character called into question and even of being ostracized by the community.

Still, it is possible to effect change. One of the best examples is provided by the young people's dance troupes sponsored by the UPWA (and other community groups). In a sense, those troupes summarize what the organization is about. In the first place, they help preserve a treasured folk art expressing the spirit of the people. Second, they act as cultural ambassadors, educating audiences about Palestinian culture and providing an image to counter the bloody ones more often associated with Palestinians. Another advantage is that the troupes bring together young people, both male and female, in friendly companionship. Finally, the troupes, which sometimes perform out of town, give girls more freedom, most dramatically by challenging the taboo against an Arab daughter's ever spending a night away from home, even if chaperoned. At first, some parents simply refused to let their daughters travel; but in time, girls as young as fifteen and sixteen were doing so on a regular basis. As one woman explained, "Most parents are proud to see their kids developing a strong sense of Arab identity and culture."

Once again, then, what makes change possible is the fact that the activities in question occur within and on behalf of the Palestinian community. The Palestinian cause may sometimes have inhibited women's freedoms, encouraging a reactionary insistence on the status quo. But it has also been the means for ordinary women, both under occupation and in exile, to expand their horizons, reinterpret their role in the family, and broaden their sphere of action outside the home.

MONA

"My generation redefined honor. The political generation, the Palestinian active generation, we defined it for ourselves."

Mona (a pseudonym), the daughter of Palestinian immigrants from Jordan, has been a leader among young people in her community. She is also an outspoken feminist. According to Mona, the first time in her life she felt the difference between men and women was in 1979, when she was nine years old and accompanied her family on a one-month visit back to Jordan.

I found my uncle's eight-year-old daughter wearing the *hijab* and a full-length dress. All you could see was her face. And her brothers treated her like crap . . . "Do this! Do that!" But me and my brothers were friends.

And I remember my uncle was constantly putting down my dad by lecturing him and embarrassing him on how in America he hasn't kept up the culture and the language and especially the religion [Islam].

It was during Ramadan that we went to Jordan, the holy month of fasting. Ramadan was really nice there because the atmosphere is so close and warm. My brother Hassan—he was eleven at the time—he started getting really into the religion and the praying. Me and my brother were very close, so whatever he would do, I wanted to do. My uncle was so happy. "You both want to pray?" But I remember my uncle spending more time with my brother than he would with me, explaining what the prayers meant.

Then, I remember the first time I came to pray with them. I think my arms were showing and my hair was down. My uncle said, "*Haram* [shame]! Go get covered, go get something on your hair, go get something down to here [the wrists]." So I said, "Okay, fine." I went and got the *hijab* and wore the thing. Then I put my [prayer] rug next to my brother.

My uncle was looking at me again. Then he asked me, "What are you doing?" I said, "I'm going to pray with you." He said, "You have to get behind us." I said, "Why?" He said, "Because [not to do that] is *haram*." I said, "Why is it *haram*? I want to be able to read the prayers with you." Then my uncle started explaining to me that "in the Koran it is written down that we must respect and protect women, and by you being beside the men it doesn't give you respect." I said, "How is that so?" He said, "If women kneel in front of men, it's very distracting. Men might start thinking something [bad], the devil might come between them." I told him, "Well, it doesn't make sense"—I'll never forget this because I got in so much trouble for it—I said, "It doesn't make sense because then we really should be next to each other because if women distract the men, what about the men kneeling in front? Isn't that distracting to the women?"

He exploded! "Oh, how dare I say such a thing!?" To them, that's a very open sexual remark, that we view men sexually. He yelled for my dad, "Hassan, Hassan, come here and get your daughter! *Yil'an abu ameerka* [Curses on America]." I got so scolded, and finally they made me go in the back and just pray.

That double-standard mentality continued for the whole time we were there; and, you know, at nine you're very impressionable. So when we came back to America, I continued wearing the *hijab* for about a month. My mom and sister were just very embarrassed and didn't want me to be going out in public. I remember what started turning me off [was] my brother started telling me things like "Well, go get my shoes." He even tried to continue and make me pray behind him. I took it at first, but then I got sick of it all, and I took the *hijab* off.

So after that experience, I stayed away from Arabs except for my family. I had the impression that all Arabs are like my relatives from our village, very restrictive of females and old-fashioned. My parents used to worry. "How is she going to ever assimilate into our culture?" But at the same time, they knew that I didn't like the American culture either. The area we were living around was full of very broken American families, very drug infested and very, very dysfunctional. I remember in fourth grade, one of my best friends had a very messed up family. I went [to her house] once, and they were all smoking marijuana and drinking, and I was very appalled by it all.

Another extremely big factor why I didn't accept the American culture was that from first grade, me and my brothers encountered racism in school. Things like "Camel jockey!" "Sand nigger!" "Where's your veil?" "Where's your bomb?" And just continually, continually, "You *A*-rab." So we learned that we were not a part of the American culture.

Then, there was a huge drug culture in our high school that I was not attracted to and just the kids' whole bohemian life style. They viewed everything short term, meaning you live for now, and they were superficial in terms of being very materialistic, being very individualistic—me, myself, and I—very little caring for others. The opposite of where we in the Arab culture, I felt, have human compassion, we sincerely want to help. Like if you needed a dollar, if you're short, nobody in school—or very few—would offer you a dollar. Whereas I'd say, "Here's a dollar and five more, I don't want you to worry about it. When you have it, just pay it back."

So I constantly saw the two worlds [Arab and American] clash. But one thing that appealed to me was the freedom Americans got. Freedom and so-called equality that wasn't in our culture. [For instance], I was constantly watched. I was constantly told not to hang around with the boys, to be careful of those boys. And you think "What's wrong with those boys?" We biked, we played football, we weren't sitting around playing spin-the-bottle.

When I started menstruation at age twelve, my mother began telling me, "Now you have to be more careful, you're carrying the family honor." My reaction was "Well, just because I'm menstruating, it doesn't make me stupid or careless. So don't worry." And in school, that's when everyone was going through puberty, they were all either girl crazy or boy crazy. But I didn't go through that because I thought if you did, then you were stupid, weak, and would just fall into that trap of being labeled as "female."

So then as time went on, I just started rebelling. "I don't want these restrictions. Why don't you care what my brothers are doing, and why don't you care what time they come home or if they're with girls?"

I was so, so tomboyish. My talk and my manner were very masculine. My hair was just a mess. My clothes were always just either sweats or jeans and an old raggedy T-shirt. It was like I was telling my parents, "I don't have any sexuality, so you don't have to worry about me." For instance, I used to be embarrassed to wear make-up, whereas my sisters begged to wear it at as young as eight. I didn't want it because I didn't want anything that made me look female or highlighted my gender because I knew that automatically meant restrictions.

I carried that tomboyish look and attitude up until, I'd say, age eighteen. At eighteen I started to come to terms with it's okay to be female. You do have sexuality, you do have feelings, you do get attracted to men and vice versa; but at the same time, you are still a person and you can do whatever you want without all the restrictions of being "female."

[Even as Mona was working out her identity as a female, she was also beginning to come to terms with her identity as a Palestinian. The two matters were not unrelated.]

I always knew about the Palestinian struggle. I mean, I knew that Palestine was under Israeli occupation, because we used to talk about politics a lot in my family. The 1982 invasion [of Lebanon] really hit home because my brother was back there, and one of our friends, who used to work with us in the [family] store, got killed over there. I remember my mom constantly crying. The news would come on, and it was very distressing. I didn't fully understand it. But I knew it was [the fault of] the "damn Americans" and Israel.

So from 1982, I started becoming more aware of what was happening in the Middle East and really resenting the American government. But I never really was involved in politics until I was sixteen and I went to a picnic of a Palestinian organization. At first, I didn't want to go because I thought they would all be like the people from my village.

But when I [got there], I was totally shocked. You had all these youths from fifteen to thirty, and everybody was just so socially open. You had males and females, mothers and fathers, all sitting together like one family, all laughing together and playing together, and some of the younger men and women were playing volleyball, and some were in their bathing suits, going to go swimming. I didn't know there were Arabs and Arab Americans like this. I felt like this was where I belonged.

From then on, I became involved [with this Palestinian club]. I was going back and forth to the Palestinian community center, and my family were so relieved and so happy that I was getting back in touch with the Arab culture and identity. But I was still tough, and the men viewed me as tough. I didn't leave any room for flirting.

It didn't take me long to become politically driven. I was constantly around political literature and pictures of our massacred people, of our country—I began to absorb it all unconsciously. Plus, just the whole atmosphere was political: the discussions were always deep and very hot and very educational. I felt like, "Wow! This is so different than at school," where they used to talk about hairstyles or who's dating who. Then, my junior year in high school, the *intifada* broke out, and my involvement just took off!

My parents couldn't accept it. I was becoming very active and very public and working very close with men politically. They told me, "Even though we trust you, [other] people see you as an unmarried public girl who works with men in politics. You're going to be burned socially. You're going to be viewed as too strong, like you're not female. And you're not going to get married." I told them, "I don't care."

Anyhow, the *intifada* just sparked the hell out of everybody. I remember going to school, and I would be a zombie. Before that, I didn't fit in, but now I *extremely* didn't fit in. I didn't want to talk to people in school because they were just so superficial. During the Gulf War, I felt it again, like "Oh my God, I really don't belong. Don't you know what's going on in this world? Don't you care? Who gives a shit about clothes and boys? Don't you care about what's happening to other humans? And we're funding this?" Everybody in my eye was nothing. "You're all collaborators, you're all part of oppression, and I have no reason to respect you or to trust you or to listen to you."

I remember especially the first year of the *intifada*. Every day after school let out, I would automatically go to the club, to organize, prepare posters, call people, and then take off and go demonstrate. Now I became "Palestinian," period. I wouldn't even let anybody call me "Palestinian American." I would love when somebody would say, "She's more Palestinian than the people from back home." That was the best.

I still denied my femininity and sexuality because I wanted to let everyone know that when I leave the house it's for politics, nothing else. Because they [the Arab community] think if women are politically involved, then they will have easy contacts to men, politics will lead into a friendship and then into a relationship, automatically sexual and automatically dishonoring the family. So I wanted to prove to them that I was sincere, I wasn't trying to use politics as a means to an end, a way to meet men or a way to get out of the house. And all the time, my parents were telling me, "We're Arab, and Arab girls are not like this [public and active]."

Here I was, just wanting to be Palestinian, and they're telling me if you're doing what you're doing, you're not Palestinian, you're not Arab, you're just the opposite.

But then as time went on, I started realizing that being Arab doesn't mean just what they mean. I found my honor through my political work. And that was [because of] the *intifada*, too. I mean, back home in Palestine it redefined the structure of the society, it redefined the role of women. That's why women went into the streets, because now the honor was the homeland, how much you were giving to the cause, not the woman's sexuality. That's why my family may have cringed [at my activism] and gave me problems, but they could never really do anything about it because at the same time, it was an honor now. We redefined honor, my generation defined it, the political generation, the Palestinian active generation, we defined it for ourselves.

Now I accept being called "Arab American" because I realize that it's just a matter of fact, it's an identity, and it's not a bad identity. The reason I hated "Arab American" so much when I was younger is because I thought that label meant you're not a good Arab and you're not a good American. Therefore, to make life simpler, you're either just a good Arab and follow their rules, or a good American and have their mentality—"Oh, let my parents go to hell, I'm going to move out." I also realized it was actually good to be Arab American because you get the best of both worlds. Politically, as [Arab Americans], we know how to work with the mainstream and do outreach; we have an advantage over the Arabs back home.

[As far as Mona's social and personal life is concerned, she has arrived at a formula that is neither fully "Arab" nor fully "American."]

We've reached a compromise in my family. I will not date just to date. I do not want a boyfriend just for the fact of having a boyfriend, or just for going out, or just because I meet someone who's good looking and says, "Hey, you want to do something?" No, I won't do that. But if he's interested in a commitment, and he thinks that I might fit the bill, if he's looking for a sincere relationship and not just a good time, then we'll explore, we'll get to know each other. It's dating but not dating in the American sense. And my family will be automatically involved. This is what I prefer because superficial relationships don't do anything for me.

See, for me it's deeper than just social. I'm a political leader in the community; I'm looked upon as a leader for the youth. So I'm out to prove, not just for other people but also for myself, that as females we can do it all and still keep our respect.

15

COLLAGE

I

When a daughter is born, the very threshold of the house weeps forty days.

Arab proverb

No, no, the parents just feel bad for a week.

Hannah Shakir, Lebanese

My father didn't want me to be born. He only wanted boys. So with his first born, he was very happy, it was a boy. The second one, my sister, it was okay. The third time it was terrible, twin girls. But they were premature and one died. My mother told me, "I'll bet he was happy. I cried but I bet he was happy." After that, my mother didn't want more children, but she got pregnant with me. She cried, she went to the *hammam* for hot baths, she carried heavy stuff and drank salt laxatives, but she couldn't get rid of me. So when she delivered and it was a girl, my father was so mad he didn't come to see me for several days.

My mother would tell me these things, and I felt bad.

Karima Roudesli, Algerian

My father doesn't have any sisters, so he wanted a girl badly. I was very privileged, the only daughter among three brothers. For instance, one time my father bought me a keyboard. All my brothers can play music, but I'm the only one who got [a present like] that. And when I went to college, I got a car. My brother went to the college four years and he took the bus! But I got a car the first year. And I didn't do any housecleaning until I was in college, but my brothers did. When they were in intermediate school and then high school, I saw them cleaning in the house with my mother. They would wipe, they would dust. I was just sitting there playing, making a mess.

Asmahan S. (a pseudonym), Palestinian raised in Kuwait

So many times I would be asked to fix my brother's bed. I was told, "He is a boy." And I would say, "He has arms and legs." Or sometimes he would be sitting, and he would say, "Go get me a glass of water." I would say, "Never! Get your own." My family would say to me, "Your head is so strong, it cannot be broken with a hammer."

We lived in Beirut from October through June, but come the summer, we all went up to the village. My uncle was the caretaker of the village church, and he would tell us [girls], "Now don't you go behind the altar." The boys had free rein, they could go wherever they wanted. But [menstruating] girls were not clean enough to be in a spiritual place. So one day I thought, "Okay, I'm going to go behind that altar." I was really scared, but at the same time feeling defiant and risk taking. So I went behind the altar and then I came out. Nothing happened. I wasn't struck by lightening. So I did it again. And then I went home having this huge sense of accomplishment.

Hayat Weiss, Lebanese

My mother would insist, "Come and look at the grass, come and look at the flower, feel it, touch it." And even when she was standing in the kitchen cooking, she would tell me, "Come and see, come and touch." That's the way I was taught to appreciate things as they are.

I owe my mother a lot. She was intelligent, she spoke French and English fluently, and Arabic. And she encouraged my father to be more open to the world. She came as a teacher from Beirut, which is a metropolitan city, and moved to Mosul [in Iraq], which was at that time and still is very traditional. I can see how difficult it was for her. Yet every summer, when we had the last day of school, she would pack us up and take us to Beirut. She tried to provide the same sort of atmosphere inside the house. It was like an island, a beautiful island. All my memories are beautiful.

Shameem Rassam Amal, Iraqi

I was raised by my grandmother. She didn't have a chance herself at education because she got married when she was twelve years old. Her daughters didn't have a chance because they had to work early to survive. And she kept that in her heart. But after independence [from France], the drive for education was there in the country, so we had *carte blanche* to go to school to any level we wanted. It was wonderful the support my grandmother gave us. She always made sure that we got up early and went to school, and if we had an exam, she would wake up at five o'clock in the morning and make coffee. But she also wanted us to be as perfect as we could be as wives and mothers. Her word was, "I don't want anyone ever to say to you, 'Cursed be the person who raised you.' "

Dalila Messaoudi, Algerian

I was born in Kuwait and lived in Saudi Arabia for my first five years. When I was six and it was time for me to wear the *hijab*, my dad decided to leave. In Saudi Arabia, my mother had to cover her hair and her body with that black garb they wear, and neither of my parents wanted me to wear it. So my family went back and planted itself in Jordan, and I went to Catholic school there for twelve years.

Mai N. (a pseudonym), Palestinian Jordanian

When I was nine or ten years old, we woke up one morning, my sister and I, and my mother is telling us, "From now on you are wearing the *chador* [black drapery worn outside the home and covering a woman from head to foot]." So that means that I cannot any more play with boys in the street, I will have to be treated as an adult woman. My sister—she is two years younger and we have different personalities—she enjoyed that, for her that was like playing house. But I resented it. And the pressure inside me was building and building.

In high school we were studying Marxism, and I was reading books by feminist authors. The values of freedom and a woman's equality were instilled in me at that time. So when I was about sixteen or seventeen, I remember I left that *chador* in school and I went home, just like that. It was a revolution! My mother was going to have a heart attack! She called my uncles on me. They came, they were angry, they yelled and screamed, my mother cried. But I said, "No, I'm not wearing it any more."

Suad Mohamed, Yemeni

I became known as the crazy person in the family. If I got angry, I would shout, and my mother would say, "Don't shout. The neighbors will hear you. Nobody will want to marry you." Or I used to walk around the house singing. My family thought that was not very proper. "Stop heehawing like a donkey," they would say.

I knew I wasn't crazy, but it was tough to be able to be myself. The way I dealt with it was to create an internal world. Starting age fifteen, I started reading the French existentialists, and Simone de Beauvoir was my ideal. I read everything by her and Jean Paul Sartre, too. In books I could find my soul mates.

One summer I had had it. I decided I was not going to speak any more. So I was silent. They would talk to me, I would smile, I would do whatever it is I'm supposed to do, offer coffee to visitors, pass around the chocolate candy and the almond candy. But I never spoke, for at least a month. It drove everybody nuts.

I wasn't allowed to go to the movies at all because movies corrupt girls. I was going to the most prominent French school in Beirut; I was reading *avant garde* literature, newspapers, and magazines that came straight from France; yet I was not allowed to have my own thoughts. In other words, I had to be intellectually great in the school, but at the same time, when I came home, I had to be this traditional woman. At some point, it didn't jibe any more. My first movie was at age sixteen, when I had my own money and could physically take myself on the *service* [public taxi] for a quarter each way. I saw *The Carpetbaggers* with George Peppard. He was young, and I thought he looked really good.

So I was enjoying the movie in one part of myself, and I was very afraid in the other part and thinking, "What am I going to tell them back home?" It was maybe nine o'clock, and to them that was late. So I lied to them, I said I got hit by a car. To prove that I was hit by a car, I snuck first into my room, I took scissors, and I cut myself. I cut a piece of flesh out of my left thigh.

I must have been desperate. I must have been really scared. I did it in slow pieces so at the beginning it didn't hurt, and then it started bleeding. But they didn't even look. I did it for nothing!

Hayat Weiss, Lebanese

When we were very little kids, my two cousins and me would sit around playing with Lego and we would make [a model of] *Hamra*, the most popular street in Beirut. Our dream was to go to AUB [the American University of Beirut]. A whole generation of the intelligentsia in the Arab world had graduated from there and their experience was just so glorified. So the three of us were going to have our little apartment, become doctors or whatever, and never get married.

We got those ideas from our mothers. Neither of them had finished any higher education. They both had some aspirations which never matured because they had to get married. They married good men, but that wasn't all they wanted out of life. I mean, I don't even remember the first time my mother started talking to me about alternatives to marriage. I was really little when she started.

But all of a sudden, when I turned nineteen, twenty, she started seeing that, well, it wouldn't be so bad if I found a comfortably rich Palestinian from a good family. I'm telling her, "Mom, they're a hard catch. And it's [especially] hard to get one I can deal with." Because if you marry one of those guys, you have to become their mother. You have to start being able to bake real tiny, puffy pastries with just the right amount of sesame.

When I turned twenty-two, I went home [to Jordan] and I found she had already made my wedding quilt. Usually the mother and daughter make it together, and usually it's a real hot color—bright pink, lavender, red. When I found out she had made it, I couldn't decide whether it was out of encouragement or despair, or just this is her duty and now she's done it.

Mai N. (a pseudonym), Palestinian Jordanian

I chose my own husband. My family did not approve because he was fifteen years older than me. Also, I think, because he was darker. But I was a teenager, madly in love. He was just everything to me, he was my teacher, my mentor, my little god. I told my family, "If you don't allow me to marry him, I will run away." They were terrified of a scandal, so they said, "Okay, let her get married, the hell with her!" One of my uncles whom I loved very dearly—he was a very, very good man—he never, never spoke to me again until the day he died.

Suad Mohamed, Yemini

When I was in college in Beirut, I met Joe, my husband. He was an American teacher. Almost hell broke loose because my parents didn't approve of me dating anybody, let alone an American. They called him "the thief."

But the Lebanese are very polite. Not a word [to him] and not any inkling of them not liking him. Once he sets his foot in the door, he is the king; hospitality goes into high gear. So it was fresh-squeezed orange juice, and dinners, because he's living alone, poor American.

We got married in 1971, and once we got married, they gave him the key to the house, and they said, "Welcome to the family, you are one of us now."

We thought we would come to the States to finish our education and then we would go back and live in Lebanon and start a family. But the [civil] war broke out in 1975, and we were never able to go back.

Hayat Weiss, Lebanese

My fiancé had a scholarship to come to America. So I married him, this handsome guy, and the next day we came to the United States. My parents were crushed, but I was very happy. To me, it was adventure and freedom and opportunity to learn something and just be in the Western world. From the start, my husband said that he would not go back, he was absolutely adamant about it. But, of course, we did not tell my parents that.

Karima Roudesli, Algerian

In 1955, when I came to study in America, Iraqis of some means—mostly Christian—sent their daughters to college in Beirut or Egypt. I remember at a meeting of the Arab Students Association here, you could count the women on the fingers of one hand, the hall was filled with men. A lot were here on government scholarship. And all of us, our intention was to go back and help our developing society develop further. But we were young, it was the time of falling in love and mating. A lot of the men married Americans and stayed. And I did the same.

Hind Rassam Cullhane, Iraqi

When I left Egypt in 1976, I knew that I was leaving for good. Because it was very hard for me there. My father could tell me, "Oh, don't do this," and I would stop. I couldn't make a decision about my own life. The fact is I spent a year convincing him to let me come to the States to work on my master's degree. If he had said no at the end, I wouldn't have come, even though I was a grown woman [married and divorced].

If my father was not there, my uncle was going to be the ruler. He can decide for me if I should get married again or not. The family can decide for me if I go out or I don't go out.

Hawa T. (a pseudonym), Egyptian

I was twelve years old, and I was going to move with my family to the United States. I was going to see—like on TV—people who are on drugs or kill each other, or women being abused. So I was very, very scared. But my other image of the United States was the land of opportunity, and I was wondering, "How can the land of opportunity have so much violence?"

Mary Yazbeck, Lebanese

I thought coming here was a stinking idea. I had just become a Brownie, and I thought that this was absolutely the best thing that had ever happened to me. We had songs, we had cute brown uniforms. I didn't want to go away.

Nimet Habachy, Egyptian

II

I'm twenty years old, but I feel like I'm thirty-five. The war tends to make you grow up. In my school, the high school and junior high were in charge of the kindergarten and elementary school. We took the children [in case of air raid], put them in the shelter. We knew how to stop the bleeding and prevent shock in case somebody got shot. Once one child got hit.

Once I got stuck in my school because they were bombing. I stayed two days without seeing my parents. Another time, in the summer vacation, my brother got shot. He was translating for the UN, and he got hit by the Israelis. They shot him, and they didn't let the United Nations ambulance reach him for six hours.

Adults look at the children [and think], "They don't know what's happening." Yes, they do know. They're growing up much faster. They no longer play in playgrounds, they play in shelters, trying to plan, "How can I get even with this person who's killing my parents, my cousins, my family?"

Nada Mansi, Lebanese

My brother was the first one to come here. The militias were after him to become active, so my parents said, "You're out of here!" Then about a year after the [Lebanese civil war] started, the rest of us just packed up and left. My parents had a very, very comfortable existence in Lebanon. I was nine, but I knew enough about what we used to do, who our friends were, what my parents used to do socially in comparison to here, where my mother might not leave her home for a week. I always refer to my parents as the disposable generation because they sacrificed everything just so their kids can have a better life.

Lena B. (a pseudonym), Lebanese

My husband never had any interest at all in politics. But his two brothers, who were older, got involved in problems with the government of Syria, the Assad regime. One brother fled to Kuwait, and the other brother, who was a lawyer, was kidnapped by the Syrian regime in 1981 and ever since we have no idea if he's alive or dead. We were in Kuwait, but we were under constant threat of having to leave there; they even fingerprinted us. And in Syria, with the situation of his family, if my husband goes there, he will be imprisoned.

We decided we would be better off if we moved to the States. So here we are, accepted in a country that's very nice, wonderful people, open. But my three-year old had the hardest time, his world was changed, his whole life was upset. He kept saying, "Why did we come? We have to go back."

Abla Shocair, Syrian

In Baghdad, we worked under machine guns because the radio and the TV stations were the most important facilities under government control. So we had the tanks there all the time and special units from the army. Radio and TV means control of everything. That's where you reach the remote places in Iraq if you overthrow the government. It's where you issue your first communiqué.

The director of television and radio would have his machine gun on his desk when I would go to his office. That's how they treated us.

You learn to survive, you don't want to see yourself in one of the jails; you don't want to see your family in one of the jails; you don't want to see your neighbors. So you don't argue politically, you don't tell people that you know better, you don't think.

In the studio, there's several telephones in front of the one who's in charge that night. This telephone is from the palace, this telephone is from the vice president, this is from military security, this is from internal security.

Now this is what happens. A telephone rings. The man in the studio would do like this [rises to attention]. "Yes, sir!" And he's so scared he's almost going to urinate on himself. Then he runs. He doesn't even know what the caller said; all he remembers is it's the president's voice or vice president's or prime minister's and he said something about the show that's on the air right now. The man runs out, "Stop that show!" They stop it, just like that. Then whoever is doing that show, he's suspended from even appearing on TV, and nobody knows why.

That is what happened to me. I had a program. The prime minister calls in. He says, "Why is Shameem smiling so much?" For seven months I was suspended from being on the air. Then one day, my husband ran into the prime minister. The prime minister said, "How come I haven't seen Shameem for some time on TV?" My husband said, "Because of you. It seems you called the TV and made a comment." The prime minister said, "Oh no, I didn't mean to take her off the air. I just said she was smiling." My husband said, "I think you should make another call."

My mother and my husband were the people I trusted in my life. My husband was my first supporter, he pushed me a lot, he was my best friend. When he died, I lost somebody that I can talk to confidentially.

[During the Iraq-Iran War], the rockets would come or a missile would fall. Before an air raid, you would hear the alarm. What can you do? You can count, five to seven minutes, because that's the time it takes airplanes to cross the border and come to Baghdad. You learn where is the safest part of the house; you stand at the corner of two cement walls. I did that at first. Then after a while, I would go on with my daily chores. Out of nervousness, I would start cleaning the house or washing dishes. Even if they're clean dishes, I'll wash them. All the time, I'm counting the minutes. When it's over, I thank God.

Once there was a big explosion, the radio station was attacked. It was a big lorry with dynamite—one of those suicides; he crashed himself into the building. It was around ten o'clock in the morning, we were having coffee, and then all of a sudden we heard the explosion. So the Civil Defense came to take us out of the buildings, and I remember we were standing in the courtyard, and the Republican Guard on the roofs of all the buildings had their guns aimed at us because they didn't know who's behind it. Then you see your colleagues coming out of the building, all in blood, and falling in front of you, and you cannot help them. You're not supposed to move. The soldiers are shouting at you, "Don't you ever move!"

My sister called me from the States and said, "Why don't you come here for the summer?" A week after I was here, the war started with Kuwait. My brother said, "It's not wise for you to go back."

I heard there were several reports written about me back home, accusing me to be a traitor. I thought, "That's it, you're going to stay." I was granted political asylum. Then I'm starting from scratch, I'm starting from no money. I had [only] seven hundred dollars with me; I left everything else behind: my three houses, my cars, my money in the bank, my stock. I said, "Why do I have to pay for what that man [Saddam Hussein] is doing?"

I wanted my children to grow up in Iraq knowing my friends, knowing the back streets of every Arab country. I wanted my daughter to grow up to know what my culture is, my tradition as a woman. And maybe to have new ideas to improve that. I wanted my son and daughter to be close to their father's tomb, to visit it often. I wanted, myself, to see the palm trees growing in my backyard, to smell that odor of every day. I said, "Why do I have to give it up for that man? He has ruined my life."

Shameem Rassam Amal, Iraqi

III

I was not used to such cold, I didn't have the clothes for it. I didn't think to buy boots early enough, so when it snowed, I was wearing high heeled shoes and just couldn't walk. And going to the grocery store was almost an all-day affair because I didn't know what to buy. Shelves of bread, cans of things, all kinds of things. I would pick up every can and read the ingredients on it.

In Lebanon you just buy from the merchant on the street. You're walking, you see tomatoes, "Give me two tomatoes." Or the donkey comes to the door, and the [driver] shouts, "Potatoes! Fifty cents a kilo!"

Hayat Weiss, Lebanese

I came to this country being an MD already. That surprised people. They had the built-in idea that [because] I'm a woman and Arab and Muslim, I shouldn't be a doctor who is outgoing, very independent, and very Westernized. But if you don't look at fanatic groups—fanatic groups in any religion are going to give you the wrong impression—women are encouraged in Islam, they're encouraged in the Koran.

Mawya Shocair, Syrian

When I came, that's when I began wearing the *hijab*, in the third grade. The kids were very mean. "Take that towel off!" "Take that sheet off!" I'm a tough person, but sometimes I felt like quitting school, that's one thing I felt. But taking it off? Never! It's part of my religion.

Zeainab Karnib, Lebanese

I think there are some problems in the schools in terms of counselors. If a girl comes in dressed in traditional dress with the *hijab*, I don't think that counselor provides the same kind of alternatives for that child as she would for someone else.

Lena B. (a pseudonym), Lebanese

I was in a class for international students, [and] we introduced ourselves all around. It was during the hostage thing, and I say I'm Lebanese. So one fresh kid got up and said, "Oh, you're from that terrorist country." I didn't like his remark. I said, "Oh, so all Lebanese are terrorists, all Colombians are drug dealers, all Cubans are Communist. That's very open minded." And I sat down.

Nada Mansi, Lebanese

In high school here, making fun of people is the big thing, especially making fun of someone who can't speak English. So the first year I didn't speak any English, and the second year I spoke only when I had to. I was determined not to speak to anyone until I had fluently learned the language and didn't have an accent, because otherwise I'd be humiliated in the halls.

There was one African American girl, and she would bug me. She would sit next to me on the bus and just try to talk to me. I was like, "Oh no, God don't let her sit here." I didn't understand her, and I didn't want to make her feel bad by not talking. But she tried so hard and I came to like her a lot. There are always special people trying to reach you even though you want to be secluded.

Wijdan Azzou, Iraqi

I lived in a college dormitory, which was my first experience with Americans. The girls just seemed to me so oversexed. I would sit my roommates down, and I would give them lectures in morality about the shorts they're wearing, that they're very short, and not becoming to a lady to wear.

Back in Jordan, I was a member of the basketball team and I wore shorts to games. I was a part of the *avant garde*, wearing shorts where men were, and it was a scandal across the country. Eventually they illegalized it. Now the girls have to wear long pants. But *there* we were fighting for something; *here* they're just selling it.

The first week in the dorm, I had a little map of Palestine in bronze over red velvet in the center of my door, and this guy comes in, totally drunk, and he screams, "Israel!" So me and my cousin just pounce on him. At the time I had no problem attacking someone physically. I attacked one boy for creeping into my cousin's room to steal a bra of hers. I was there when he did it, and he got beaten up almost into a pulp. So people knew I would do these things, and it just reinforced the whole idea about terrorism and Palestinians.

You know, one of my freshmen roommates eventually converted to Judaism and became an Israeli supporter. That was very stunning. Here is a person I came so close to, the person I gave a moral lecture to about showing her thighs. Here I give her the jewels of my culture, and she goes and becomes a Jew. My God *[laughing]*, it hurt! You can't help but wonder— was it something in me that pushed her overboard?

Mai N. (a pseudonym), Palestinian Jordanian

Ours was a very privileged emigration, living quite nicely in New York, [and I was] going to a very nice private school. But I felt very often like the Indian in a bad Western. I remember silly, ugly things. Years ago, in the late 1950s, we're driving, our car gets stuck in the sand on a beach. We are kindly helped out by a gentleman who says somewhere along in the conversation, "Where are you all from?" We announce we are Egyptian, and he says, "If I'd known that, I'd have left you there."

Nimet Habachy, Egyptian

Because of the way Americans see Arabs, for a long time I didn't feel like saying where I'm from. I resented anybody that asked me. I just didn't think that was a conversation opener.

Fatan M. (a pseudonym), Jordanian

I'm thinking that my whole life in the United States has been punctuated by nothing but misery and bad news of the Middle East, news of wars, conflicts, killings. If it's not Iraq, it's Lebanon; if it's not Lebanon, it's Egypt. And after the wars, the prejudice against us because we are Arabs and the whole media portrayal of "these terrorists." During the Arab Israeli wars in the 1970s, my sons were beaten up in grade school and in high school because they were half Arab. My son says, "Sometimes I don't want to say I'm an Arab." I feel badly for children that they have to hide their identity. I'm a psychologist, and I think that hostility here [against Arabs] has led to depression; I think it has led to shaky identity. People have not even done studies on what it's done to our identity as an ethnic group.

Hind Rassam Cullhane, Iraqi

The FBI watch us even though we are political refugees and they know what side we're on. They question us, they question all Libyans. They threatened my husband over the phone. They said they would kick him out of the country if he didn't cooperate and give them information about his friends.

Look, I hate Khadafy, but I do not condone what America did to the Libyan people. The places America bombed were in downtown Tripoli. I know somebody here who phoned home; there was no reply. When she eventually called her husband's parents, someone told her that they're at the funeral of her dad and mom and sister. One of my best friends, her father died, her mother lost her eye, and her brother is paralyzed as a result of that bombing.

Mufida H. (a pseudonym), Libyan

My biggest shock was watching the [Gulf War] from a CNN TV screen. I don't think I will ever recover from that experience. It's safe to say I was pretty much on the verge of a nervous breakdown because I had no idea how to contact my family. For six months, I did not know whether my parents were dead or alive. And the whole media hype. They had to show Saddam as a villain, but not just Saddam; the whole Iraqi people had to look like villains.

I feel like I have to explain myself the whole time. Even here in school, people always want to ask me questions about my country, its politics, the culture, the religion, everything. I get tired, I get very tired. People are interested in a sort of scientific way; they don't understand how emotional this whole thing is to me. They say, "Oh, how interesting, let me write it down." Because they want to use it in a paper or something.

Leila K. (a pseudonym), Iraqi

IV

We came here because of war and suffering in our country. America is good, it's very good. Anyone who says America isn't good, he's not good. America protects the poor and it protects the rich—people live well and easy. It provides them with a living. It protects children from war. And it educates them, even ones without money.

But we are older. What are our problems here? It is this sitting at home. We can't stir without a car. An older person, seventy-five, can't speak the language right away or go out among people and do her shopping unless she has younger people to help her. Isn't that right, my dear?

Over there we used to go for a walk; we used to wander freely, buy our vegetables, carry them on our heads in a box. Yes, we'd carry them on our heads, vegetables and food for our children, and we didn't mind it. Here if you walk in the street, you feel ashamed. People think, "Don't they have children to give them a lift?"

Here each day [when] you get up, your body feels run down, from being cooped up at home, from the [central] heating. In the weather back home we live ten years longer than here. [It's] because we live here within four walls. Where can we go? Over there, you walk, you visit your mother's sisters, your father's sisters. You go out, you pick by hand from your own garden the apricot, the olive, the grape. We used to eat bulgur, chick peas, lentils, everything from our own land. We would grind the bulgur with our own hands and dry it on our roofs. Here you don't know where anything comes from. Here you sit idly, and everything you eat is artificial; you don't see the sheep or the cow slaughtered in front of you. Over there, you go to the brook, you take your fishing pole with you, you catch your fish and you bring them home and you cook them and eat them. Here you buy fish, you don't know how old it is.

But America is good. A person can't say anything bad about it. No, you have to speak the truth, my daughter. Because if you don't tell the truth, your God will hold you to account for it.

It was a lot of work [in the village], a lot, a lot. A woman like me who has twelve children, what could she do, my dear? She would pile up firewood, put on a wash basin and boil her children's clothing, wash them by hand. We would go down to the brook, we'd carry the laundry in a big bucket on our heads, we'd take a brush and scrub the clothes, the men's pants. After that, we'd take the laundry home and hang it to dry on the roof, then gather it, iron it, and fold it. And the children's diapers, for twelve children, I swear! I would sew them all by hand, on the machine, two full drawers of them. I would wash them and iron them. Here in America, mothers don't know how hard we had it.

I was fifty years old. My son my darling Ghassan, told me, "I'm not going to let you keep washing by hand." He bought me a washing machine because he loved me so much.

Thank God, I raised twelve children without ever striking them. And their father never hit them. I swear, never did I speak a harsh word to my children.

Seven girls and five boys and thank God, still in my hand [none have died].
I don't understand how they beat children, [like] what I've seen in some
houses. For shame, for shame! Children are wonderful. I say anyone who
doesn't have children is wretched.

For instance, my husband died three years ago. If I didn't have children,
how could I pay the mortgage on the house? I told my son, my heart's
beloved, "This house is too big for me and your sisters and we can't pay for
it. We'll take a smaller house, my son, and live in it." He told me, "Look
mama, my beloved, my father lived in this house for a year with you and he
was very happy in it. This house is to remain yours as long as you live. You
don't have to worry about the payments, I will make them directly to the
bank. You didn't bear us so that we will forget you."

Older people get scared. When we are gathered at a house, someone says,
"Today a thief came to so-and-so's house in the city." Yesterday we heard
about a Lebanese man who was killed [at his gas station]. My son has a gas
station. He works with his two grown sons, God bless them. When I heard
about the Lebanese man, I got scared for my grandsons and my son, and
for my daughter-in-law, too. She works there two nights [a week]. These
things, they wear down one's nerves.

In Lebanon, too, there was no safety. But here it is harder. We feel more
fear than during the war in Lebanon. We didn't have thieves and such.
When they'd shell, you'd feel frightened at the moment, but then it would
pass. You'd sit in a shelter an hour, two hours, then you'd go to the bakery
for your bread.

Each day I get up in the morning, I pray, I bless the Prophet, and then I
go back to bed. About ten or eleven I get up again. If I have the strength
and I feel good, I clean the whole house. From top to bottom, I sweep and
dust, and I clean the kitchen. Some days I cook two dishes. When I don't
have the strength, my daughter comes and does the housework. At one
o'clock, I have to watch my serial [soap].

I won't lie about it, I like television a lot. In our religion they've come
out with propaganda that it's wrong to watch it. I asked, "Why is it wrong?"
When you are in your own house, after you've said your prayers and wor-
shipped and bathed yourself and performed your ablutions and you sit down,
what do you do? You can't just keep at your prayer beads. One gets tired.

There is a serial, I watch it every day from one o'clock to two o'clock. I
understand who did this and that. Today he did such and such. Tomorrow
I watch to see what he did next.

In the evening, my daughters come and put the news on. I understand a
little [of it] and they encourage me to ask when I don't understand. My
husband, God rest his soul, used to sit beside me and explain, he used to

translate for me. We used to sit together every day, him and me, until four or five when the children come home.

When a woman's husband dies, she does feel more and more lonely. And when a woman loses her husband, the lord of the house, everything hurts her feelings. From her daughter, her son, from everyone—everything offends her. If I ever got angry at my children, my husband would come and sit beside me and say, "What do you care about them? Why should they bother you? Whatever you want, I get for you; whatever you wish, I serve up to you; and whatever you like, I do for you."

Days now I sit and cry and cry and cry enough to fill this box full of tears. My son, the one who's here, sometimes I wouldn't see him for a week when his father was alive; he was busy with his own affairs. [And it was all right.] Now if he comes to see me three times a day, I'm not satisfied or consoled. I'm telling you the truth, it's good to be frank. Their father was there to cushion things for me and calm me down. He liked to talk to me, and I would talk to him. Now, poor me, I sit alone, my face to the wall. I don't talk to anyone, and nobody talks to me.

One day we were sitting on the veranda, some fifteen men and a lot of women, too. In the summer, talking. One man said to me, "You have sons and they support you. Do you love them more or do you love *Bu Naji* [your husband] more?" I said, "By God and by your leave, I have twelve children. But the shoe my husband takes off at the doorstep is worth all twelve children." He said, "Why??" I said to him, "Because first of all, he is the lord of the house. And what I reveal to my husband, I don't tell my daughter or son. And without him, where would these twelve children have come from?" The man is the one who brings the children. He's the one who made them, he's the one who brought them into being through the power of God's will.

My husband and I grew up together. From when I was five, I liked him a lot. And I never got mad at him and went back to my family. He never put me out of the house or laid his hand on me. I lived with this man fifty-five years, and I never went to bed one night angry at him. There is nothing better in the whole world than a man. Now from the time my husband died, my spirit is tired. Nothing delights me. If I wanted to pray, he would wait for me. God help him, he was always waiting for me. He used to get up before me in the morning, go downstairs, make the coffee—both American and Arabic—and put it on the table. If the neighbors came, he wouldn't call up to me, but he would climb the stairs, open the bedroom door, and tell me, "Get up, *Imm Naji*, just wash your face and come down." I'd go downstairs and sit outside on the veranda with them while he prepared coffee. His daughters would leave for work or school, and he would say to them, "God be with you." He would see their cars leave and he would call on God to protect them. This word of blessing comes from God.

I have lost all of this, my dear. He has been dead three years, poor man. And I look at this house, and it looks at me.

Imm [mother of] Naji, Lebanese

If my daughter-in-law doesn't come to see me for two days or three, I'm offended. I say to myself, "When I was in the village, she'd come every day." She wouldn't dare not to because of her husband, and he'd be afraid of his father. Now his father is gone. You see how it is?

How much we used to work! I had five cows. Every day, with this hand, I used to milk them, getting forty kilos of milk a day. Men used to come and take my milk and sell it for me. Four kilos for me, one for them. In the night I'd get up, do the milking, boil the milk. If I had to cook, I cooked; if I had to bake, I baked. I was done before the field workers came in the morning. I had ten or fifteen workers. I'd go out with them. We planted tomatoes, beans, cucumbers. I used to spend my whole day in the field, and I'd be pregnant. I had one child after another, fourteen children. Nine are living.

After school and during vacations, we'd tell the children, "Get up and come with us to the fields." But when they had a test, I'd tell their father, "No, I won't let them go."

My husband died four years ago. He had a face this wide and shoulders this broad. They examined his lungs, there was something like a sack in his lungs. The smoke would go down in his lungs and congeal. You see how it was. From this he died. And he used to be strong as a lion.

My children brought me here. What am I to do? I tell them I want to go back. They tell me, "No." If I go back, I wouldn't be able to plough or plant. I can't do it any more, a woman of seventy-eight. It takes a man.

Hajjeh Nadia (a pseudonym), Lebanese[1]

V

Over here the woman rules the man. She takes everything he has, calls the police on him, and puts him out. The man is the lord of the house, my dear, the man is the lord of the house. He is the one to rule, not the woman.

Imm Naji, Lebanese

My husband loved me more than anything in life, but it's just his own way of possessiveness, like Pygmalion. Because he couldn't stand the idea that I was really changing, he will blame anything. It could be school, it could be my American friends, it could be America. "I brought you to America and now you're a different person." But he never really understood the underlying issue that "I am not yours, I am who I am." When I left him, I just took my desk, my daughter's piano, one bed, and my books.

Suad Mohamed, Yemeni

My husband and I were very compatible in many ways, but the real conflict between us was his refusal to accept my own independent identity as a person, as equal to him. Once he told me, "I'm the man, and in a family one person has to be in charge." I told him then, "Look Yusuf, if I see this is white and you come and tell me this is black, if *God* comes down and tries to tell me it's black, I'm going to insist it's white." He said, "Then we're not going to be able to get along together," and a couple of months later we were divorced.

Helen Khal, expatriate (Lebanese American)

Me and my husband are friends, we're not competing against each other. We do disagree on a lot of things, and a lot of times he cannot convince me, nor can I convince him. But if I'm wrong, I just go and say, "I was wrong and I admit it," and he does that, too. Arab men, and I think also Arab women, we are raised in an environment where pride is everything. We say, "Oh, he was mean to me and I won't forgive him!" I think that's why we have holidays—for instance in my religion, Islam—where we are supposed to be forgiving and forgiven, and to make peace with family and friends.

Dalila Messaoudi, Algerian

I had a friend from Saudi Arabia, I respect him a lot; me and my husband we used to have fun with him. Then he decided to get married. He called his mother in Saudi Arabia and told her. She arranged for him to come and see someone. He went over there and two weeks later he was married and he came back with her. So even though he's in the States and he's doing his Ph.D., he still thinks the old-fashioned way.

But he's happy, he's very happy. He goes out with the guys, but his wife is sitting at home. I don't know if she's happy, but I think she is.

Asmahan S. (a pseudonym), Palestinian

When we came here, I just stay in the house. To me, it was okay, as long as there's no war because I was very scared in Lebanon—very, very scared. We did not even sleep night after night.

[Then] I started to go out, one block at a time, taking the kids for a walk. One day I found a place, I see Arabic writing [in the window]; I felt so good. But I did not know what was the place. They talked to me, they brought someone who speaks Arabic. Her name was Abla. She gave me her phone number. I [found out I] was in health center for low-income family. She said, "Whenever the kids get sick, you call me and you can bring them over here." That was great. For me it was like winning the lottery.

When I told my husband, he got crazy, he start shouting, "Why did you do that [go out]? Do you know it's dangerous if someone kidnap you and kidnap the kids?" Because he works in gas station in bad area for the prostitute, and he doesn't want me to see something I don't have to. I said, "If I'm gonna be scared, I should go back to Lebanon."

I used to wait for my husband to come home to take me to the store to buy a can of salt or a can of tomato paste. It was very hard. So I discovered the store, I went to the store by myself. They asked me for the money, I put money in my hand and they'll take the amount. They were very honest with me. Let me tell you this, I love the American people. They are the very specialest, very dearest people to me because the way they helped me—no other people would.

Then I find out there's a school [English as a Second Language] downtown. I can take the bus. I told my brother, I told my Arabic friend. They said, "You crazy? You want to take the bus goin' downtown [Detroit]?" So one day I said, "I'm gonna find out for myself." I took change with me, I waited for the bus, and I told the bus driver, "I wanna go school international." So he showed me where it is. I went to the school, I register. Beautiful, no problem whatsoever.

The first two weeks my husband did not know I went to school. Then I told him. He said, "No way you're gonna go. No more money!" I said, "No more cookin'!" He said, "We'll see." I said, "We'll see." I did not cook, I did not wash his clothes. He said, "You're fightin' me." I said, "I'm not fightin' you. I'm just tryin' to explain to you I need this." Then he give up.

One day I told my kids, "You wanna go shoppin'?" They said, "Oh, yes, we'll go!" We took some money, we took the bus [to the mall]. It was so beautiful. We had ice cream, we had hamburger. I mean, to you it sound like that's nothing, but to me it was everything. I did it on my own. So I called my sister from the mall. "Guess where I am!" She said, "Don't worry, stay where you are, we're gonna call someone to come and pick you up." I said, "Why? I'm not ready to come home!" We came home on our own, safe and sound.

My husband used to buy the children candy, which I did not like. I said, "I don't want them to be hyper." I read about the nutrition, I read about healthy diet, I read about the environment, what is good and what is bad. I educate myself. I did not stop. I love to read anything that I find. Newspapers, magazines. You know what I did? I used to copy newspaper, just copy it out. I didn't know what I was reading.

My husband didn't like America, he did not like it at all. Well, that was bad because I liked it, I enjoy it. I mean, I discover something about myself. It's special feeling. When I was in Lebanon, I didn't even know how to buy tomatoes. My husband does all the shopping, he even buys clothes for me and the kids. I was very happy. But now I look back and I say, "How stupid I was!"

Mary B. (a pseudonym), Lebanese

Right now we're having married women come [into the clinic] with sexually transmitted disease. We tell them, "You got this while you've been practicing sex with your husband." And they're, "No, no, no, no, my husband doesn't have any infections, he's clean, he's good." I mean, they live in denial. We have a few females who admit that they know that their husbands have extramarital sex—some of them are really furious but they can't do anything, they don't have other options. Some of the husbands are really abusive, the female cannot discuss this issue with them. Other women feel like it's easier for the husband to go outside. One woman said to me, "My husband has a different need, he likes anal sex. And you know it's *haram* [forbidden] and I don't like it, so he sees other women."

Amine Kleit, Lebanese

VI

It scares us, the lifestyle that kids have over here, the drugs, the sex. It scares us to listen to the news or watch TV. My daughter says, "Oh, look, they're always kissing and they're having sex." She's five and a half years old! My Tunisian friend and her husband went back home; they didn't want their daughter to grow up in this environment. People start worrying when their children are five or six. If they get to twelve, you're lost; it's too late.

Dalila Messaoudi, Algerian

Being a woman doctor, I see more [American] girls than the average doctor. I find them suffering all kinds of psychological consequences from the traumatic experiences [with sex] they've had very early on. So I worry about my daughters [small children at the time of the interview]. I see how they might get very busy trying to attract a man instead of concentrating on their studies. There is a golden opportunity for them at a certain age that they can lose trying to chase a man. I see girls in college, at the ages of 20 and 22, and they still don't know what they want to do. I want my kids to have a definite sense of direction and not to be distracted by things they might later regret.

Mawya Shocair, Syrian

The girls here acted so air-headed. I couldn't pin it down. Part of it was that they never had nuns in their lives [like I did] who kept talking about seriousness and pursuing something professional. [In school back home] the girls that didn't do good academically were put down publicly. On the other hand, the girls that did were complimented and given advantages. The nuns weren't interested in wasting their energies; they wanted to produce a good crop.

Mai N. (a pseudonym), Palestinian Jordanian

[In Lebanon] I used to go home and study for like four to six hours straight, no TV. And I was a little girl then. It was homework every single night. If you had ten days of Christmas vacation, you got ten days of homework. During the summer, you had workbooks to do and you have to pass them in the first day of school. So it was definitely hard; they challenged you more. Here I do my homework in one hour, two hours tops. And I'm a senior in high school.

Barbara L. (a pseudonym), Lebanese

There was no easy classes, it was just study, study, study. By seventh grade you have to reach algebra and geometry. No question about it, you have to do it. You reach pre-calculus when you're in eighth grade; you study Shakespeare when you're in seventh grade. I started English when I was three years old.

Nada Mansi, Lebanese

The truth is I absolutely, absolutely love the schools here. They are so great. At home, the teachers are so into discipline, you are always afraid of them. Here teachers treat you like a friend; you can always come over and talk to them, just for them to help you. Just work hard and that way you get respect from them and you show them that you respect them and that you appreciate their teaching.

Mary Yazbeck, Lebanese

It was like being surrounded by children. There was this one girl, she would come into class and put her feet on the desk, and she was chewing gum. I thought, "Oh, my God! This is incredible!" That would absolutely not have been allowed at home. The girls here weren't polite; they were rude to the teachers and to each other. Also the emphasis on looking good and dressing nicely, preppie or whatever was in style at the time. Of course, I was a nerd, I'm sure that's what they thought of me. And also the emphasis on sports. You have to take a gym class, and that was so hard for me to go to the gym, dress in front of other people, taking a shower with all these other girls that I didn't know. And then swimming; I needed to wear a bathing suit, having never worn a bathing suit before in my life.

And also the emphasis here on dating. Everyone asked me if I had a boyfriend, and I thought, "Of course not!"

Wijdan Azzou, Iraqi

I would not be comfortable with it [dating] now. Because I think it will be a waste of time. He'll want attention; he'll want this, want that, and I'm really not ready for that. I have a full-time job, too. I just don't find it amusing in any way. If I want to ever date, I want to be mature enough to choose and to make a commitment out of it. I don't want a fling. It's not going to happen. And, of course, I will not do anything without the approval of my parents. They mean too much to me that I would do anything against them.

Nada Mansi, Lebanese

My parents don't have a problem with dating. I've dated. The only thing is they want to know who the guy is. They have to meet him, they have to get to know him and to really like him. As long as I'm honest with them, they don't care.

I see a lot of my friends now deciding to go to college, and a lot of them want to live on campus just for the parties. But I don't want to get away from my parents. Usually our tradition is nobody moves out until they get married. I like that, I don't have a problem with it.

Barbara L. (a pseudonym), Lebanese

I guess I'd miss my mom's cooking. Not only that. I'm just eighteen years old, so I have years ahead of me that I can be alone, away from my family. Now I'm so young that I should enjoy the little shelter that I get from my mom. I think after I graduate [from college], I can make it on my own, but I'm still too young to leave home.

Mary Yazbeck, Lebanese

I have a cousin who has been living with us for six years. She came to go to school. I find myself acting with her like my grandmother [did with me]. She can go out, fine, with some friends that *I* know, but not beyond a certain hour, and she's not supposed to stay overnight at a girlfriend's house unless it's somebody I really trust and know. She's not a kid, she's twenty-six. But it's just the way our parents would [act]. Even though you are thirty, you're under their roof. Most people couldn't conceive having their kids living on their own, unless they go to a different city.

Dalila Messaoudi, Algerian

You know, today I live in the United States, but I can hear my mother all the time. Now everything my mother told me not to do, I don't do it. I mean, she is after me—she's here! At some point in our life, we get rebellious, we try and break the rules; but then at the end, we become an image of our parents. The basic things they taught us are the things we live by. We change our clothes, but we can't change them.

Hawa T. (a pseudonym), Egyptian

People keep thinking that if you go to the United States, the United States will corrupt you. It's not true. I tried hashish before I came here. And I slept with someone before I came here.

I was completely convinced that sex was okay. So it's not a matter of guilt. But there was the fear that others won't respect me, won't like me, or would harm me. I was never afraid of my brother. But I was afraid of my father. Even when I was here, thousands of miles away, I would be in a room, making love, and I would be afraid he would come in that door. For a long time, many years. Then I realized at some point, no, it's not going to happen, the possibility is not there.

[And yet] I don't think my background was very strict, we didn't hear horror stories, and my father wasn't violent with us.

Fatan M. (a pseudonym), Jordanian

When you look at [other] teen programs across our state, they're providing family planning, condoms, and contraception—things we can't do. If that's what we did at our clinic [for low-income Arab families], we would have parents on our door shutting us down. As it now is, teenagers go to other clinics for services having to do with being sexually active because they don't feel they can trust us. [They know] we know their mothers, their parents. But we get calls from these other clinics saying, "Your patients are coming with gonorrhea, they're coming here with STD's, [so we know] that some of our kids must be more sexually active than they let on to be.

Lena B. (a pseudonym), Lebanese

I knew a couple of girls like that. I couldn't believe why you want to waste your time with such a thing, knowing the diseases that are going on. See, to me, I think it's a sense of religion. If you lose that, if you lose the fear of God, you just lose track of your life.

Nada Mansi, Lebanese

Men are dogs, ninety percent of them.

Wardi T. (a pseudonym), Lebanese

VII

Sometimes I think of men as no good. But part of my religion is to get married. It's how God wanted it to be. Marriage is something you have to do, whether you like it or not. But then, in a way, you like it afterwards.

Marriage was in my mind when I was like thirteen. I turned thirteen, I was like I want to get married, I want to get a house. But then things change. I seen how school was, what I could become. And then marriage moved far from my head. Girls usually get married at seventeen. If you reach nineteen or twenty and you're not married, people are going to say, "Oh, my God, either that girl did something bad or something is wrong with her."

[This is how you get married.] It starts if the guy sees you or someone tells him about you. First, he talks to you. A girl that is good, she'll tell him to go talk to her parents.

I don't make no important decision except for my parents. Because the parents' decision is very important. And then if my father finds he's Okay, he'll tell me about him. Then I'll get to know him as long as I want, and if I find him he's not my type, I just say it didn't work out. I don't get married in arranged marriage. And I don't marry a man that doesn't fear God.

[But] I plan to go to college. I want me to be the first one to finish college out of my family. But I wouldn't wait that long to get married. Honestly, no. I feel like [I'll be] too old to get married. And it depends on the guy. You know, the guys that want their wives to stay at home, those are the ones that are not educated. But some of them that are educated, they would love for their wives to go to college. I would really like that. But if it doesn't come, I wouldn't mind because if I graduate college and go to work, who's going to take care of my kids? I want to raise them up how I think they should be raised. I want them to know their mother. You know, if you're married and you work and you have a family, it's very hectic. Because I plan to have kids—if God is willing to give me—I plan to have kids. And I'm not gonna give up kids for work. I want to raise up my kids to be the best kids.

Zeainab Karnib, Lebanese

I'd like to get married when I have my career set. My parents are like, "Think about your career, get your degrees, [then] set up with any guy you like." If it's up to my dad, he'll marry me off at thirty or forty.

Nada Mansi, Lebanese

I'm marrying my cousin, my uncle's son. I've never met him, but I'm ready to get married, and this is the kind of person I want to spend my life with.

My mom traveled to Yemen three years ago, and that's when he asked her for my hand. When she told me, I was flattered. I knew he was educated—that was the top thing for me—and his age was right, seven years older than me. I wouldn't want to marry somebody the same age because I feel I'm more mature, and also, after I have kids, I'm going to get older faster than the man I marry. You have to think ahead. And he was Muslim, that's very important to me. He spoke Arabic and he read and wrote it. I wanted that for my kids. And it was a special thing that he was my relative. So everything kind of fit.

The only concern I had was how was he going to be with the idea of me working. But he said to my mom, "I'm willing for her to work." And he said to me [on the phone], "Send me your resume, I can start looking [for you] now." So that was good. And his sisters work. Also he lived in Europe for seven years, so that was a plus for him.

I didn't wait this long to just get married to anyone. As to living in Yemen, I always thought that even if I married here, I would like to go back to live— we left when I was six. I always thought, "Yeah, I can go back, it's my country." Actually, I have the option for him to come here, but I think that's a selfish way to do because he's got a very good job there. I mean, why would I want to bring him here and struggle?

Mayyada Yehia, Yemeni

I was born in Allentown, Pennsylvania, but in 1946—when I was twenty— I went on a very indefinite, open-ended visit to Lebanon with my mother. Her father was still living there, and her family. That's when I enrolled in the Academy of Fine Arts in Beirut. A year later, just about the time my mother was getting ready to come back and I was supposed to come back with her, I met this young man and fell in love and got married. So my mother came back by herself, and I stayed in Lebanon.

I was married for sixteen years and then divorced. But I don't regret at all my life in Lebanon, even with all the ups and downs of my marriage. Beirut was wonderful, absolutely wonderful during the 1950s, 1960s, and early 1970s. Golden years. It'll never be the same.

The war in Lebanon, the uprootedness that it caused, I'm sure has had a very profound effect on my work. My colors [here] are more quiet, more gray, they don't have the sunlight in them that they had there. Another thing is that I used to like to do portraits, and I projected into them, I think, a belief in the goodness of people—a kind of altruistic, romantic idea of humanity. I think that the war and the terrible things that happened there have destroyed that somewhat; I don't have the same purity of vision. Maybe that's because I'm not believing any more.

The most meaningful years of my life were spent in Lebanon, and I feel that I am a displaced person here [in the United States] even though I was born and I grew up here. I don't know whether I can still go back to Lebanon or not. Whether because of [the fighting] or because the Lebanon that was there before is not there now.[2]

Helen Khal, Lebanese American

VIII

My husband said, "Let's go back to Lebanon and try to live there." He went and built a house. I went for one year, and I enjoyed it, I loved it, it's my country. But I seen that the kids there they play with pretend guns, they fight, they shout. The war took Lebanon twenty years backwards. The war—what I believe—is not Christian and Muslim. I know there is religious people they use the war to make people believe it's religion, but it's not. Let me assure you that there is Muslim people who use God's name and Christian people who use also God's name and Jesus' name just to fight for their own purpose, not for the good of the people. In the neighborhood I grew up in, there was very open-minded people, and we have no problem. Christian, Muslim [like my family], Druse, it doesn't matter. In the war, my Christian friends, they come to my house for safety, and I went to their house for safety, too, when I was in Beirut. But one family from our neighborhood, they were bad; they steal, they gamble, they do whatever they want to do. Now the wife is wearin' the scarf, and the husband grew a beard and spreads rumor others are bad because they're not coverin' their head or growin' a beard or goin' to the mosque to pray. Believe me, if there is God, this man he's never God's friend.

Mary B. (a pseudonym), Lebanese

When I went to Algeria three years ago, I was wearing Western dress, but decent—long sleeves, long skirt. Not to the ankle, but long enough [and no scarf]. People were frowning upon me in the street, like, "Oh, my gosh, you're naked!" One time I took the bus. I didn't notice that the women would sit in the back, so the first seat I saw, I sat down. It was the men's section. And this old guy comes on, wearing the traditional *abaya* [long, flowing robe] and burnoose. He saw the situation and started giving us a speech, telling the guys, "You will go to hell because you're looking at this woman and she's naked." I was crying. I went to my parents and said, "I'm not coming back, this is not where I belong." I felt really bad, I felt like nothing.

Karima Roudesli, Algerian

Last time when I was in Jordan, all of a sudden it dawned on me that if I was to live in that country, I wouldn't mind wearing the black stuff. Why? Because men would stop staring at you and giving you comments on the street. I feel so much anger walking down the street.

Fatan M. (a pseudonym), Jordanian

"When are you coming back? When are you coming back?" My mother and my grandmother haven't said that to me in five years. Now they say, "Wherever you are, you are better off than being here."

In the war for independence [from France], some Algerian owomen fought and died, and some were tortured. The expectation was "we sacrificed, we expect to get something in return." My disappointment is that after thirty years of independence, we're not better off as women.

My sister is a professor at the university, and every morning she has to go to work thinking she might not make it home to her kids and her husband. Actually, they almost lost their lives one night. They lived in an area where there were a lot of fundamentalists and, because she doesn't veil, some men were trying to force the door to her house. The next day, before sunrise, her husband took her with the kids and went home to my parents [in suburbs of Algiers].

I was so worried about her. I said, "Why don't you just stay home and take care of the kids while your husband works?" You know what she said? She said, "If I have to stop working, it means that they have won." I said, "If you had to wear the *hijab*, would you?" She said, "I would never wear it, never, even if I know I'm going to die for it."

Dalila Messaoudi, Algerian

I'm not covered up now, but that's how I'd like to see myself in the future. But it's not me, yet, I feel too young. There's a lot of fashion I still want to wear. If I put on the *hijab*, I have to be a totally different person, a more mature person, an older person.

But if I go back to Yemen, I'll probably feel weird walking around uncovered; I'll stand out in the crowd. I might end up covering. It's not a major issue to me.

Mayyada Yehia, Yemeni

In Syria, there's a very famous professor in my field. He keeps telling me, "You have to come so we can work together." After I came here, I went to see him, crossing from Amman to Syria. The minute I arrived at the border, they said I had to go to jail. I explained I have a sister in Damascus, but they would not listen. They were asking me questions about people I know, and they would not release me before I signed four white papers. I have no idea what they said. For ten days I had no access to anybody, moving from one jail to another. I was scared, scared.

Now every time the professor tells me to come, I tell him, "I can't."

Fatima G. (a pseudonym), Syrian

The last time I was in Iraq was in 1989, when I went to Baghdad University to lecture. I was invited by the government, and I talked about the psychology of adolescence, child psychology, parenting. Then I stayed on my own and lectured at the college of nursing. The students were so sweet and curious. A lot of them smuggled pieces of paper in my pocket. "Can you get me a scholarship to come and study in the United States?" A lot were typical teenagers, rock and roll was big, and they wanted posters of Michael Jackson.

Hind Rassam Cullhane, Iraqi

IX

My family thought life would be better here, but it's not. You don't feel like you belong in a country where you weren't born here. I don't like it. My family don't like it here either. There's not one minute that passes by that I don't think of going to Lebanon. The past nine years, every single day, I tell my dad, "Come on, dad, it's time to go back."

Zeainab Karnib, Lebanese

I miss it all the time; it's a beautiful place. My summer house was gorgeous. We had a house in the city as well, and it was right near the ocean. The weather is great, and all my relatives are there. I have like twenty-eight cousins; I grew up with them. By now a lot of them have gotten married and have kids. I've never met their kids or their husbands or their wives.

Barbara L. (a pseudonym), Lebanese

It's more choices here, there's more to see. See it, learn it, do it! You can do whatever you want, and nobody will look at you. I have learned more, I have opened my mind more. I see more cultures, more colors. It's a good experience.

[But] if it ever goes peaceful in Lebanon, I would love to raise my family there. It's more religious, more respectful.

Nada Mansi, Lebanese

I always thought, "I'll go back, I'll go back." "When I finish my BA, I'll go back," "When I finish my master's degree, I'll go back." Now I'm saying, "When I finish my Ph.D., I'll go back." But meanwhile you develop your attachments here, and I have good friends now. But I think it's really a good feeling that we have at least the alternative. It could be illusion, it could be real, but it makes you feel safe. You need that. It just gives you some kind of peace of mind for a while.

Suad Mohamed, Yemeni

We kept thinking, "Okay, we'll finish our schooling, get some kind of master's or Ph.D., and then we will go back."

But then at some point, I didn't want to go back. I had found my life here. I knew I couldn't go back and live there, as much as I would have liked for my kids to know different languages, to have aunts and uncles nearby, to have a community. I knew that was not going to be. There was a lot of pain, even until now. Just two days ago, my daughter said to me, "You love it over there, but at the same time, you don't. It's like a love-hate relationship." And it's true. When she said it, it hit me that I do love it. I love the flowers, the air. I love the people, the community. I just don't like the way I was treated, I don't like the way women are treated.

I met an American woman who took me under her wing. Whenever there was a meeting with other women—this was the beginning of the women's movement here—she would call me up and invite me. I remember one time she had brought with her lots of magazines, and we went through them and we cut out things that showed images of women and we talked about that. I had lived in my head for so long and in books—nobody that I knew would discuss things like this with me—and here I found human beings, other women [to talk to], and I thought, "My God, this is like Alice in Wonderland; I found a place where women can do what they want to do." I thought.

Hayat Weiss, Lebanese

The real positive [here] is that in my education I have more opportunities. I'm very, very encouraged to achieve my goals, go for the stars, reach for the sky. The school, the teachers, my mother, they encourage me to do so much; they want me to be independent and successful, as any parent or teacher would want. The teachers want to see that all their work paid off, like this is someone who wants to become something and wants to be recognized in this world. That's something that I really, really love.

Mary Yazbeck, Lebanese

I don't think American women are happy. I laugh when I read American magazines like *Cosmopolitan* because these magazines portray these anorexic women who are competing for satisfaction in every way; whether it's career or sex, they're always competing. But I think most Arab women or Muslim women have this peace within themselves that they do not have to compete in order to prove who they are.

Leila K. (a pseudonym), Iraqi

I know so many Americans, but I don't feel comfortable making social relations with them. They're different. Even when you first go into their house, the way they keep asking you if you would like a drink, and you keep making the point that you don't drink. Even if I talk to them about my own problems, they don't relate to those problems. I need somebody from my own culture to understand.

Asmahan S. (a pseudonym), Palestinian

I tried not to get in touch with the Arab community here. Deliberately. Because I didn't like the fact that they talk about each other and they expect you to behave in a certain way. I didn't want the stigma of "this woman goes out," I didn't want to see that in people's eyes; I wanted to see myself as I wanted to see myself.

I had one Arab guy say to me, "Any American woman here, I will bet ten dollars that I can sleep with her tonight." I said, "What! Who do you think you are!" Just one conversation like that with this guy, and I didn't want to see an Arab for ten years.

Fatan M. (a pseudonym), Jordanian

If I live there [in Yemen] as a divorced woman or if I live here as a divorced woman, what would be the advantages and disadvantages? Well, the advantage [here] is really obvious. Here I have choices—I make my own decisions, I have freedom, I have the potential to develop more, to fulfill my dreams. I follow cultural events, I extend myself, I meet different people, I enjoy male companionship, I feel like I'm growing. The disadvantage is the social deprivation here. Especially because I'm on my own, and the kids, they have their own plans for their own life, which is the right thing to do. So I find myself by myself most of the time.

When I went back home [to visit], it was a big difference. The warmth, the family nurturing, it was so incredible. I have four brothers and one sister there. You get all this attention from your nieces and nephews, you feel you are important, you have influence on the other generations. I felt like,

"Wow, there is a part of me that has been starving." Over there they repress sexuality. Here we repress a lot of the social needs, everyone is just on his own.

That's the price. There's a price for everything.

Suad Mohamed, Yemeni

I had a baby, nobody cared. If I were back home, I would be overwhelmed with people coming and visiting and with gifts and ceremonies. We have a ceremony when a baby is born; we have a ceremony when he's seven weeks old; we have a ceremony when he's forty days old. We have a ceremony when the first tooth comes out; we have ceremonies for every single thing.

Asmahan S., Palestinian

There was a time when I didn't go back for many years—five, six, seven. It was very hard because I need both places. [Now] I figured out that I can stay two years without going. The third year I have to go to get some of my juices filled up again, some of my senses, some of the things that I'm not even aware of, which freeze when I'm here. For example, I speak French over there, I socialize. People knock on people's doors, they smile at each other. It's a different way of being. So I get replenished [from being] with my sister and my cousins, the women, and Marta [our housekeeper]. Then I feel okay. When I come here, it's more isolated. All of a sudden I come to a house that is empty and there's nobody around. I have friends, but you have to call the friends. It's not a community; it's like all of a sudden I have to count on my own resources.

It's getting harder actually. The last time I went and came back, it was very hard—that was the summer of 1994—maybe because Lebanon is getting better. We were able to go walk on the Corniche in Beirut, right next to the sea. What was interesting, you had these people doing aerobics right on the beach, men and women. Some women were wearing short, short shorts, and some women were covered up on the head and with long sleeves, and they would still be exercising up and down with their arms and legs. Talk about diversity and different cultures! Then when they finished, the women in shorts and the women in head scarves would [go] hand in hand and walk along. All together.

Hayat Weiss, Lebanese

EPILOGUE

DEAR MOTHER,

Strange that I associate the word "pious" with you. You were not pious in any conventional sense, never hanging gilded icons above your bed or caring two cents about church doctrine. You judged each new priest—most *im*piously I used to think—primarily by how well he sang the service. (You liked a good performance when you looked in each year.) Otherwise, if he kept his opinions to himself, you had no quarrel with him. And if he looked forward to coffee in your kitchen, after sprinkling upstairs and down with holy water, and could tell a good story, you declared him as fine a priest as one could reasonably expect.

Pious in what way, then? Perhaps in respecting all variety of creature (flies buzzing round your dishpan lived to buzz another day) and believing, for all your humor, that some few things were to be taken seriously. Not just the looking out for family (that was nature, no special merit there) but the claims of neighbor and community. "What does she do for others?" you complained on cue, whenever the conversation turned to a particular in-law who spent her days tending her own grapevine. You never understood, I think, that some people need all their strength just to get *themselves* through the day.

And for sure, you were patting yourself on the back—remembering your years of service to the Ladies' Aid—but I never begrudged you that vanity. You tried to make a place for me, too, in the club, enrolling me at birth, paying my dues punctually year after year. Grown up, I would sometimes act the member—attend a meeting, write a press release, model hats at a fund raiser. But it was all play. I didn't have the calling.

I wonder now how seriously you would take this book, over which your spirit presides. You'd be pleased, at least, at the company I've been keeping. It irritated you that the girlfriends I brought home (and that you charmed) were Irish, German, Norwegian or, most often, Jewish (though Jews, you said, were practically our cousins). You would have settled for just one *bint arab*. Now here's a bookful for you. Or a houseful, all branches of the family converging. Doors thrown open to old and young and middle-aged, Muslim and Christian, Syrian, Lebanese, and Palestinian, Iraqi, north African and Arabian, all the kin. *"Ahlan wa sahlan*, my home is yours. My book is yours!"

As long as I'm showing to such good advantage, I might just hint that doing for others can take many forms, including this text, which (in imagination) I push over to your side of the table. "Yes," you say, paging through it with curiosity. But I see you have reservations. You know me as one knows an old antagonist and are used to looking for the corner left undusted. It will not long escape your eye, the absence of a final setting-to-rights, a housewifely conclusion that clears the dishes, sweeps the crumbs, hangs up the apron, and slips each guest a bag of goodies to be carried home.

Look, here's the best I can do. (Let's settle for a lived-in look.) This house, this text, is full of voices tumbling over one another. Point and counterpoint, yes and no. Issues worried in every room, on every story (*in* every story) from generation to generation: how to be a good daughter, sister, wife, mother, how to be a good Arab, how (pay good heed) to survive. In the house our mothers built, yes your mother too, shame lurked at every landing, so we proceeded cautiously, ears cocked to hear others (*nnaas*) whispering. Hearts divided between two urges. The need to make a getaway (crash out the back door, run for your life), the need to belong (pull up to the table with women who call you "sister" and know your people for three generations back). Mother, you remember. Clutter of right and wrong and second thoughts, curtains of laughter, candles of affection. And finally, after half a lifetime staring out the window, planting in the garden, smiling at the neighbors, passage into a new identity, neither *arab* nor *ameerkan*.

A new story to tell the children.

APPENDIX

In 1996, six years after my first conversation with Suhair, Souad, Nuha, and Nawal, I mailed each of them a transcript of that session, then followed up with phone calls. I was curious about the direction their lives had taken, but I also wanted to know how they would react to this snapshot from the past. Would they now have a different read on that period in their lives?

SUHAIR

Suhair, who did indeed graduate from college, is still married though she and her husband have had rocky times and once came close to divorce. But her in-laws, the source of many of her problems, have since moved back to Palestine, as has her own mother, together with the youngest children in the family. "My parents wanted my little brothers and sisters to have more of the Arab culture and Arab language and religion than we had," she explained. Suhair's father, who has a business in this country, pays extended visits to his wife and little ones. At twenty-nine, Suhair has one overriding preoccupation these days; it is her desire to have children and her inability, so far, to conceive.

As for our earlier interview, Suhair told me, "I was interested to read it; I wanted to see how we were at that time. As I was reading, I was wondering did I feel uncomfortable about anything in it, and I said no." But she was surprised at things she had long put out of her mind, especially the threats from her uncles. "As I was reading, I remembered how scared everybody was," she said. "But I guess after a while the [anonymous] letters stopped coming, and then after that we just forgot about it."

SOUAD

When I talked to Suhair's sister Souad, she was on her way overseas to marry a Palestinian and (like her mother) settle down in Palestine. "That's a goal I've always had," she explained. "I do want to bring up my children back home because I'm very much into the culture and politics and the history of Palestine."

About the interview, Souad said, "When I read it, I thought, 'Oh, that's me,' I recognized myself." She still advocates respecting "what parents believe and the way they grew up," and reiterated even more strongly her gratitude to her father for his support of his daughters and for his insistence; after observing Suhair's problems, that his other girls finish college before marrying.

What about the passages in the transcript that told of physical or psychological abuse? Her reply:

I was very, very happy with that interview. This is reality, this is what Arab American females are facing. There's a whole array of social problems that have emerged in the community—child abuse, domestic violence, kids in gangs, youths on drugs. I think our society needs to start realizing that.

NAWAL

Nawal, the youngest and—in 1990—the most rebellious of the four young women, is married now and the mother of two sons. "My life is very beautiful," she said, "my two kids are my pride and joy, my husband is very, very good." At the same time, she sees her youthful anger as a necessary instrument of growth and is proud of having been a fighter, despite the price she had to pay. A year or so after our interview, she was asked not to return to the Arab American Center since her behavior—at the least, drinking and dating—had sullied her reputation in the community and would undermine any cause or group she was associated with. "I was shunned by the people that I adored the most," she said.

Nawal's response to our earlier conversation was "I've grown, I haven't changed. I still agree with a lot of the stuff that I said then." About her story of being beaten, she said, "I think it's important; you'll be surprised at how many girls can connect to this, not the middle class and not the rich, but the poor Arabs." Until she was about eighteen, Nawal's family relied on food stamps and scavenged for clothes and toys in other people's trash; in their neighborhood of equally poor Latino, African American, and white families, physical abuse was common. "But I think it's harder for Arab girls," she added, "because there are so many rules and admonitions. If a Latina tells me she was abused, it was for something big—she probably swore at her parents—not [just] the fact that she was laughing in front of guys."

NUHA

Nuha, now twenty-four, works two jobs and is saving money to return to college; after transferring from one school to another and going from full-time to part-time study, she is now only a semester's work short of her degree.

Nuha's response to our earlier interview was "Oh, my God, I've changed a lot. I don't think this way any more as far as trying to please my parents and living my life for my parents." What precipitated this change was the death of her father in 1993. Since then she has found it easier to assert her independence, for instance by moving out of the house and into her own apartment (she told her mom, "You have to accept this") and by smoking, drinking, and going out openly with men.

Nuha told me that if she could give her younger self one piece of advice, it would be "Do what it takes to make you happy even though you are going to have to hurt people and disappoint people." Her own struggle to live by that philosophy, she admitted, is far from over. "My mom has a way of making me feel really guilty," she said. More specifically, there is the question of marriage. On the one hand, Nuha can barely imagine trusting a man enough to run the risk of wedlock—her independence has been too hard won. On the other, even if she does marry, she suspects it will not be to an Arab.

And that would totally devastate my family; and my brother-in-law [the one who beat Nawal] would punish me by not letting me see his kids. So that's the next thing that I need to work on for myself, to be strong enough to put my foot down and tell my mother, "Hey, listen, I might not marry an Arab." I just need to build up my strength again.

NOTES

INTRODUCTION

1. For a stereotype-shattering picture of spirited harem women, see Fatima Mernissi's memoir, *Dreams of Trespass*.

2. For all their horror of the harem, some nineteenth-century American feminists adopted (and recommended) harem women's "Turkish trowsers" precisely because such "bloomers" offered greater freedom and comfort than did Western fashions. (See Fischer.)

3. On a more aggressive note, Layyah Barakat (another immigrant from Mount Lebanon) reminded her American readers that "it was from my country that the missionaries of the Cross went to your heathen ancestors and Christianized them and made them what they are today" (1912, 22).

4. An exception to this generalization is the work of Afaf Meleis (a professor in the School of Nursing at the University of California, San Francisco) and her colleagues, who have published widely on the health care needs of Arab women immigrants.

CHAPTER 1

1. This great-aunt, also named Miriam, is a featured character in Alfreda Carhart's *It Happened in Syria*.

CHAPTER 3

1. For a detailed exposition of *Syrian* immigration to the United States before World War II, see Alixa Naff's *Becoming American*. Gregory Orfalea's *Before the Flames* has a broader sweep, tracing the history of Arab immigration up to the 1980s.

2. On weavers, see Naff 78. On the peregrinations of stone masons, see Rihbany 41.

3. According to one account, "Over a period of 22 days in 1860, over 7,000

Christians were killed, 360 villages destroyed, 560 churches ruined, 43 monasteries burned, and 28 schools leveled" (Orfalea 1988, 57, citing Kayal and Kayal 62). Lebanese Druse also suffered substantial loss of life and property.

4. For other descriptions of silkworm cultivation, see Rihbany 23–25, Carhart 27–29, and Tannous, "Trends" 109.

5. For a fictionalized account of a Catholic priest's hostility toward a Protestant (in this case, British) school and the way in which European powers, for their own political ends, attempted to promote or discredit the school, see Amin Maalouf's *The Rock of Tanios*.

6. The story is told of a Muslim man who in 1885 was planning to accompany Christian friends to the United States. He had gone so far as to buy his ticket and board the vessel when he thought to ask the captain about mosques in America. When the captain said there weren't any, the man "immediately got off the boat" rather than venture to "a land of unbelief" (Elkholy 17).

7. See Naff 91–107, on the "network of services." Naff claims that the network misrouted hundreds of *Syrians*, sometimes dividing families forever. She cites one scholar who found that agents of Latin-American steamship lines were so eager for a share of the immigrant market that they lied about their vessels' destinations.

8. Afif Tannous has described the sudden importance of the village post office:

Once or twice a week, the mail came to the village. Many hours before the arrival of the mail, people would assemble in the barber shop of Uncle Deeb . . . who was responsible for the distribution of the mail. For hours, before and after mail distribution, people would loiter there, exchanging the news of their emigrants and having a social time. Usually, Uncle Deeb preferred to put the registered letters [containing checks from abroad] aside and then give them in person to the families concerned. That was his reward—to be a messenger of joy to the village people. As he went around, he spread the news of the registered letters far and wide, until the whole village began to talk about them. ("Trends" 229–230. See also Tannous, "Emigration" 70–71.)

9. A few of those who returned, having gained some familiarity with English and with Western ways, soon found work catering to the needs of Western tourists and travelers in the Middle East. In 1901—to cite a spicy instance—a twenty-four-year-old Damascene dragoman, who had spent four years in the United States, became personal guide (and eventually lover) to the extraordinary Englishwoman Margaret Fountaine, who had come to *Syria* on a butterfly-collecting expedition. For her story of their romance (which would be carried on for twenty-eight years and across several continents) see *Love Among the Butterflies: The Travels and Adventures of a Victorian Lady*.

10. Statistically camouflaged are those *Syrians* who entered by way of Canada and Latin America.

CHAPTER 4

1. Between 1899 (the first year in which the U.S. Immigration Commission listed *Syrians* as a separate people) and 1910, 32.1 percent of *Syrians* entering the country were female, as compared to 30.5 percent of all arrivals. In the same period, women constituted only 23.5 percent of Armenian immigrants, 17.2 percent of Spanish, 4.9 percent of Greek, and 4.3 percent of Bulgarian and Serb. Philip Hitti, the source of these statistics, also pointed out that "the percentage of *Syrian* females would have

been still higher had it not been for the fact that the 1,000 *Syrian* Druse in this country brought with them only about a dozen women; and the 8,000 Muhammadans, about twice that number" (Hitti 58).

2. Writing in 1910, the *Syrian*-American journalist Afifa Karam attacked the greed of husbands who sent their wives to America to make money while they stayed safely and comfortably at home. Karam warned such men that after encountering "the hardships and suffering that inevitably face every newcomer in America," a woman will see her husband in a new and unflattering light.

She is afflicted in turn by misfortune, ignorance of the language, lack of resources, confusion, anxiety, loneliness and grief. Then she begins to realize the extent of your love for her, for instead of coming with her to protect her from these ills and to share her suffering and sweeten its bitterness, you sent her alone to struggle and strive and endure suffering in all its shapes and forms. . . . She might send you money. She might write to you and say, "Go out and enjoy yourself." . . . But the truth is that she will have started to hold you in contempt and perhaps to despise you. . . . [And] when the last trace of your love begins to fade in her heart, another might come along and find that heart empty." ("Syrian Immigration")

3. For another example of a girl deeply influenced by American teacher missionaries, see Layyah Barakat's autobiography, *A Message from Mount Lebanon*. Like Haidar, Barakat became a Protestant convert and went on to do mission work.

4. Interview with Louise Tamer, West Roxbury, Massachusetts. After giving a talk in which I repeated my cousin's story, two Lebanese American women came up to me, each with her own story of a grandmother who had blazed her family's way to America. In fact, family legend has it that one of these pioneers spent so much time in the United States and Latin America that on one of her periodic visits home she passed her own children in the street and failed to recognize them.

5. In a 1943 article, Afif Tannous told about a woman whose husband came to a Southern city (presumably Vicksburg, Mississippi) some time after the turn of the century. She had wanted to come, too, and to bring along their four children, but "he refused, saying that it would be a *shame* on him to let his wife travel to the end of the world in order to earn a living." The upshot, according to the wife, was this:

The climate here did not suit my husband, and he fell ill. I left the children with their grandmother and joined him. I tried peddling, as soon as I arrived, and succeeded very well at it, making much money. Then *I sent my husband back home* and continued my successful peddling. ("Acculturation" 271)

In the mid-1930s, Morris Zelditch studied the *Syrian* community of Pittsburgh, focusing on the earliest ten immigrants he could find who spoke English. Of the ten, all of whom had arrived in America between 1890 and 1903, two were women, both of whom came without their husbands. In 1893, Mrs. C (about twenty at the time) emigrated with her brother and a number of other men from her village. A mother of three, she took only the oldest with her, leaving the others behind with her husband while she came to see if the stories about fortunes to be made in America were indeed true. Two or three years later, her husband and younger children joined her (69). In 1895, Mrs. G came to America to join her daughter and son-in-law; her husband, "unable to come because of eye trouble," remained behind and died a few years later. Once in America, both Mrs. G and Mrs. C peddled; in fact, though already sixty or so when she emigrated, Mrs. G continued to peddle for some thirty years (77).

6. Karam also opposed the practice of married men leaving their wives behind while they came to garner wealth in the United States. Such separations, she warned, though intended to be of short duration, often stretched on for many years, creating a dangerous and unnatural state of affairs. The man exposed himself to "many things unpleasing to God," wrote Karam, and exposed his wife to "people's suspicions and possibly to something worse than that." With equal vehemence, Karam disapproved of parents who came to America, entrusting their children "temporarily" to relatives at home. "If you give your children to others to raise," she warned, "you give them the children's love, loyalty, and obedience." And there were practical implications, too. Karam added the reminder that parents, who (inevitably) missed and worried about their children back home, damaged their own health and, consequently, their capacity to work and earn money, thus undermining the very purpose for which they had left home in the first place ("Syrian Immigration" IV).

Though Karam did not directly address it, Muslim, and especially Druse, women presented a special case since they were strongly discouraged from venturing abroad. Given this circumstance, Druse leaders required men to swear an oath that they would return to their wives or fiancées within two years "or release them from obligation before their departure" (Naff 90). But in 1909, an *Al-Huda* editorial urged Druse religious leaders to discard "old and sterile traditions." "Where," it asked, "is the dishonor in a mother accompanying her son, or a sister her brother, or a wife her husband?" ("Our View" 4). Another article on the same page warned that Druse men, on their own in America, were tempted to marry foreigners and convert to Christianity or else were pressured to make a premature—and thus financially disadvantageous—return home. "So [the man] leaves his wife once more [to earn more money] while she weeps and wails, calling for the destruction of America" (Muhammad 4).

CHAPTER 5

1. Alixa Naff, speaking of the early immigrants, has said that "those who eschewed peddling entirely constituted a small minority" (12) though it is not altogether clear how long she thinks that was the case. On the other hand, Eric Hooglund has concluded that the *Syrian* peddler is a "stereotype." According to Hooglund, "the [work] experience of the early Arabs in America was as diverse as that of other ethnic groups who came in the great immigration wave during the generation leading up to World War I" (*Taking Root* 2: iv).

2. In 1903, Lucius Miller estimated that "industrious" peddlers in New York City earned "perhaps $10 to $12 a week . . . average gross returns" (41). In 1911, Louise Houghton concluded that *Syrian* peddlers across the United States earned anywhere from $200 to $1,500 annually, with "the higher class of peddlers" making considerably more (663). Naff arrives at her estimate of annual earnings by assuming that peddlers made a net profit of $5 a day and worked only 200 days a year—"allowing for illnesses, Sundays, holidays and other rest days, as well as visits to the homeland" (197).

3. For stories of other turn-of-the-century women peddlers, see chapter 4.

4. Even Houghton, however, says that *Syrians* would not be desirable immigrants if they "universally preferred peddling as a means of livelihood, rather than as a means to a higher form of occupation" (658).

5. Later in the same article, Houghton implicitly concedes that some women, or even children, may be the bread winners in *Syrian* families. But this state of affairs, she says, is due "not to the cruelty, nor even to the idleness, of the men, but to the present industrial situation [in the United States]" (662).

CHAPTER 6

1. Chronic disputes about pay finally led the garment makers' union to push for a system whereby most workers were paid by the hour rather than by the piece.

2. For instance, my own calculations, based on the 1910 federal census (Houghton published in 1911), indicate that in Boston about 50 percent of *married* Syrian men worked for themselves, either as peddlers or in their own shops and stores. But younger, single men were more likely to be wage earners.

3. From an obituary by Mary Mokarzel, apparently published in the *Lebanese American Journal* (no date or page available).

4. Ibid.

5. The prime exception is Eric Hooglund, who studied the 1910 census of ten communities, nine of them in the Northeast, and found that most *Syrians* worked not in their own businesses but for others (*Taking Root*, n.p.).

6. As Hooglund wrote, the immigrants' "[poor] language skills, ignorance of labor law, and fear of authority combined to make them generally docile workers" (*Crossing* 10).

7. Just before the strike, the Massachusetts legislature had reduced the work week for women and children from 56 to 54 hours. It was the third such reduction in twenty years and, in effect, applied to men workers, too, since the mills could not function without their female operatives. In response to previous reductions, mill owners had not lowered salaries proportionally, but this time they did. The workers first knew about the cutback when they opened their pay envelopes.

8. In 1904, a combination strike and lockout, lasting some six months, drove 7,000 experienced weavers, mostly English and Canadian, from the Fall River mills. By the following year, the city's mill owners were advertising overseas for new workers; hence, Fall River's sudden influx of immigrants—including *Syrians*—at that time (Younis, "Growth," 110).

9. These girls—most between sixteen and twenty—were conforming to a pattern that cut across ethnic lines. See, for instance, Louise Lamphere's discussion of young immigrant women in the mill town of Central Falls, Rhode Island, but note that Lamphere's remarks on *Syrians* are unreliable because they are based on few sources and limited data.

10. The strike Hannah refers to is undoubtedly that of March 3, 1936. It was one of a series of strikes in the late 1930s as workers rebelled against Depression-era reductions in wages and deterioration of working conditions.

11. More workers would have escaped had the owners not kept some doors locked in order to discourage tardiness.

For a painfully moving account of the fire, see William G. Shepherd, *"Eyewitness at Triangle,"* in the *Milwaukee Journal*, March 27, 1911 (reprinted in Stein 188–193). The horror of the scene was also captured in *New York Times* stories of March 26 and 27.

CHAPTER 7

1. In this respect, *Syrians* were in step with mainstream American thinking. As late as the 1950s, the Anglo American parents of a girl I knew discouraged her from applying for a college scholarship because (as they explained) if she won the scholarship, she would be snatching it away from some young man who would eventually have a wife and family to support. She, on the other hand, was expected to find a man to support her.

2. The largest and most influential publications, with subscribers throughout the United States and even abroad, came out of New York City. But a few other cities— Detroit, Boston, Lawrence (Massachusetts)—also supported presses and periodicals; in fact, the number of Arabic newspapers published (however briefly) in America was remarkable, considering the relatively small size of the *Syrian* community here and the number of immigrants who could neither read nor write. Through the early 1930s, it is estimated, the *Syrian* American community gave birth to between 80 and 100 newspapers and magazines (Ajami 79–80).

3. At the same time, the papers also covered political events in the homeland, taught immigrants about the history of their own people, and (through their very existence) helped for a while to keep the Arabic language alive in the United States.

4. After studying in German and American schools back home, Barakat (a native of 'Abay, Lebanon) taught for a while in Egypt before marrying and emigrating to the United States. Active in international temperance circles, Barakat was once described as possibly "the most capable *Syrian* public speaker in English" (Barakat 15).

5. See also an article by Wadia Faris Rashed, in which she accuses many *Syrian* women of having their heads turned by the "new riches acquired through emigration." Infatuated with her new circumstances, the *nouveau riche* woman forgets her previous "state of miserable poverty," "imagines she is superior to all her relatives and acquaintances," and "boasts unceasingly of her husband's wealth or her costly dress." In her ignorance, she wears her finest clothes and jewelry whether in her kitchen at home or at a party. "Such a woman," says Rashed, "desires to imitate American ladies but has no idea how to do it properly" (39).

A native of Damascus, Rashed emigrated to the United States with her mother. According to a brief biography, she was "devoted to good works and respected for her refinement and modesty" (Rashed 37).

6. A native of Lebanon, living in Cuba, al-Barid was said to be fluent in Arabic, French, and Spanish. To these accomplishments, wrote the editors of *al-Huda*, "she added a sizeable fortune by her skillful management of a store patronized by the daughters of the finest families [who] elected her secretary of the largest and most famous of their societies in Havana" (al-Barid 169).

7. In effect, said Karam, a husband could say to his wife,

I am the man! My will is inviolable law, and my ruling will be enforced with no appeal. My ease and comfort is your only concern. . . . You will not grumble when I get drunk, you will not complain when I betray you . . . if I am angry, be content; if I strike you, smile; if I curse and blaspheme, bless me, for I am the man and I hold absolute power. ("Between Two Men" 4)

In a return to a favorite theme, the selfishness of husbands who stayed home while allowing their wives to forage for wealth in America, Karam added,

If the *Syrian* woman were cultivated and educated, the man would not have been able to twirl his mustache and hop from tavern to tavern and from house to house, after sending his wife to roam in the wasteland, exposing herself and her reputation to shame, that she might bring him back gold, and on her return not ask "Where have you been?" but instead, "What have you brought?" ("Between Two Men" 4)

It would be a mistake to read Karam's inflammatory rhetoric as an accurate depiction of prevailing custom among *Syrians*. There is too much evidence to the contrary. But it can be assumed that the cruelties she pointed to were real, even if not as widespread as she seems to imply. As the "Defender of the Syrian Woman," Karam was fiercely committed to exposing the oppression visited on women and on promoting their rights.

8. Philomena Yusuf al-Barid also noted that the phenomenon of women writing for newspapers did not sit well with everyone. "Many of us [*Syrians*]," she wrote, "deride women and girls who take up writing and who, in the pages of newspapers and magazines, treat useful women's topics that improve the minds of *Syrian* women" (170).

CHAPTER 8

1. For a more detailed description of such clubs and their members' energetic fund raising, and of *Syrian* American clubs in general, see Naff 287–288, 305–319.

2. The Ladies' Aid of New York, still in existence today, continues to help Arab refugees and immigrants and also contributes to a host of charities and institutions both here and in the Arab world. I am grateful to Helen Sahadi, Madelyn Abousleman, and Pauline Haddad for bringing me up to date on the Society's history.

Other women's groups (only a sample) mentioned by Houghton in 1911 are the Women's Society of the Syrian Presbyterian Church in Brooklyn (at least some of whom were also members of the Ladies' Aid), the Women's Benefit Society in St. Paul, Minnesota, and the Guardians of Education in Chicago.

3. Much of my discussion of the Ladies' Aid of Boston is drawn from my article "Good Works, Good Times."

4. Mrs. Asma Traboulsi, another early essayist, understood that charitable clubs benefited not only the poor but also the members themselves. They "would learn social graces," she wrote, "and would become used to speaking in a disciplined fashion on social and cultural topics, and through discussion and reading, would become more aware of their duties toward their husbands and homes and children, as well as towards society at large" (132).

Traboulsi, a resident of Montana and native of Beirut, had studied at a Jesuit school in Lebanon, where she learned French and Latin; later she emigrated with her brother to the United States, where she learned English (129).

5. Afifa Karam was one of those who urged "the need for women to participate with men in theatrical performances that are moral, literary, and improving." Not everyone agreed. "Some people were furious at me," she said, "and a few individuals resorted to hurling taunts, gibes, and invective at me" ("Girls" 60).

CHAPTER 9

1. Women interviewed by Alixa Naff reveal vastly different outcomes of arranged marriages forced on daughters. For instance, Najla Simon (b. 1898, imm. 1913), a native of Damascus, married a man who proved to be a tyrant, working her hard, virtually keeping her a prisoner in the house, and once abandoning her for two years. She was so unhappy, she prayed for death.

A contemporary, Bahieh Kappaz (b. 1897, imm. 1912), also of Damascus, was more aggressive than her husband, whom she described as "weak" and "quiet." He gave her his salary each week and babysat their children while she went to the movies. "Men have to be trained," she said.

2. In a 1944 book based on research he had done in the Lebanese village of Munsif, anthropologist John Gulick described (more dryly) a similar process.

The traditional culture provides an escape for couples who face severe family disapproval. This is equivalent to elopement.... Generally, the prospective groom, with the help of friends, secretly removes the girl from the village. He then returns to the village to attempt negotiations, through an intermediary, with her father. All attempts are made to gain his approval, but if they fail, the wedding is likely to go ahead anyway.... Marriages by elopement are nothing new. (82)

3. Parts of the discussion that follows are drawn directly from my article "Syrian-Lebanese Women Tell Their Story."

4. In the newspaper *Al-Huda*, writer Philomena Yusuf al-Barid campaigned against arranged marriages, which were often (she thought) based on deceit, greed, and ignorance. She cited the example of a young man "who returns from America with, say, a hundred pounds in his pocket, which he makes out to be ten thousand" or another good catch who has only "his father's fortune and social position to plead his case for him." According to al-Barid,

If someone says that this young man is immoral, his supporters would say that like all young men, he will mend his ways after marriage. Thus a girl is forced to marry someone she does not love only to honor the wishes of her parents, who are eager to get her out of the house before she grows any older, and who are unaware that such a marriage will be a cause of misery and hardship rather than happiness and bliss. They cannot understand that it is better for the girl to be an old maid in her parents' home than to marry someone she does not love and whom she does not regard as a suitable mate. (172–173)

5. As everyone in the family knows, Saleemy became a dear and valued member.

CHAPTER 10

1. Given the religious make-up of the Middle East, these figures mean that Christians are still coming to the United States in disproportionate numbers.

2. For a while in the 1970s and early 1980s, Elaine told me, the Anti-Defamation League published lists of people it labeled "anti-Semites." Included in the list were both Arab Americans and others—such as Senator William Fulbright and Under Secretary of State George Ball—who were sympathetic to the Palestinian cause. These lists were distributed to Jewish student organizations, together with advice. According to Elaine, the advice was "if these people are coming to campus, try to

block them; if you can't block them, don't let them speak about Palestinians; and if they insist on talking about Palestinians, bring up terrorism and then just keep filibustering."

In 1986, Helen Samhan wrote that "many of the most respected Jewish organizations and leaders have reacted to the [new] maturity and visibility of the Arab American community with such alarm that discrediting Arab American activity has become a disproportionate part of their agenda" (18). For a detailed account of political racism directed at Arab Americans, see her article "Politics and Exclusion: The Arab American Experience."

3. According to one journalist, rumors about Mary Rose "reached absurd levels when it was implied that oil-rich Arab nations were making $50,000 contributions to her campaign." The truth was that she raised, in all, only something under $100,000, that $17,000 of that was in loans, and that the campaign (though successful) left her $37,000 in debt. See Goldman, specifically pages 12–13, 27.

4. Later, after the incident made the newspapers, Kennedy apologized to Abourezk and said he would gladly accept the donation. But Abourezk had already passed it on to Mel King, who was Kennedy's opponent in the Democratic primary.

5. See Esther Scott, *The Palestinian Flag Controversy at Lakeland High School*, which was researched and developed by Paula Hajar.

CHAPTER 12

1. Adding insult to injury, Jeanne Barkey misidentified Carol as Azizah Al-Hibri, another Lebanese American participant in the conference.

2. Arab women, especially those born and reared in the Arab world, may oppose abortion not only because of a cultural preference for many children (sons, above all) or even because of religious scruples, but also, among Palestinians, because of a sense that their survival as a people is at risk. In the face of that perceived peril and in order to swell the ranks of resisters and fighters, Palestinian leaders—like Zionists before them—have told women that it is their patriotic duty to bear children. At a less rhetorical level, hundreds of Palestinian women subjected to attacks of Israeli tear gas have aborted involuntarily; thus, the reproductive right they may be most concerned about, even in this country, is not the right to terminate a pregnancy but rather the right—without being molested—to carry it to term.

CHAPTER 13

1. For a concise and cogent account of Muslim immigrants and their children, taking into account not just generation but era, see Sharon Abu-Laban's "Coexistence of Cohorts" (1989) or her reworking of that article in "Family and Religion Among Muslim Immigrants and Their Descendants."

2. For a discussion of the Americanization of the mosque and the reform movement that has attempted to reverse it, see the work of Yvonne Haddad, in particular her article "Arab Muslims and Islamic Institutions in America: Adaptation and Reform" and her book *Islamic Values in the United States*. Also relevant is an article, "The South End: An Arab Muslim Working Class Community," by Sameer and Nabeel Abraham and Barbara Aswad. For a comparison of an acculturated and a

traditional mosque, see Abdo Elkholy's ground-breaking book, *The Arab Moslems in the United States.*

3. Of relevance to Khadija's history is an article on women in the Arab world who adopted Islamic dress in the 1980s. Written by Lama Abu Odeh, an Arab feminist who would never choose such dress for herself, the article acknowledges the empowerment that so-called veiling bestows on women, allowing them to go to work or school with less likelihood of being harassed on the street or in a bus and, if they are harassed, enabling them to protest more forcefully and (since their dress is so modest) to win unqualified support from bystanders. Of particular interest is the author's attempt to deconstruct monolithic notions of the "veiled woman" by dividing such women into several categories based on the extent to which other impulses complicate or subvert their wearing of traditional dress. The category of which Khadija is most reminiscent consists of women who "wear the veil [in this case, cover all but face and hands], but retain a fiercely ambivalent relationship with it, so that wearing it is a conscious decision that is made almost every day. It is not uncommon to find them wearing it some days and taking it off others" (35).

CHAPTER 14

1. The actual size of the Palestinian community in this country has always been difficult to determine. Census counts are unreliable, as are records of the Immigration and Naturalization Service, which did not separate out Palestinians from other *Syrians* until 1922 and then, after 1967, no longer allowed people entering the country to identify themselves as Palestinian or to name Palestine as their country of birth. Another impediment is that Palestinians have often followed a circuitous route to the United States, passing time first in other Arab countries. Thus in the mid-1980s, historian Gregory Orfalea estimated that in the years since 1967, half of all immigrants from Lebanon, Syria, Iraq, and the Gulf states had actually been Palestinian, as had two-thirds of those from Jordan (1988, 325). In any case, educated guess has it that Palestinian Americans now number well over 100,000.

2. Sometimes children are made aware that they are Palestinian but warned not to tell others. For a poignant illustration, see Hajar, 198.

3. According to health care professionals, conflicting pressures (from American vs. Arab communities, from husband vs. children) exerted on Arab women immigrants—Palestinian or not—put them at high risk for both physical and mental illness. See, for instance, such excellent articles as Afaf Meleis, "Between Two Cultures: Identity, Role, and Health," and Marianne Hattar-Pollara and Afaf Meleis, "The Stress of Immigration and the Daily Lived Experiences of Jordanian Immigrant Women in the United States."

4. See, for instance, Fadwa Kazaleh's comment that "popular opinion and a study of Palestinians now living in Ramallah reveal that those who emigrated to America hold more to traditional ties and patterns of behavior than do their counterparts in Ramallah itself" (11).

5. Najeebi is mistaken. There is no such injunction in the Koran.

6. Circumstances affecting a girl's fate may include not only the general temperament and religious fervor of her kin but also, according to anthropologist Gideon

Kressel, the social aspirations and relative social status of the two families involved and the extent to which the indiscretion becomes known within the community (151). But in a reply to Kressel, Joseph Ginat of the University of Haifa asserts that even when the sexual transgression becomes public knowledge, most girls are *not* killed. "Those who have conducted field studies know that there are many more cases of this latter kind" (Kressel 153).

7. But ordinary people may sometimes confuse religion with ancient traditions having nothing to do with Islam. For that reason, says Wakin, some Muslims mistakenly believe that Islam prohibits birth control.

In any case, it is significant that "honor killing" is not a feature of life in all parts of the Islamic world, nor is it a practice peculiar to Muslims or even to Arabs. Rural societies in the Mediterranean and elsewhere have similar traditions; at one time or another, says anthropologist Frank Stewart, "the idea [of 'honor killing'] was quite widespread in Europe" (personal communication). See also Stewart's book *Honor*.

8. Amal's comments (edited by her) are drawn from an interview on Nov. 15, 1996, with the *Arabic Hour* television program in Boston and are reproduced with its permission.

9. Amal's comments (edited by her) are drawn from an interview on Nov. 15, 1996, with *The Arabic Hour* television program in Boston and are reproduced with its permission.

10. In the 1920s and 1930s, news notes and articles in *The Syrian World* (and likely in other publications) kept readers informed about the struggle for women's rights in Arab lands. See, most notably, Ameen Rihani's article, "Woman in the Near East."

11. This question of priorities is crucial. Many Arab women are frustrated by their inability to persuade Western feminists that the suffering of women living under military occupation or in a war zone belongs high on the agenda of feminist debate. In her keynote address at the Second International Congress on Women's Health Issues, Afaf Meleis attempted to bring home this point: "Feminism in third-world countries is defined not in terms of freedom from male oppression; rather it is freedom from foreign oppression, from hunger, poverty, illness, malnutrition, and from other forms of deprivation" ("Women in Transition" 206).

12. The greater emphasis on local needs has probably been accelerated by disillusionment with political events in the Middle East. Many Palestinians believe that the alliance between Yasir Arafat and the Israeli government (perhaps now called into question by the election of Benjamin Netanyahu) has retarded rather than furthered the creation of a democratic Palestinian state. Thus, with politics back home firmly in the hands of the politicians and reduced funding available from the community here (which has had large new demands made on its resources), the UPWA has sharply curtailed its activities at the national level, leaving individual branches to raise their own funds and to address the needs of their local constituencies.

13. As it attempts to address these needs, the UPWA moves closer to the kind of work done by ACCESS (Arab Community Center for Economic and Social Services) in Dearborn, a city which is home to the largest Arab American community in the United States. From its beginnings in a storefront in 1971, ACCESS has expanded dramatically, now occupying several sites that offer dozens of services, including emergency food and shelter programs, prenatal care, AIDS education, family counseling, classes in English, and after-school tutoring for children. A staff of 40 full-time workers and 150 volunteers serves over 30,000 clients annually. In 1992,

President George Bush presented ACCESS with his Points of Light award for outstanding volunteer service to the community.

CHAPTER 15

1. *Hajjeh* is a term of respect for women who have made the pilgrimage to Mecca. Hajjeh Nadia has now returned to Lebanon. For a different analysis of how immigration may cheat Arab women of the status and power that have traditionally accrued to them in their later years, see Meleis, "Between Two Cultures," as well as my essay "Pretending to be Arab: Role-Playing in Vance Bourjaily's 'A Fractional Man.' "

2. In 1995, Helen Khal moved back to Lebanon.

BIBLIOGRAPHY

ENGLISH SOURCES

Abinader, Elmaz. *Children of the Roojme: A Family's Journey*. New York: Norton, 1991.

Aboud, Albert G. Letter. *The Syrian World* 3.7 (Jan. 1929): 46–47.

Abraham, Sameer Y., and Nabeel Abraham, eds. *Arabs in the New World: Studies on Arab-American Communities*. Detroit, MI: Wayne State U, 1983.

Abraham Sameer Y., Nabeel Abraham, and Barbara Aswad. "The Southend: An Arab Muslim Working-Class Community." In *Arabs in the New World: Studies on Arab-American Communities*, edited by Sameer Y. Abraham and Nabeel Abraham. Detroit, MI: Wayne State U, 1983.

Absi, Matilda G. Letter. *The Syrian World* 3.9 (March 1929): 47–49.

Abu-Laban, Baha, and Michael Suleiman, eds. *Arab Americans: Continuity and Change*. Belmont, MA: Association of Arab-American University Graduates, 1989.

Abu-Laban, Sharon McIrvin. "The Coexistence of Cohorts: Identity and Adaptation among Arab-American Muslims." In *Arab Americans: Continuity and Change*, edited by Baha Abu-Laban and Michael Suleiman. Belmont, MA: Association of Arab-American University Graduates, 1989.

———. "Family and Religion Among Muslim Immigrants and Their Descendants." In *Muslim Families in North America*, edited by Earl H. Waugh, Sharon McIrvin Abu-Laban, and Regula Burckhardt Qureshi. Edmonton: U of Alberta P, 1991.

Abu Odeh, Lama. "Post-Colonial Feminism and the Veil: Thinking the Difference." *Feminist Review* 43 (Spring 1993): 26–37.

Ahmed, Leila. "Western Ethnocentrism and Perceptions of the Harem." *Feminist Studies* 8.3 (Fall 1982): 521–533.

Ajami, Joseph. "The Arabic Press in the United States since 1892: A Socio-Historical Study." Ph.D. diss., Ohio U, 1987.

Associated Charities of Boston. *Twentieth Annual Report, 1899*.

Barakat, Layyah. *A Message from Mount Lebanon*. Philadelphia, PA: The Sunday School Times Co., 1912.

Barkey, Jeanne. "Perspectives by American Women of Color." *Off Our Backs* 12.9 (October 1982): 3.

Beshara, Tafeeda. Interview. Naff Collection, Smithsonian Institution, Washington, D.C., 1962.

Blatty, William Peter. *Which Way to Mecca, Jack?* New York: Lancer, 1960.

Bliss, Frederick. *The Religions of Modern Syria and Palestine.* New York: Scribner, 1960.

Bourjaily, Vance. *Confessions of a Spent Youth.* New York: Bantam, 1961.

"Breach of Promise." *Ash-Shaab* (April 1930). Rpt. in *The Syrian World* 3.11 (May 1929): 46.

Cainkar, Louise. "Palestinian Women in the United States: Coping with Tradition, Change, and Alienation." Ph.D. diss., Northwestern U, 1988.

Carhart, Alfreda Post. *It Happened in Syria.* New York: Fleming H. Revell, 1940.

Cole, Donald. *Immigrant City: Lawrence, Massachusetts, 1845–1921.* Chapel Hill: U of North Carolina P, 1963.

Cole, William I. *Immigrant Races in Massachusetts: The Syrians.* Boston: 1921[?].

Conklin, Nancy Faires, and Nora Faires. " 'Colored' and Catholic: The Lebanese in Birmingham, Alabama." In *Crossing the Waters: Arabic-Speaking Immigrants to the United States before 1940*, edited by Eric Hooglund. Washington, D.C.: Smithsonian Institution P, 1987.

Denison House: The College Settlement in Boston. Annual Report for the Year Ending Oct. 1, 1915.

Denison House: The College Settlement in Boston. Annual Report for the Year Ending Oct. 1, 1916.

Elkholy, Abdo. *The Arab Moslems in the United States: Religion and Assimilation.* New Haven, CT: College and UP, 1966.

Ferguson, Mary. Letter. *The Syrian World* 1.3 (Sept. 1926): 56–57.

Fischer, Gayle V. " 'Pantalets' and 'Turkish Trowsers': Designing Freedom in the Mid-Nineteenth Century United States." *Feminist Studies* 23.1 (Spring 1997): 111–114.

Fountaine, Margaret. *Love Among the Butterflies: The Travels and Adventures of a Victorian Lady.* Ed. W. F. Cater. New York: Penguin, 1982.

Geha, Joseph. "Everything, Everything." *Through and Through: Toledo Stories.* St. Paul, MN: Graywolf P, 1990. 19–31.

Gibran, Jean, and Kahlil Gibran. *Kahlil Gibran: His Life and World.* New York: Interlink, 1991.

Goldman, Caren. "Mary Rose Oakar: Cleveland's Congressional Maverick." *Sunday Plain Dealer Magazine*, April 10, 1977, 9ff.

Graham-Brown, Sarah. *Images of Women: The Portrayal of Women in Photography of the Middle East 1860–1950.* New York: Columbia UP, 1988.

Granqvist, Hilma. *Marriage Conditions in a Palestinian Village.* Helsingfors: Societas Scientiarum Fennica, Commentations Humanarum Litterarum 3.8 (1931) and 6.8 (1935).

Grant, Madison. *The Passing of the Great Race: The Racial Basis of European History.* New York: Scribner, 1916.

Gulick, John. *Social Structure and Culture Change in a Lebanese Village.* New York: Warner Green Foundation for Anthropological Research, 1955.

Haddad, Carol. "Arab American Women: Caught Between Two Worlds." Paper presented at the American-Arab Anti-Discrimination Committee, 1st National Convention. Washington, D.C., 16 March 1984.

————. "Arab-Americans: The Forgotten Minority in Feminist Circles." Paper presented at the National Women's Association, 4th Annual Convention. Arcata, CA., 17 June 1982.

Haddad, Yvonne. "Arab Muslims and Islamic Institutions in America: Adaptation and Reform." In *Arabs in the New World: Studies on Arab-American Communities*, edited by Sameer Y. Abraham and Nabeel Abraham. Detroit, MI: Wayne State U, 1983.

Haddad, Yvonne, and Adair T. Lummis. *Islamic Values in the United States: A Comparative Study*. New York and Oxford: Oxford UP, 1991.

Hagopian, Elaine C., and Ann Paden, eds. *The Arab-Americans: Studies in Assimilation*. Wilmette, IL: Medina UP International, 1969.

Haidar, Princess Rahme. *Under Syrian Stars*. New York: Fleming H. Revell, 1929.

Hajar, Paula. "Arab Immigrant Parents and American Schoolpeople: An Ethnography of a Cross-Cultural Relationship." Ed.D. diss., Harvard U, 1993.

Hakim, A. [Salloum Mokarzel]. "On the Marriage Problem Among Syrians [in three parts]." *The Syrian World* 3.5 (Nov. 1928): 27–32; 3.6 (Dec. 1928): 20–25; 3.7 (Jan. 1929): 18–23.

Hattar-Pollara, Marianne, and Afaf I. Meleis. "The Stress of Immigration and the Daily Lived Experience of Jordanian Women in the United States." *Western Journal of Nursing Research* 17.5 (1995): 521–539.

Hentoff, Nat. "You Can't Tell a Terrorist by the Cover of Her Book." *Washington Post*, 2 June 1986: A23.

Hitti, Philip. *The Syrians in America*. New York: George H. Doran, 1924.

Hooglund, Eric, ed. *Crossing the Waters: Arabic-Speaking Immigrants to the United States before 1940*. Washington, D.C.: Smithsonian Institution P, 1987.

————, ed. *Taking Root: Arab-American Community Studies*. Vol. 2. Washington, D.C.: ADC Research Institute, 1985.

Houghton, Louise. "The Syrians in the United States." *The Survey* 26.1–4 (1911): 480–495, 647–656, 786–802, 957–968.

Ireland, Patricia. Luncheon Keynote Address. Papers presented at the American–Arab Anti-Discrimination Committee, 11th National Convention. Arlington, VA., 15 April 1994.

Jessup, Rev. Henry Harris. *Women of the Arabs: With a Chapter for Children*. New York: Dodd & Mead, 1873.

Kadi, Joanne, ed. *Food for Our Grandmothers: Writings by Arab-American and Arab-Canadian Feminists*. Boston: South End P, 1994.

Kappaz, Bahieh. Interview. Naff Collection, Smithsonian Institution, Washington, D.C., 1980.

Kayal, Philip M., and Joseph M. Kayal. *The Syrian-Lebanese in America: A Study in Religion and Assimilation*. Boston: Twayne, 1975.

Kazaleh, Fadwa Ann. "Biculturalism and Adjustment: A Study of Ramallah-American Adolescents in Jacksonville, Florida." Ph.D. diss., Florida State U, 1986.

Khalaf, Samir. "The Background and Causes of Lebanese-Syrian Immigration to the United States before World War I." In *Crossing the Waters: Arabic-speaking Immigrants to the United States before 1940*, edited by Eric Hooglund. Washington, D.C.: Smithsonian Institution P, 1987.

Kressel, Gideon M. "Sororicide/Filiacide: Homicide for Family Honor." *Current Anthropology* 22.2 (April 1981): 141–158.

Lamphere, Louise. *From Working Daughters to Working Mothers.* Ithaca, NY: Cornell UP, 1987.

Maalouf, Amin. *The Rock of Tanios.* Trans. Dorothy S. Blair. New York: George Braziller, 1994.

Makdisi, Jean Said. *Beirut Fragments.* New York: Persea, 1990.

Mansur, Rev. A. W. "Problems of Syrian Youth in America." *Syrian World* 2.6 (Dec. 1927): 9.

"Marie El-Khouri, Designer, was 74." *New York Times* 28 September 1957: 17.

Meleis, Afaf I. "Between Two Cultures: Identity Roles and Health." *Health Care for Women International* 12 (1991): 365–377.

Meleis, Afaf Ibrahim, and Marianne Hattar-Pollara. "Arab Middle Eastern American Women." In *Health Issues for Women of Color: A Cultural Diversity Perspective,* edited by Diane Adams. Thousand Oaks, CA: Sage, 1995.

Meleis, Afaf Ibrahim, and Sandra Rogers. "Women in Transition: Being Versus Becoming or Being and Becoming." *Health Care for Women International* 8 (1987): 199–217.

Melman, Billie. *Women's Orients: English Women and the Middle East, 1718–1918.* Ann Arbor: U of Michigan P, 1992.

Menconi, Evelyn, ed. *William G. Abdalah Library Newsletter,* West Roxbury, MA, January 1988.

Mernissi, Fatima. *Dreams of Trespass.* Reading, MA: Addison-Wesley, 1994.

Miller, Lucius Hopkins. "A Study of the Syrian Communities of Greater New York." *Federation: Quarterly of the Federation of Churches and Christian Organizations in New York City* 3.2 (October 1903): 13–57. See also pp. 11, 12, and 58.

"Moslem Couple Gets Death Sentence for Murdering Daughter," *Agence France Press,* 20 Dec. 1991.

Naff, Alixa. *Becoming American: The Early Arab Immigrant Experience.* Carbondale: Southern Illinois UP, 1985.

"NOW's Approach to Arab-American Women." *ADC Times: News and Opinions of the American–Arab Anti-Discrimination Committee.* 15.4 (May 1994): 5.

"Nursery for Syrian Babes." *New York Times* 21 May 1899: 20.

"Nursery for Syrian Babies." *New York Times* 19 March 1899: 20.

Orfalea, Gregory. *Before the Flames: A Quest for the History of Arab Americans.* Austin: U of Texas P, 1988.

———. "There's a Wire Brush at My Bones." In *Crossing the Waters: Arabic-Speaking Immigrants to the United States before 1940,* edited by Eric Hooglund. Washington, D.C.: Smithsonian Institution P, 1987.

Rihani, Ameen. "Woman in the Near East." *The Syrian World.* 5.1 (Sept. 1930): 5–13.

Rihbany, Abraham. *A Far Journey.* Boston: Houghton Mifflin, 1914.

Rizk, Salom. *Syrian Yankee.* Garden City, NY: Doubleday, Doran, 1943.

Said, Edward. *Orientalism.* New York: Vintage, 1979.

Said, Laila. *A Bridge Through Time: A Memoir.* New York: Summit, 1985.

Saliba, Najib. "Emigration from Syria." In *Arabs in the New World: Studies on Arab-American Communities,* edited by Sameer Y. Abraham and Nabeel Abraham. Detroit, MI: Wayne State U, 1983.

———. *Emigration from Syria and the Syrian-Lebanese Community of Worcester, MA.* Ligonier, PA: Antakya P, 1992.

Samhan, Helen Hatab. "Politics and Exclusion." *Journal of Palestine Studies* 16.2 (1987): 11–28.

Scott, Esther. *The Palestinian Flag Controversy at Lakeland High School.* Case Program, John F. Kennedy School of Government, Harvard University. Cambridge: Harvard UP, 1994. Researched and developed by Paula Hajar.

Shakir, Evelyn. "Good Works, Good Times: The Syrian Ladies' Aid Society of Boston, 1917–1932." In *Crossing the Waters: Arabic-Speaking Immigrants to the United States before 1940,* edited by Eric Hooglund. Washington, D.C.: Smithsonian Institution P, 1987.

———. "Syrian-Lebanese Women Tell Their Story." *Frontiers* 7.1 (1983): 9–13.

———. "Pretending to be Arab: Role-Playing in Vance Bourjaily's 'A Fractional Man.' " *MELUS* 9.1 (Spring 1982): 7–21.

Simon, John. Letter. *The Syrian World* 1.4 (Oct. 1926): 55.

Simon, Najla. Interview. Naff Collection, Smithsonian Institution, Washington, D.C., 1980.

Solomon, Mary. Letter. *The Syrian World* 3.7 (Jan. 1929): 47–49.

———. Letter. *The Syrian World* 3.9 (March 1929): 45–47.

Stein, Leon, ed. *Out of the Sweatshop: The Struggle for Industrial Democracy.* New York: Quadrangle/New York Times, 1977.

Stewart, Frank. *Honor.* Chicago: U of Chicago P, 1994.

Tannous, Afif. "Acculturation of an Arab-Syrian Community in the Deep South." *American Sociological Review* 8 (1943): 264–271.

———. "Emigration: A Force of Social Change in an Arab Village." *Rural Sociology* 7 (1942): 62–74.

———. "Missionary Education in Lebanon: A Study in Acculturation." *Social Forces* 21 (March 1942): 338–343.

———. "Social Change in an Arab Village." *American Sociological Review* 6 (1941): 650–652.

———. [spelled "Tannus"] "Trends of Social and Cultural Change in Bishmizzeen, an Arab Village of North Lebanon." Ph.D. diss., Cornell U, 1940.

Twentieth Annual Report of the Associated Charities of Boston (1899).

Vecoli, Rudolph J. "Born Italian: Color Me Red, White, and Green." *Soundings* 6.1 (Spring 1973): 117–123.

Waugh, Earl H., Sharon McIrvin Abu-Laban, and Regula Burckhardt Qureshi, eds. *Muslim Families in North America.* Edmonton: U of Alberta P, 1991.

Woods, Robert. *City Wilderness.* Boston: Houghton Mifflin, 1898.

"Young Women's Christian Association of Greater Lansing (Michigan). Nationality Communities Department." Archival papers, Immigration History Research Center, U of Minnesota.

Younis, Adele. "The Coming of the Arabic-Speaking People to the United States." Ph.D. diss., Boston U, 1961.

———. "The Growth of Arabic-Speaking Settlements in the United States." In *The Arab-Americans: Studies in Assimilation,* edited by Elaine C. Hagopian and Ann Paden. Wilmette, Illinois: Medina UP International, 1969.

Zelditch, Morris. "The Syrians in Pittsburgh." Master's thesis, U of Pittsburgh, 1936.

ARABIC SOURCES

al-Barid, Philomena Yusuf. "The Condition of Syrian Women [*Halat al-Mar'a As-Suriyya*]." *Miscellany*, 169–174.

Barakat, Layyah. "The Eastern Woman in the West [*Al-Mar'a As-Sharqiyya fi al-Bilad al-Gharbiyya*]." *Miscellany*, 15–20.

"How Afifa Karam was Raised and Lived [*Kayfa Nasha'at wa-'Ashat*]." *Al-Akhlaq* 5.7 (July 1924): 5.

Karam, Afifa. "The Articles of Afifa Karam [*Magalaat Afifa Karam*]" [an unpublished scrapbook].

———. "Between Two Men [*Bayn Ar-Rajulayn*]." *Al-Huda* 4 Dec. 1908: 4, 6.

———. "Girls [*Al-Fatat*]." *Miscellany*, 60–65.

———. "Marriage [*Az-Zawaj*]." *The New World [Al-Aalamu aj-Jadid*] 4.3 (March 1913): 323–329.

———. "Reply to a Critique [*'Radd ala I 'tirad*]." *Al-Huda* 9 Jan. 1909: 4.*

———. "Syrian Immigration [*As-Suriyyun wa al-Muhajara*], Part III: Women Emigrating Alone [*Muhajarat al-Mar'a Wahdaha*]." Part IV [untitled]." Karam, "Articles."

A Miscellany of Essays [Nithar al-Afkar]. New York: Al-Huda, c. 1911.

Muhammad, Saeed. "A Look at Druse Immigration [*Nathrah fil Muhajarah ad-Durziyyah*]." *Al-Huda* 6 Feb. 1909: 4.

"Our View of the Druse Woman [*Al-Mar'a ad-Durziyyah wa Ra'yuna*]." *Al-Huda* 6 Feb. 1909: 4.

Rashed, Wadia Faris. "New Riches and the Syrian Woman [*Al-Mar'a as-Suriyya wa Hadathat al-Ni'ma*]." *Miscellany* 37–42.

Salim, Hannah Shakir. "Moderation [*At-Tawassutwa al-i'tidal*]." *Al-Huda* 17 Dec. 1908: 4.*

"The Syrian Woman in the United States [*Al-Mar'a as-Suriyyah fil Wilayat al-Muttahida*]." *Al-Huda* 5 March 1899: 15–17.

Traboulsi, Asma. "Women's Clubs [*Al-Jam'iyyat an-Nisa'iyya*]" *Miscellany*, 129–133.

*Asterisked items were translated for me by Shirine Hamadeh. All other articles were translated by Alex Baramki.

INDEX

AAUG (American-Arab University Graduates), 85–86, 96

Abinader, Elmaz, 32–33

Abinader, Mayme, 32–33

Abortion, 106, 209 n.2 (chap. 12)

Abourezk, James, 87, 209 n.4

Abraham, Nabeel, 209 n.2 (chap. 13)

Abraham, Sameer, 209 n.2 (chap. 13)

Abu-Laban, Sharon, 116, 209 n.1 (chap. 13)

Abu Odeh, Lama, 210 n.3 (chap. 13)

Abuse of women, 6, 67. *See also* Violence against women and girls

ACCESS (Arab Community Center for Economic and Social Services), 211–12 n.13

Acculturation. *See* Assimilation

Acting on stage, women, 62–63, 207 n.5

Activism, political, 85–87, 93–94, 96–103, 105, 110–11, 119, 151, 153–57, 162–64. *See also* Clubs and organizations, women's; *Intifada*

ADC (American-Arab Anti-Discrimination Committee), 93, 96, 104, 105–6

Adjustment to the United States, problems in, 173–80. *See also* Emigration, Arab women, resistance to American society; Palestinians, resistance to American society; Racism, anti-Arab

ADL (Anti-Defamation League), 86, 208–9 n.2 (chap. 10)

Ahmed, Leila, 3–4

Ajami, Joseph Georges, 206 n.2

Albany, New York, 45

Al-Barid, Philomena Yusuf, 54–55, 206 n.6, 207 n.8, 208 n.4

Algerian women, 165, 166–67, 169, 181, 183, 185, 189, 190

Al-Huda, 41, 55, 56, 204 n.6, 206 n.6

Alia (pseudonym), 144–45

Alice, 73

Amal, Shameem Rassam, 166, 171–73

American University of Beirut (AUB), 23, 84, 95, 168

Amireh, Amal, 144, 156–57

Ansara, James: grandmother of, 38–39; wife of, 39

Arab American Institute, 96–97

Arab women: deference to brothers, 18, 19; power, 6–8, 29; social restrictions, 133–34, 137–38, 148, 159, 161–62, 167–68, 170, 185, 193, 199; stereotypes, 1–6, 8, 104, 155, 173–74; traditional tasks, 7, 13–14, 49, 177, 180. *See also* Emigration, *Syrian women*; Harems; Honor

Arafat, Yasir, 211 n.12
Arranged marriages. *See* Marriage
Ashrawi, Hanan, 105
Asma, 67–68, 70
Asmahan S. (pseudonym), 165–66, 181, 193, 194
Assimilation, 82, 95, 107–8, 114–15, 116–18, 126, 135, 136. *See also* Emigration, Arab women; Palestinians, resistance to American society
Aswad, Barbara, 209 n.2 (chap. 13)
Aunt Mary, 28, 38
Azzou, Wijdan, 174, 184–85

Baldensperger, Phillipe, 7–8
Barakat, Layyah, 41, 54, 201 n.2 (intro.), 203 n.3, 206 n.4
Barbara L. (pseudonym), 184, 185, 191
Beauty, concerns about, 81, 107–8, 112–13, 117–18
Beirut, 24, 88, 166, 168, 188, 194; golden age, 16, 168, 188
Bible. *See* Holy Land
Bigotry, anti-Arab. *See* Orientalism; Racism, anti-Arab; Religious bigotry
Birmingham, Alabama, 81
Birth control, 211 n.7
Bishmizeen, Lebanon. *See* Tannous, Afif
Blatty, William Peter, mother of, 39
Bliss, Frederick, 7, 8
Boston, Massachusetts, 15, 18, 35, 39–40, 45, 50, 59–60, 80–81, 82, 205 n.2
Bourjaily, Vance 8, 30, 83, 212 n.1; grandmother of, 39
Bread and Roses Strike, 48, 205 n.7

Cainkar, Louise, 126
CAIR (Council on American Islamic Relations), 116
Carhart, Emily Post, 201 n.1 (chap. 1), 202 n.4
Carter, Jimmy, 86
Catherine (pseudonym), 106–7, 113
Cedar Rapids, North Dakota, 61
Chador, 167. *See also* Dress
Chastity, 10, 67, 144, 146, 149, 186. *See also* Honor

Chicago, Illinois, 207 n.2
Child labor, 52–53
Christian emigration and immigration, 24, 126, 208 n.1 (chap.10)
Christian women, 1–2, 6, 8
Cincinnati, Ohio, 45
Citizenship, *Syrian* eligibility for, 81
Clubs and organizations, women's, 59–64, 82, 111, 153, 157–59, 207 nn.1–4
Cole, Donald, 48
Cole, William, 45
Color, *Syrian. See* Beauty, concerns about; Racism, anti-Arab, ethnic
Communities, Arab American. *See individual cities and towns*
Community: loss of, 194; pleasure in, 89–90, 94, 108, 111, 132; rejection of, 193
Conklin, Nancy Faires, 81
Courtship, 65–76, 121–22, 128, 169, 187; double standard for sons and daughters, 72; modified in America, 70, 71–72, 74, 164–169; rapid, 68. *See also* Dating; Elopement; Marriage
Cullhane, Hind Rassam, 170, 175–76, 191

Damascus, 24, 85
Dating, 10, 69–70, 71, 72, 75, 121, 135, 144, 149, 164, 185. *See also* Courtship; Single women
Dearborn, Michigan, 211–12, n.13
Denison House, 59–60
Divorce, 159, 180–81, 193
Douma, Lebanon, 89–90
Dress: modest, 145, 150, 184–85; Muslim, 116, 119–22, 137, 139, 155–56, 157, 158, 160–61, 167, 174–75, 189–90, 194, 210 n.3 (chap. 13). *See also* Veiling
Druse, 17, 201 n.3 (chap. 3), 202 n.1, 204 n.6

Education, female, 52–58; denial of, 146, 158, 168; desire for, 54, 138–39, 146, 168, 187, 192; encouragement of, 14, 52, 54–56, 131, 144, 151, 166–67, 168, 187, 192; exceptional, 54–56;

misgivings about, 54, 56; neglect of, 53–54; sex, 55–56. *See also* Schooling, Middle East vs. America

Egypt, 84, 85, 126, 175

Egyptian women, 170, 175, 186

Elkholy, Abdo, 202 n.6, 209–10 n.2 (chap. 13)

El-Khoury, Marie Azeez, 46

Elopement, 66, 74, 208 n.2 (chap. 9). *See also* Courtship; Marriage; Single women

Emigration, Arab women: balancing losses and gains, 136, 139–40, 176–78, 180, 192, 193–94; decision to emigrate, 15, 18, 29, 169–170, 171; health problems, 201 n.3 (intro.), 210 n.3 (chap. 14); new opportunities, 181–83, 191, 192; older women, 176–80, 212 n.1; political motives, 171–73; resistance to American society, 174–75, 183–86, 193. *See also* Emigration, *Syrian*; Emigrtion, *Syrian* women

Emigration, *Syrian*, 20–26, 201 n.1 (chap. 3); ambivalence about, 25–26; causes, 14, 20–25, 35; economic considerations, 21–22; impact of World War I, 25, 28, 32; misrouting, 24, 202 n.7; missionaries' influence, 23, 24; numbers, 20, 25, 202 n.1; political motives, 24–25; religious makeup, 24, 202 n.6, 202 n.1, 204 n.6; separation of families, 25, 32–33, 202 n.7, 203–4 n.6. *See also* Emigration, *Syrian* women; Return, dream of; Sabbagh, Miriam Ashook

Emigration, *Syrian* women, 27–34, 35; corrupting influence, 54, 206 n.5; hardships, 31, 203 n.2; impact of World War I, 28, 32; independent exodus, 28–31, 203 nn.4, 5; missionaries' influence, 23, 28–29, 203 n.3; new opportunities for, 10, 18, 28–29, 30–31, 35; numbers, 28, 202 nn.10 (chap. 3), 1 (chap. 4); sexual risks and temptations, 31. *See also* Emigration, *Syrian*; Sabbagh, Miriam Ashook; Shakir, Katreen Dibs

Entrepreneurs, *Syrian*, 43–46, 205 n.2

Exploitation of women and girls, 40, 52, 53–54, 55, 73, 203 n.2, 206–207 n.7. *See also* "Honor killings"; Marriages, arranged; Violence against women and girls

Fadwa (pseudonym), 155–56

Faires, Nora, 81

Fall River, Massachusetts, 45, 47, 48–49, 205 n.8

Family conflicts: husbands and wives, 138–39, 159, 180–81, 182–183; parents and children, 10, 72–73, 119, 137, 139–40, 142–43, 145–52 passim, 160–69 passim, 198, 199. *See also* Exploitation of women and girls; Family harmony

Family harmony: husbands and wives, 172, 179–80, 181, 198; parents and children, 72, 136, 144–45, 177–78, 185. *See also*Family conflicts

FAN (Feminist Arab Network), 105

Fatan M. (pseudonym), 175, 186, 190, 193

Fatima G. (pseudonym), 190–91

FBI (Federal Bureau of Investigation), 86, 176

Feminists: American, 3–4, 60, 89, 104–6, 112, 120–21, 158, 192, 211 n.11; Arab and Arab American, 3, 104–6, 108, 111, 120–21, 157–60, 167, 192, 211 n.11

Fort Wayne, Indiana, 38

Fountaine, Margaret, 202 n.9

Garment industry, 43–44, 50–51, 97–98, 205 nn.1, 10, 11

Geha, Joseph, 112–13

Gibran, Kahlil, 30, 36, 46

Ginat, Joseph, 211 n.6

Graham-Brown, Sarah, 5

Granqvist, Hilma, 6–7, 8

Grant, Madison, 80

Greater Syria, 1, 5–8, 20, 49

Gulf War, 150–51, 163, 173, 176

Gulick, John, 208 n.2 (chap. 9)

Habachy, Nimet, 170, 175
Haddad, Carol, 104–5, 113
Haddad, Yvonne, 115–16, 209 n.2
    (chap. 13)
Hagopian, Elaine, 85–87, 96, 208–9 n.2
    (chap. 10)
Haidar, Rahme, 5, 28–29
Hajar, Paula, 29, 33–34, 89–94, 95, 210
    n.2
Hajjeh, Nadia (pseudonym), 180, 212
    n.1
Harassment of Arab Americans, 86–88,
    150–51, 161, 175, 175–76. See also
    Racism, anti-Arab; Religious bigotry
Harems, 3–5, 22, 201 n.1 (intro.)
Hattar-Pollara, Marianne, 210 n.3
Hawa T. (pseudonym), 170, 186
Hentoff, Nat, 88
Hijab, 116, 119–22, 157, 160–61, 167,
    174, 190, 194. See also Dress
Hitti, Philip, 81, 202 n.1
Holy Land, association with, 5–6, 14,
    22, 23, 36, 125, 201 n.2 (intro.)
Honor, 10, 31, 41, 49, 62–63, 66–67,
    110, 133–35, 137–38, 144, 147–49,
    162, 163–64. See also Chastity;
    "Honor Killings"; Sex
"Honor killings," 6, 140–42, 143–44,
    151, 210–11 nn.6, 7. See also Chastity;
    Honor; Sex
Hooglund, Eric, 204 n.1, 205 nn.5, 6
Houghton, Louise: on children's
    schooling, 52–53; on entrepreneurs,
    45; on peddling, 40–41, 42, 204 n.4,
    205 n.5; on women's clubs, 61, 207
    n.2
Hussein, Saddam, 173, 176
Hyder, Happy, 106

Identity, concealment of, 127, 175, 176,
    210 n.2.
Ihsan (pseudonym), 131–34
Immigration, immigrants. See Emigra-
    tion, Arab women; Emigration, Syr-
    ian Emigration, Syrian women
Intermarriage, ethnic and religious, 72–
    73, 114, 116–17, 118, 122, 126, 140,
    169, 170, 199

Intifada, 93, 99–100, 101–3, 128, 129–
    30, 153–55, 156–57, 163–64; inspira-
    tion to women and girls, 156, 164;
    role of women and girls, 99, 100, 153–
    55, 156, 164
Iraq, Iraqis, 84, 126, 171–73; Iraqi
    women, 166, 170, 171–73, 174, 175–
    76, 184–85, 191, 193
Iraq-Iran War, 172
Ireland, Patricia, 105–6
Islam. See Muslim emigration; Muslims;
    Muslim women and girls
Israel, 82; establishment, 90, 100, 126,
    127. See also Activism, political; Pal-
    estine; Racism, anti–Arab, political

Jackson, Jesse, 79
Jerusalem, 24, 127–28, 132, 133, 147
Jessup, Henry, 6, 9
Jewish Defense League, 86
Jews, dialogue with, 86–87, 130–31
Jordan, 84, 175
Jordanian women, 167, 168–69, 174–75,
    183–84, 186, 190, 193, 210 n.3 (chap.
    14)
Journalists, women, 54–56, 207 n.8. See
    also Al-Barid, Philomena Yusuf; Bar-
    akat, Layyah; Karam, Afifa; Rashed,
    Wadia Faris; Salim, Hannah Shakir;
    Traboulsi, Asma

Karam, Afifa, 30–31, 40, 55–56, 68; 203
    n.2, 204 n.6, 206–7 n.7, 207 n.5
Karima (pseudonym), 144
Karnib, Zeainab, 174, 187, 191
Kazaleh, Fadwa, 210 n.4
Kennedy, Joseph, Jr., 87, 209 n.4
Khadaffi, Moammar, 176
Khadija (pseudonym), 117–22, 210 n.3
    (chap. 13)
Khal, Helen, 181, 188–89, 212 n.2
Kleit, Amina, 183
Kressel, Gideon, 210–11 n.6

Lansing, Michigan, 59, 81–82
Lawrence, Massachusetts, 29, 39, 48.
    See also Bread and Roses Strike
Lebanese Syrian Ladies' Aid Society.

See Syrian Ladies' Aid Society of Boston

Lebanese women, 165, 166, 167–68, 169, 170–71, 173, 174, 176–80, 181–83, 184, 185, 186–87, 188–89, 191, 192, 194

Lebanon, 1, 10, 20; civil war (1975–1990), 16–17, 140, 169, 170–71, 178, 181, 188–89; golden age, 16; Israeli invasion (1982), 84, 88–89, 93, 104–5, 107, 110, 111, 162; World War I, 25, 32–33. *See also* Beirut; Mount Lebanon

Leila K. (pseudonym), 176, 193

Lena B. (pseudonym), 171, 174, 186

Lesbians, 106–11

Libya, Libyans, 176

Lowell, Massachusetts 38–39

Lucille (Ablan), 71

Lummis, Adair, 115–16

Maalouf, Ameen, 202 n.5

Magazines, women's, 55. *See also* Journalists, women

Maha (pseudonym), 135–36

Mai N. (pseudonym), 167, 168–69, 174–75, 183–84

Makdisi, Jean Said, 83–84

Malouf, Mary Kfouri, 32

Mansi, Nada, 170–71, 174, 184, 185, 186, 187, 191

Mansur, Rev. A. W., 80

Marriage: arranged, 65–69, 70–71, 72, 134, 135, 146–47, 181, 187–88, 208 nn.1 (chap. 9), 4; early, 146, 148, 158, 187; first-cousin, 146, 187–88. *See also* Courtship; Dating; Elopement; Single women

Mary, 66–67, 70

Mary B. (pseudonym), 181–83, 189

Meir, Golda, 135

Meleis, Afaf, 201 n.3 (intro.), 210 n.3 (chap. 14), 211 n.11, 212 n.1

Melman, Billie, 4

Menconi, Evelyn, 48

Mernissi, Fatima, 201 n.1 (intro.)

Messaoudi, Dalila, 166–67, 181, 183, 185, 190

Middle East conflicts: American policies, 10, 79, 126, 162, 163, 176; impact on Arab Americans, 82–85, 87–89, 90, 110–11, 156–57. *See also* Activism, political; Hajar, Paula; Racism, anti-Arab, political; Simon, Linda

Miller, Lucius: on Arab licentiousness, 40; on businessmen, 45; on children's schooling, 52–53; on peddling, 38, 39, 204 n.2

Mill hands, *Syrian*, 46–49, 205 nn.7, 8, 9; strike participation, 48; women, 49; working conditions, 47

Minneapolis, Minnesota, 45

Missionaries to the Middle East, 5, 6, 9, 22–23; influence on emigration, 23, 28–29; mission schools, 22–23, 54, 202 n.5, 203 n.3

Modesty, female. *See* Honor

Mohamed, Suad, 167, 169, 180–81, 192, 193–94

Mokarzel, Naoum, 55

Mokarzel, Salloum, 71–73, 95

Mona (pseudonym), 160–64

Montagu, Lady Mary Wortley, 4, 8, 9

Montana, 18

Mount Lebanon, 2, 13–15, 20–26; civil bloodshed (1860), 17, 20, 24, 201 n.3 (chap. 3); economy, 21–22; exodus of eligible men, 30; silk industry, 21, 49, 202 n.4; World War I, 25, 32–33. *See also* Lebanon

MS Magazine, 105

Mufida H. (pseudonym) 176

Muslim emigration, 24, 114, 202 nn.6, 1, 209 n.1 (chap. 13). *See also* Muslims; Muslim women and girls

Muslims: assimilation, 114–15, 116–17, 126; bigotry toward, 113–14, 174; born again, 118; history in U.S., 114–15; mosques, 115–16, 209–10 n.2 (chap. 13); numbers in U.S., 114; revivalists, 114–115, 209–10 n.2 (chap. 13). *See also* Muslim emigration; Muslim women and girls

Muslim women and girls, 3–4, 6, 7–8, 9, 61, 117–22, 160; contentment, 193;

discrimination against, 116; dress, 116, 119–22, 137, 139, 155, 210 n.3 (chap. 13); emigration, 114, 202 n.1, 204 n.6; power, 6–8; role in mosques, 115–16; stereotypes, 2–6, 155–56, 173–74. *See also* Dress; Muslim emigration; Muslims

Nackley, Alice, 37
Naff, Alixa: on emigration, 24, 201 n.1 (chap. 3), 202 n.7; on peddling, 36, 37, 38, 42, 45, 204 nn.1, 2; on women immigrants, 28; on women's clubs 61, 207 n.1
Najeebi (pseudonym), 137–43, 144, 210 n.5
Naji, Imm, 176–80
Nasser, Gamal Abdul, 83
Nawal (pseudonym), 145–52, 198–99
Netanyahu, Benjamin, 211 n.12
Newspapers, Arab American, 54, 206 nn.2, 3. *See also* Journalists, women; Magazines, women's
New York City, New York, 36, 38, 39, 45, 46, 59, 61, 204 n.2
NOW (National Organization for Women), 105–6
Nuha (pseudonym), 145–52, 199

Oakar, Mary Rose, 87, 209 n.3
October 1973 War, 92–93
Operation Boulder, 86. *See also* Racism, anti-Arab, political
Orfalea, Gregory, 32, 33, 36, 201 n.1 (chap. 3), 210 n.1
Orfalea, Nazera Jabaly, 36
Orientalism, 2–5, 8, 9

Palestine, 5, 10, 22; first Arab-Israeli war (1948), 100, 125, 127–28, 131, 133, 137; idyllic memories, 132–33; occupation, 99–100, 102–3. *See also* Holy Land, association with
Palestinians, 125–164; concealment of identity, 127, 210 n.2; early merchants to U.S., 23–24, 125; emigrant history, 84, 125–27; image in U.S., 125, 126, 130, 135, 144, 159, 161,

175; numbers in U.S., 210 n.1; political consciousness, 149–50, 152–53, 162–63; refugees, 126–27, 128, 133, 137, 153; resistance to American society, 126–27, 134–36, 139–40, 142–43, 149–50, 151, 158, 161, 164, 210 n.4; sense of exile, 127, 133, 134, 135; sense of grievance, 127, 128, 131, 135, 162. *See also* Emigration, Arab women; *Intifada*; Palestine; Palestinian women
Palestinian women: activism, 153–55, 156–57, 163–64; individual women, 165–66, 167, 168–69, 174–75, 181, 183–84, 193, 194, 197–99; pressures on, 135, 210 n.3 (chap. 14), under occupation, 209 n.2 (chap. 12). *See also* Emigration, Arab women; *Intifada*; Palestine; Palestinians
Peace process, Middle-Eastern, 94, 131, 211 n.12
Peddlers, *Syrian*, 35–42, 204–5 nn.1–5, 205 n.2; criticism of, 39; depots, 45; earnings, 38, 204 n.2; hardships, 36–37; wares, 36. *See also* Peddlers, women
Peddlers, women, 35–42; acculturation, 42; advantages over men, 38; benefits enjoyed, 40, 41–42; criticism of, 39–41, 42; exploitation of, 40; individuals, 28, 29, 36, 37–39, 203 nn.4, 5. *See also* Peddlers, *Syrian*
Pittsburgh, Pennsylvania, 45
PLO (Palestine Liberation Organization), 128
Portland, Maine, 45

Qamar, Cheryl, 107–11

Rabin, Yitzhak, 99
Racism, anti-Arab: ethnic, 40, 79–82, 161; political, 79, 82–94, 111, 126, 130, 151, 174, 175–76, 208–9 nn.2, 3, 4 (chap. 10). *See also* Orientalism, Religious bigotry
Ramallah, Palestine, 128, 135–36, 210 n.4
Rashed, Wadia Faris, 206 n.5

Religious bigotry: anti-Catholic, 113; anti-Muslim, 113–14, 174
Reputation. *See* Honor
Return, dream of, 24, 25–26, 169, 170, 180, 189, 191–192, 198, 202 n.9; accomplished, 197, 198, 202 n.9, 212 nn.1, 2; to raise children, 151, 183, 197, 198; trial, 189. *See also* Visits "home"
Rihani, Ameen, 46, 211 n.10
Rihbany, Abraham, 5, 8, 9, 22, 36, 201 n.2 (chap. 3), 202 n.4
Rita (pseudonym), 154–55
Rizk, Salom, 32
Roudesli, Karima, 165, 169, 189

Sabbagh, Adele, 69, 70
Sabbagh, Alexander George, 25–26, 47
Sabbagh, Elias George, 13, 15, 22, 43, 47, 63, 69, 70
Sabbagh, Jiryas, 14–15, 24, 43, 69
Sabbagh, Litfallah George, 13, 47, 52, 63, 67, 68–69
Sabbagh, Miriam Ashook, 13–16, 19, 21, 22, 25, 27, 48, 69
Sabbagh, Munnee, 69
Sabbagh, Naseeb George, 13, 23, 25–26, 43, 47, 53, 63, 70
Sabbagh, Rashid George, 43, 45, 47, 68–69
Sabbagh, Saleemy, 69, 70, 208 n.5
Said, Edward, 2
Saliba, Najib, 30, 61
Salim, Hannah Shakir, 56
Samhan, Helen Hatab, 79, 95–97, 209 n.2 (chap. 11)
Saudi Arabia, 3–4, 167, 181
Schooling, Middle East vs. America, 183–85
Second-generation women, 54, 70–74, 81–82, 85
Sewing factories. *See* Garment industry
Sex, 31, 120, 138, 140, 144, 149–50, 160–61, 162, 163–64, 166, 174–75, 183, 186, 203–4 n.6. *See also* Chastity; Honor; "Honor killings"
Shakir, Hannah Sabbagh, 10, 14, 15, 42, 195–96; on courtship and marriage, 48, 65–66, 67, 68–70, 75–76; as entrepreneur, 43–45, 51; on labor unions, 50, 205 n.10; on mill work, 47, 52; on Miriam and Katreen, 18–19; on women peddlers, 35; on preference for sons, 165; on Protestant schools in Mount Lebanon, 22, 23; on schooling, 53, 56–58; on separation of families through emigration, 25–26, 27; on silkworm cultivation, 21; on the Syrian Ladies' Aid Society of Boston, 59, 62, 63–64
Shakir, Josephine Tamer, 37–38
Shakir, Katreen Dibs, 17–19
Shakir, Shikri, 37–38
Shakir, Wadie Elias, 18, 19, 44, 56, 57, 59, 69–70
Shame. *See* Honor
Shamir, Yitzhak, 130
Shihadeh, Emily, 127–31
Shocair, Abla, 171
Shocair, Mawya, 173–74, 183
Silencing of Arab Americans, 90, 91–92, 107. *See also* Racism, anti-Arab, political
Simon, Linda, 97–103, 104
Single women, 72–74. *See also* Courtship; Dating; Elopement; Marriage
Six-Day War, 1, 83–84, 85, 92, 96, 125, 126, 153
Sons, preference for, preferential treatment of, 165–66
Sophie (Malouf), 71
Souad (pseudonym), 145–52, 198
Stage plays. *See* Acting on stage, women
Stereotypes. *See* Arab women, stereotypes; Harems; Muslim women and girls, stereotypes; Palestinians, image in U.S.
Stewart, Frank, 211 n.7
Stitchers. *See* Garment industry
St. Paul, Minnesota, 207 n.2
Suhair (pseudonym), 145–52, 197
Syria. See Greater Syria
Syria, Syrians, 1, 84, 85, 126, 171, 190–91. *See also Greater Syria*; Syrian women

Syrian Ladies' Aid Society of Boston, 2, 59, 61–64, 153, 158
Syrian Ladies' Aid Society of New York, 61, 207 n.2
Syrian women, 171, 173–74, 183, 190–91.
Syrian women. *See* Emigration, *Syrian*; Emigration, *Syrian* women
Syrian Women's Union of New York, 61
Syrian World, 54, 70–73, 80, 95, 135, 211 n.10

Tamer, Louise Ayoob, 29, 203 n.4
Tannous, Afif, 22, 30, 49, 62–63, 66, 67, 202 nn.4, 8, 203 n.5
Third-generation women, 82, 85, 95–96
Toledo, Ohio, 45
Traboulsi, Asma, 207 n.4
Triangle Shirtwaist fire, 50, 205 n.11

UPWA (Union of Palestinian Women's Associations), 153, 157–59, 211 nn.12, 13

Vecoli, Rudolph, 81
Veiling, 5, 7, 116, 155–56, 210 n.3 (chap. 13). *See also* Dress
Vicksburg, Mississippi, 203 n.5

Violence against women and girls, 6, 67, 148, 151–52, 155, 159, 190, 197, 198, 199. *See also* "Honor killings"
Visits "home," 147, 150, 160–61, 189, 190–91, 193–94. *See also* Return, dream of

Wage earners, *Syrian*, 46–51, 205 nn.2, 5
Wakin, Jeanette, 144, 211 n.7
Wardi T. (pseudonym), 186
Weiss, Hayat, 166, 167–68, 169, 173, 192, 194
Westerners in the Middle East, 5, 22. *See also* Missionaries to the Middle East
Woods, Robert, 80–81
Worcester, Massachusetts, 61

Yazbeck, Mary, 170, 184, 185, 192
Yazgie, Saleemie, 29, 33–34
Yehia, Mayyada, 187–88, 190
Yemeni women, 167, 169, 180–81, 187–88, 190, 192, 193–94
Younis, Adele, 205 n.8

Zahle, Lebanon, 17, 18, 23
Zelditch, Morris, 203 n.5
Zionism, Zionists, 18, 83, 86, 98, 125, 136, 153

About the Author

EVELYN SHAKIR, the daughter of Lebanese immigrants, has been writing for many years on the subjects of Arab American women and Arab American literature. She is Associate Professor of English at Bentley College.